THAT MAN
BARNHOUSE

That Barn

MARGARET N.

TYNDALE HOUSE PUBLISHERS, INC.

Man
house

BARNHOUSE

WHEATON, ILLINOIS

Unless otherwise indicated, Scripture references
are taken from the *King James Version* of the Bible.

Fourth printing, April 1985

Library of Congress Catalog Card Number 82-74279
ISBN 0-8423-7033-1
Copyright © 1983 by Margaret N. Barnhouse
All rights reserved
Printed in the United States of America

Unto Him
　who loved us
and
　unto those
　　everywhere
　　whom He loves

CONTENTS

FOREWORD

The name Donald Grey Barnhouse was not known to me the Sunday morning in 1947 when I wandered into Tenth Presbyterian Church in Philadelphia in the middle of his explanatory remarks before reading a portion of the tenth chapter of Hebrews. His authoritative voice held my attention, his physical appearance was arresting, and his preaching was teaching of the highest intellectual order. I sat under that teaching for almost two decades and always learned from him a deeper understanding of the Word of God.

I became a Christian through that teaching and then had the privilege of serving the Lord with DGB (as we who were close to him usually called him) as an elder of Tenth Church, and as president of the Evangelical Foundation, more recently known as Evangelical Ministries.

DGB stood in awe of the grace of God, and I always marveled at the simplicity of the faith of this very intelligent and learned man. As I met others over the years who first recognized Christian truth through DGB, they all seemed to recognize the simplicity of his faith, his unswerving belief in the sovereignty of God, his reliance on the inspiration and authority of Scripture, and his humility before Jesus Christ.

On a day when DGB was en route to Washington to appear before a Congressional committee in testimony, he stopped by the Evangelical Foundation office in Philadelphia in order to sign some letters. He was clothed in white from head to toe. As he lifted his pen from his desk set and brought it toward him, the ink showered his white shirt and suitcoat with large blotches of blue ink. No expletive left his lips. Instead, he said: "I guess the Lord did not want me to appear before that committee looking too well groomed." And off he went to Washington. Sovereignty, humility, graciousness, and purpose. I loved the man, as did the author of this book. I think you will, too, when you come to know him in these pages.

C. Everett Koop, M.D. ScD.

PREFACE

*I am Alpha and Omega, the beginning and the end, the
first and the last. . . . I Jesus. . . .* Revelation 22:13, 16

The beginning and the end of this book is the Lord
Jesus Christ. Between the first page and the last you will see
Him at work, by His Holy Spirit wooing us indifferent,
sinful humans—loving us, calling us, and using us as channels to convey the love and forgiveness of God the Father.

In particular you will see Him at work in and through
Donald Grey Barnhouse—and frequently in spite of him.
Here was a man mighty in intellect and physical stature
who radiated a joy and confidence that sometimes came
across as over-optimism, dogmatism, and even arrogance.
But through his God-given gift of illustration this dynamic
Bible expositor could make the Scriptures "living, and
powerful, and sharper than any two-edged sword."

I first knew Donald Grey Barnhouse as his student,
during which time he intrigued me, challenged me, and,
yes, angered me; then as his wife for six-and-a-half years
until his death in 1960.

In those ten years, he preached his way through the Epistle to the Romans, verse by verse, on coast-to-coast radio.
Gradually, through those verses, the Holy Spirit began to
speak not only through, but to him, causing him much
inner struggle. His former manner of sounding forth the

gospel was revolutionized. But while his methods, attitudes, and tone of voice changed during this period, his message remained the same: the sovereignty of God, the authority of the Scriptures, the person and work of Jesus Christ as only Savior and Lord.

Because audience reaction to him so frequently was the same as my own first reaction to the man, I tell the story from that point of view—Mrs. Average American Housewife, nominal Christian, whose life was changed because of a remarkable man of God. So if those of you with no evangelical background are outraged or intimidated by Donald Grey Barnhouse, know that I understand—so was I! And if those of you who have been steeped in the Bible since childhood have been reawakened by Donald Grey Barnhouse to a new excitement in studying the Scriptures, I share with you that joy and exhilaration.

Through it all, let us look beyond this teacher of the written Word and focus upon the living Word Himself, the Lord Jesus Christ, and *listen,* as His Holy Spirit speaks to us, filling us with His *dunamis* power, instructing us in walking, running, and mounting up with wings as eagles.

Margaret N. Barnhouse

I

The Dynamite of God

ONE

"Donald Grey Barnhouse. Who's he?"

Mrs. Northen looked up from the stack of books she was placing on the coffee table in preparation for our newly organized Bible class. "Why, honey," she said, amused, "he just happens to be the most famous Bible expositor in the whole United States, and to my mind, in the whole world."

The title stared up at me: *Teaching the Word of Truth,* Donald Grey Barnhouse.

"Never heard of him." I dismissed him with an airy wave of the hand. As I leafed through one of the books, I was sure some mistake had been made. This was obviously for young children. Didn't Mrs. Northen realize I was an intelligent forty-two-year-old woman with a teenage son and daughter?

Seeing my face, Mrs. Northen laughed aloud and said, "Look at the Preface!" The Preface read, " . . . for young Christians of any age."

"You see," she said, "you are what the Bible calls a 'babe in Christ.' I know of no quicker way to grow up spiritually than by using this book as an outline. At least give it a try."

I looked once more at the large, slim red book. *Teaching the Word of Truth,* Donald Grey Barnhouse.

With that, Donald Grey Barnhouse entered my life.

Before the class began that night, Mrs. Northen passed out slips with Bible references on them, telling us to mark the place in our Bible and be ready to read it when we came to it in the lesson. My slip read, "Heb. 12:14." That meant Hebrews, I was sure. I thought: *the New Testament is for Christians, the Old Testament for Jews, so of course Hebrews would be in the Old Testament.* I riffled through the Old Testament pages in my Bible, but could find no such book. I looked again. Embarrassed, I peeked at the index, and to my amazement discovered Hebrews was in the New Testament. My pride was stung as I realized the others had found their references easily. But I had an A.B. in English Literature from Bryn Mawr, and some of these had never been to college!

" . . . You will notice that there are references in both the Old Testament and the New Testament," Mrs Northen was saying. "Never make the mistake of thinking, as some do, that the Old Testament is for the Jew and the New Testament for the Christian." (Well!) "The whole book hangs together. 'The New is in the Old concealed; the Old is in the New revealed.' The Bible is God's revelation of Himself to mankind. As we read it, I want you to remember that *this is God speaking.*"

We started with Lesson I from the Barnhouse book: "SIN: What It Is." For the first time in my life I was confronted with God's holiness. Like most of my friends I was a good, ethical citizen with high moral integrity according to human standards. My verse in the Book of Hebrews said, "Follow peace with all men, and holiness, without which no man shall see the Lord." Before class, when I had finally found and read the verse, smugness had salved my wounded intellectual pride: *I* "followed peace with all men"; *I* was "good" and, surely, "holy." But I became more and more uneasy as the lesson progressed. Donald Grey Barnhouse brought us inescapably under God's own words in Romans 3:23, "All have sinned, and come short of the glory of God." *All? Surely not I, God!*

Week after week we followed the outline: *Sin: its extent; its effects. Salvation: the need for salvation; its basis in the death of Christ; its completeness; the condition upon which it is received.* These were concepts I had heard before but only dimly understood or had misunderstood. Intellectually, I had assented to all of it and hid my uneasiness in a great splurge of church activity. Then, about the ninth lesson, I was given Isaiah 64:6. In my best Bryn Mawr accent I read aloud, "But we are all as an unclean thing, and all our righteousnesses are as filthy rags." I did a double-take. I realized *I* was included in that "we ... our...." *All* my *righteousnesses ... filthy rags? Wait a minute, God! You don't know me very well!* I never heard the rest of the lesson, for my mind was flipping through verses I had already learned in the class, searching for some refuge. I found none. That man Barnhouse! I wished I had never encountered him and his book.

Via radio, that man Barnhouse was even to invade our home. My husband, Doug Bell, leader of the group of men who had started the Bible class, learned that Dr. Barnhouse's radio Bible studies in Romans could be brought to Florida's west coast, where we lived, if it could be underwritten for the first year. Our home was in Bradenton; the class met in Sarasota; the group was composed of people from both communities. The class decided to go out on a limb and bring the program to a St. Petersburg station that blanketed the area. What had been an author's name on a disquieting book now became a radio voice, to which I listened at first unwillingly, then with more and more appreciation as comprehension began to come.

"Through the Lord Jesus Christ we come unto Thee, our Father and our God, and in the Holy Spirit...." He spoke with clarity of diction, dignity, authority of voice. I envisioned an elderly gentleman, vigorous for his years, expounding these great doctrines by means of fascinating illustrations. And always, in closing: "And our God and Father, we pray that Thou wilt give *rest-less-ness* to all who have not been born again. But upon all Thy believing own may Thy grace, Thy mercy, and Thy peace abide. And unto Thee be the glory and the majesty, the dominion and the power, now, until our Lord Jesus comes again, and forever. Amen."

Rest-less-ness. That described me.

I was soon to see in person "the most famous Bible expositor in the whole United States." Doug's group learned that Donald Barnhouse would be speaking in Florida and made arrangements to have him come to Sarasota for a week of meetings. They decided anyone that famous would need the Civic Auditorium, with a seating capacity of 1,000, so they rented it for a week. Then they began to run into puzzling problems. How naive were we baby Christians who had not yet learned that denominational differences were not merely a matter of differing church governments! Many local ministers were evasive or outright hostile and would not advertise the meetings in their churches.

We were unaware that the "modernists" and "fundamentalists" were warring against one another. Modernists denied the virgin birth of Jesus Christ and put their emphasis on His humanity, teaching the universal fatherhood of God and brotherhood of man. I didn't *deny* the virgin birth, but in my ignorance I couldn't see why it was important enough to fight over. Wasn't it enough to know and love Jesus as a person? The universal fatherhood of God and brotherhood of man was something I had accepted all my life without ever really thinking through the implications. Because we had discussed this to some extent in the Bible class, I was beginning to see there was much more to it than appeared on the surface. Apparently Dr. Barnhouse was in the camp of the "fundamentalists," who believed every word of the Bible was literally true because God was

speaking in and through it, whereas "modernists," I discovered, thought the Bible was man groping after God, and
not to be taken literally.

To me it was all beside the point. A great Bible teacher
was coming, one who through radio and books had made
the doctrines of historic Christianity come alive for us.

The group advertised the meetings in the papers; they
had handbills and bumper stickers printed; enthusiasm ran
high.

The first meeting was scheduled for Sunday morning in
Sarasota's First Presbyterian Church. We in the Bradenton
group sat together, feeling a bit guilty at not being in our
own church for Sunday worship.

The minister and some others walked onto the platform.
But where was that "elderly gentleman, vigorous for his
years"? That great giant of a man, with the thick thatch of
curly reddish hair, who looked as if he had slept in his
clothes and needed more sleep still—was *that* Dr. Barnhouse? From the top of his forehead to the cleft in his strong
chin his whole face sagged with fatigue. (We later learned
that, on deadline for a radio sermon, he had fallen asleep
over his typewriter around 4:30 A.M., awakening with time
only to shave and dash without breakfast to the church.)
As the regular Sunday morning service got under way his
eyes began to sweep the audience, row by row; then he
bowed his head as if in prayer. Once announcements had
been made and introductions were over, this large man
rose, full of sudden inner strength, and strode to the pulpit.

"It is with great joy that I minister to you here in Sarasota
this week." The words were formal, but, oh, the smile that
swept his audience into one intimate group! *Joy*. It radiated
from him. His face, so sleep-heavy a moment ago, had become alert. His words then sliced through air charged with
expectancy.

"I was born and brought up in California. In my state is
the lowest point in the whole United States, Death Valley,
282 feet below sea level, and the highest point, Mt. Whit-

ney, soaring to almost fifteen thousand feet above sea level.

"Now suppose a man is at the lowest point in Death Valley. He is wretched, miserable, rest-less; the air is hot and still; the water in the brackish pool beside him is undrinkable. He raises his eyes to the encircling cliffs. 'I think I'll leave California,' says he, and starts to climb. After many weary days he has made his way out of Death Valley and finds himself looking out over the Pacific Ocean, at sea level. 'At last!' he cries, 'I have left California!' But has he? No, he has climbed 282 feet up, but he is still in California. Rest-less, rest-less, he looks at distant Mt. Whitney. 'I'll climb to the top—then I shall have left California!' he says. So he equips himself with mountain-climbing gear and struggles up, up, up, slipping back a few feet, hanging perilously over a cleft in the mountain, on again, until he finally reaches the top. He has climbed as far as it is possible to go. But he is still in California.

"So it is with human character. A man is born in what God calls a state of death. What is death? Death is separation, and there are two kinds of death. Physical death is the separation of the soul and spirit from the body; spiritual death is the separation of the soul and spirit from God. And although the human race is walking about, laughing and talking and physically alive, God says in Ephesians 2:1 that humanity is spiritually dead—'dead in trespasses and sins....' "

Suddenly what we had been studying all those weeks made sense. *Dead*—separated from God!

"So here we have a man in the state of death and sunk about as low as a human being can get.... One day he shakes himself out of a drunken stupor and decides to reform. The gutter bum pulls himself up and becomes an acceptable average citizen. He owns his own home, he pays his taxes, he marries and starts a family. But he is still in the state of death. 'Well!' says he, 'we'll fix that!' So he educates himself and polishes himself and becomes an eminent jurist with all sorts of honors and degrees, about as high as a man can go."

All this time Dr. Barnhouse had been busily pantomiming: his right fist, as first dangling at arm's length, had with great effort raised itself shoulder high, then upward, his left hand "polishing" it as it arose, then giving it a final boost at the elbow to bring it to a full upward stretch.

"Has he left the state of death? Listen. The only way you can leave California is *out,* not up.

"The only way you can leave the state of death is *out,* by the way God Himself has provided: the cross of Jesus Christ.

"Now, we are told that Jesus made His friends among the poor and the outcast and that it was the 'good' people who put Him to death." Dr. Barnhouse paused, and his eyes twinkled, although the expression on his face remained the same. "You must never forget," he continued, "that Jesus was crucified after a joint meeting of the Jerusalem ministerial association and the Jerusalem bar association!"

Everyone laughed, and I saw my husband Doug nudge the man sitting beside him—a judge—and they both grinned.

"And why did they put Him to death?" Dr. Barnhouse's voice boomed through the auditorium. "Because in the Sermon on the Mount He addressed the Death Valley bums and said, 'Except your righteousnesses shall *exceed* the righteousnesses of those who have reached the peak of Mt. Whitney—the scribes and the Pharisees—you shall in no case enter into the kingdom of heaven.' And then he thundered, 'BE YE THEREFORE PERFECT, EVEN AS YOUR FATHER WHO IS IN HEAVEN IS PERFECT!' and the leaders were enraged. You see, over the years they had whittled down God's law and had put wedgies in their shoes and by great effort had stretched up toward the whittled-down law, saying, 'I pass! I pass!' And Jesus had exposed them for what they really were. . . ."

Dr. Barnhouse leaned over the pulpit. "Where does that leave you and me? You're not perfect; I'm not perfect. What are we going to do?

" 'Oh, but,' you say, 'surely God won't be too hard on

me.' " Dr. Barnhouse smiled a too–sweet, seraphic smile.
" 'I'm good!' you say. 'I'm not a sinner.' " His voice dripped
with self–righteousness. I squirmed.

"But what is sin?"

The words were millstones falling into the stillness.

"There is one group that says original sin is sex. Rubbish!
God commanded man and woman to be fruitful and mul-
tiply, so it couldn't be sex. What then was their sin? They
deliberately partook of the fruit, knowing perfectly well
they were disobeying God. The fruit, by the way, as far as
I'm concerned, was just that: fruit, nothing more, nothing
less, but it was a test of their obedience to the known will of
God. Do you know the shortest definition of sin? I'll quote
a verse, and you finish it for me. Isaiah 53:6: 'All we like
sheep have gone astray; we have turned every one to....' "

Here and there timid voices arose in unison, "... his
own way."

"That's it! That's it! 'His own way.' That's the shortest
definition of sin. Have any of you ever gone your own way?
You know you have. And when you know it isn't God's
way but you do it anyway, that is sin. God's Word says,
'The soul that sinneth, it shall die'—that's Ezekiel 18:20. A
holy and a righteous God *must* strike sin or He would be a
liar. But He loves the sinner and created him to fellowship
with Him. So He devised a plan whereby He could in righteousness take unholy sinners like you and me into His holy
heaven without dirtying it. How?"

Dr. Barnhouse picked up a hymnal from the pulpit and
placed it on his outstretched right hand.

"Let this represent my sin, on me. If I die, physically, and
appear before God with my sin on me, God *must,* in righteousness, strike my sin." Dr. Barnhouse struck the hymnal.
"In so doing He would strike me away from Him forever.
But if, instead, Jesus has taken my sin upon Himself," Dr.
Barnhouse paused, passing the hymnal from his right hand
to his left hand, "then when the wrath of God pours out on

my sin, it strikes Jesus instead of me." Dr. Barnhouse's enormous right fist smashed down upon the hymnal. "And that's exactly what happened at the cross. For you have never understood the death of Jesus Christ until you realize *God the Father put Him to death*. Oh, sure, the Jews delivered Him and the Gentiles nailed Him—but it was *God the Father* who put His beloved Son to death to pay for your sin and mine. *That's how much He loves you."*

A small brief sob jarred the deathly stillness of the audience. Tears prickled behind my own eyelids, for suddenly I saw myself as God saw me. I thought: *Lord God, I am a sinner! I am a sinner! Lord God, did You love me that much? I knew You were my Savior, but I didn't realize what it was You saved me from!*

"Have you believed this? Because if you have, God says in John 3:16 that at that moment you have passed through the cross, out of death, and into everlasting life. He puts within you His very life, and you shall never perish. And when He rose from the dead, *in Him* you rose to newness of life. That is what the Bible calls 'justification.' Jesus shed His blood and died to pay for your sin; you have believed this, *so it is paid for,* once for all and forever. Through faith you have received new life, and that new, holy life of Christ, which 1 John 3:9 says *cannot* sin, wants to pull you upward to God. *But* the old nature is still there wanting its own way, and the struggle begins: the flesh lusts against the Spirit and the Spirit against the flesh (as we're told in Galatians 5:17), and these are contrary one to the other."

With this, Dr. Barnhouse slapped his left hand into his right hand so that his fingers interlocked. He pulled his right hand down and his left up; the struggle seesawed up and down, up and down. Light dawned. I *had* believed— yes, weeks ago—but *because the struggle was there I could not be sure.*

"Now which one is going to win? The one that is the stronger, naturally. The world is geared to feed and fatten the flesh, that old nature which wants to rule its own life. But the only thing that will feed and strengthen this new life is Bible study."

He held up his Bible, a large black leather volume, worn smooth at the edges from years of study. With what strength and joy he held it out to us. It spoke loudly, without words: *Here, my friends, is the source of life.*

"God calls this the milk of the baby Christian, the meat of the mature believer, the water of life, the bread. Have you received new life? Then this week come and feast on His Word *and grow!*" His voice, so joyously confident, made me eager to come to that feast. His face shone as Moses' must have when he had been in the presence of the Lord.

He held his hands wide in benediction and bowed his head.

"And our Father and our God, do what we cannot do. We have spoken the short distance to man's ears. Do Thou take these words the long distance from the ear to the heart. Go with us as we go. If there be any here who have not been born again, accompany them with rest-less-ness, that they may know no peace until they rest in Thee. But upon all Thy believing. . . ."

I didn't even hear the end of the benediction in the wonder of realizing that *my* rest-less-ness was gone.

TWO

That afternoon the Civic Auditorium was less than half full, which disappointed us, even though that was almost five hundred people. Right on the dot of 3:30, Dr. Barnhouse, accompanied by the sponsors and some of the local ministers, came to the platform. His step was buoyant; he looked refreshed. His intensely blue eyes once again made measured sweeps of his audience, row by row, as he sat relaxed, waiting for the opening hymn to be sung and the introductions to be over. Then he came to the podium.

"Before we begin, I've been asked to say a few words about the book table and my books.

"I wrote them. They're there. Come and browse after the meeting. I believe you'll find them a blessing in leading you deeper into the riches of God's Word.

"There are also samples of our monthly magazine, *Eternity*. This has Bible study helps, articles on the Christian life, and current events in the light of the Bible—which is, of course, the only way to look at them.

"Now a word about the offerings. I make no charge for my ministry. There will be an offering taken at each meeting, out of which the expenses of this conference will be paid: hiring this hall, publicity, and so on. After these have been met, whatever is left goes toward maintaining the work of the Evangelical Foundation, the group of men who run the business end of my ministry. We are a non-profit corporation under the laws of the Commonwealth of Pennslyvania, with no endowment: the offerings I receive at these meetings must pay the salaries of our secretaries, the utilities and other expenses of our building, and my own travel expenses.

"We are about to take the offering for this meeting. In my own church, when we take the offering, I always say, 'If you are not a Christian, you are not invited to give. The offering is like the communion table: it is for Christians only. . . .' Lord, bless now the gifts and the givers. May they give as unto Thee. In Jesus' name, Amen."

Doug's eyes danced. Here was a man after his own heart.

The offering received, Dr. Barnhouse launched into his sermon.

"This afternoon I am going to speak on assurance: how you can know beyond a shadow of a doubt that you are saved, once for all and forever.

"I am just as sure that I will be in heaven as I am that Jesus Christ is in heaven. Now, that is either the rankest arrogance or simple faith.

"I am going to read a passage of Scripture to you and I am going to make two mistakes. If you do not recognize these mistakes one of two things is true: Either you are not saved or you are a *baby* baby Christian and you need to grow up. Now I know some of you know your Scriptures backward and forward. Please do not poke your neighbor and whisper the true words in a loud voice to show off how much you know. It is of utmost importance for those who do not know to realize they do not know, without your telling them. Ready?"

Dr. Barnhouse opened his Bible and held it in such a way that it was impossible to see just where in it he was reading. Then in a sonorous, pulpit voice he proclaimed:

" 'He that believeth on the Son of God hath the witness

in himself: he that believeth not God hath made Him a liar. . . .' "

I shuddered. Did the Bible really say that? "Liar"? The word lashed like a whip.

" 'These things have I written unto you that believe on the name of the Son of God; that ye may hope that you will have eternal life, and that ye may believe on the name of the Son of God.' "

He stopped and looked up. There was an almost audible sigh, as if the whole room had been holding its breath. "Now, doesn't that sound nice and King James-y? You know, there are people who think that if you use King James English—'thou knowest,' 'he doeth,' and so forth— that it is completely orthodox. But I made two terrible errors as I read it, and if you did not spot them, either you do not truly know Jesus Christ as your Savior, or else you are still a *baby* baby Christian."

A woman on the aisle seat in front of us was leaning forward, eyes glittering with anticipation. I knew she *knew* and was bursting to tell. But *I didn't know.* I hadn't the faintest idea. It all sounded perfectly proper to me. Suddenly, I had a terrifying thought: *Maybe I wasn't saved.*

"Both these errors were in the last part. Let me read it to you again: 'These things have I written unto you that believe on the name of the son of God; that ye may hope that you will have eternal life, and that ye may believe on the name of the Son of God.'

"Is that what it says? *No! No!* Thank God that is not what it says! Here is what it really says: 'These things have I written unto you that believe on the name of the Son of God; that ye may *know* [not "hope"] that ye *have* [not "will have"] eternal life, and that ye may believe on the name of the Son of God' (1 John 5:13).

" 'Oh, but,' you say, 'does it make any difference?' " *(How did he know I was wondering?)* "DOES IT MAKE ANY DIFFERENCE! Listen: suppose a couple of tramps are down under a railroad bridge building a little fire to heat a can of water for some coffee. One says to the other, 'I hope I will have a thousand dollars one of these days.' The other says, 'I'll raise you; I hope I will have *two* thousand dollars!' Well,

If wishes were fishes, we'd have them fried;
If wishes were horses, beggars would ride.

"Now come with me to an oak-paneled room on Wall Street where five gentlemen are seated around a polished mahogany table. One of them says, 'Gentlemen, this meeting has been called because our government urgently needs a ball-bearing factory to expedite the war effort and bring the present war to a speedy close. We have been asked to raise $20 million.'

" 'I'll put in $5 million,' says Mr. DuPont.

" 'You can count on me for $5 million' says Mr. Rockefeller, and so on, around the table, and the government soon has its $20 million for the ball-bearing factory.

" 'But,' you might say, 'don't you gentlemen mean you *hope* that you *will have* $5 million?'

" 'No, we *know* that we *have* it,' they reply.

"They do, too. Now, if there is no difference between 'I hope that I may have' and 'I know that I have,' then there is no difference between a tramp and a Rockefeller.

"Now listen to me. There are hundreds of Christians who are spiritual millionaires, with all of God's spiritual resources at their disposal, who are living like tramps because they do not *know* what they have. Are you going to make God a liar? If God says that I may *know* that I have eternal life, then I may *know* that *I have it. How* may I know? *Because God's Word says so.*" Dr. Barnhouse picked up his Bible and tapped it to emphasize each word.

"A minister's wife once came to me after a meeting like this, and she said, 'Dr. Barnhouse, I have gone through life wishing I could really be sure. But no matter how hard I try, I just know that I am not good enough.' I turned to John 3:16 and had her read it.

" 'Does it say,' I asked her, '... have everlasting life if you're good enough?'

"She looked at the verse in the Bible. 'No,' she said.

" 'Does God love you?'

" 'I hope so.'

" 'Does He say He does?'

" 'Yes.'

" *'Is God a liar?'*

" 'Oh, *No!'*

" 'Well, does He *say* He loves you?'

" 'Hmmm, yes?'

" 'Now, is that any kind of answer, "Hmmm, yes?" If your husband asked, "Do you love me?" would you have answered, "Hmmm, yes?" ' She laughed. I pressed the point: '*Does* God love you?'

" '*Yes!'*

" 'That's better! Do you believe He gave His Son to die for you?'

" 'Yes!'

" 'Then, what does He say you have?'

" 'Everlasting life?'

" 'No! EVERLASTING LIFE. Period! Not question mark! Is God a liar?'

" '*No!'*

" 'Then, *do* you have everlasting life, right now, present possession?'

" 'Oh, *yes!'* she answered and pressed my hand and went away with shining eyes.

"Now, suppose you had asked the Apostle Paul that question: 'Paul, are you saved?' What would have been his answer? 'I hope so... I'm trying to be... I'm doing the best I can... I hope that maybe someday.... perhaps.' "

Again, as in the morning session, laughter swept over the audience. Again, we were brought up short.

"No! No! 'Paul are you saved?' 'I *know* whom I have believed, and am persuaded that he is able to keep that which I have committed unto him against that day.' 'There is therefore now no condemnation to them that are in Christ

Jesus. . . .' 'For I am persuaded that neither death nor life, nor angels, nor principalities, nor powers, nor things present, nor things to come, nor height, nor depth, nor any other creature shall be able to separate us from the love of God which is in Christ Jesus our Lord.' "

The words rang out with crystal clarity. I could almost hear the Apostle Paul himself saying them with confident assurance, and an answering echo began to swell within my own heart: Yes! Yes! I don't just "believe" it, I *know!*

After his message, our whole group crowded down the aisle eagerly to shake Dr. Barnhouse's hand, to tell him what his message had meant to us. Then, waiting for Dr. Barnhouse to be free to go with us for ice cream, we looked over the publications on the book table. Doug picked up a couple of *Eternity* magazines from a large stack, promising to return them the next day. The titles of the books intrigued me: *Guaranteed Deposits; His Own Received Him Not, BUT . . . ; God's Methods for Holy Living; Man's Ruin,* the first of his series on Romans. I remembered that we had bought *God's Methods for Holy Living* at the Christian bookstore several months before, but for some reason I had not been able to get into it, although from time to time I had picked it up and started to read it.

Dr. Barnhouse was autographing a Bible for a little boy, the last in line. As we went over to tell him that he would be riding with Doug and me, I heard him say, "I make a charge for my autograph." The youngster looked stricken until he continued, "You have to learn my Bible verse. Will you do it?"

"Oh, yes sir!" the boy cried, relieved. Happily, he looked at what had been inscribed in his Bible. When I asked to see it, he held it out. I read:

It is not what you do for Christ that counts;
it is what you let Him do through you.
                    Donald Grey Barnhouse   Phil. 3:10

Philippians 3:10. It didn't ring a bell. I'd have to look it up.

Doug handed Dr. Barnhouse his hat and coat, and we joined the others of our group waiting in the parking lot, already in their cars. Within moments we were on our way to a place where we could get ice cream and have a discussion. Ice cream! Just over a year ago not a man in the group would have considered he had done his duty as a host if we had not headed for the country club for a drink, yet this afternoon it never even occurred to them, so completely had the inflowing life of Christ replaced in that one short year the need for the crutch of liquor.

After we had ordered, questions flowed. Dr. Barnhouse always answered from the Bible. I asked a question. "That's Ephesians 2:10," he said. As he was answering, I had pushed my Bible toward him on the table. He pushed it back. "You look it up; I know where it is," he said and turned to the next questioner.

I could feel the heat of smoldering anger creeping up the back of my neck. I realized he was right in forcing me to find out for myself, but I didn't like being rebuffed and shown up for being biblically ignorant. What's more, I remembered that I had been offended by his casual, earthy words in the pulpit: "Death Valley bums," indeed! Laughter, in *church!* Where was the measured dignity of his radio voice? How dared he be so positive about everything?

My little universe, centering around my own ego, was beginning to crumble under the onslaught of the Word of God, and I didn't like it. And I preferred to think maybe I didn't like this man Barnhouse very much. The glow and excitement of knowing that Jesus Christ had forever claimed me for His own was still with me, but rising through it was an uneasy realization that this could lead to a greater commitment to Him on my part than I was then willing to give. I was glad someone else was scheduled to take Dr. Barnhouse to his motel.

Before and after the service at our church in Bradenton that evening everyone talked about Dr. Barnhouse and his teachings. Some were ecstatic; others in violent disagreement. It was impossible for me to keep nursing my wounded pride, especially since in the excitement of having questions answered no one had noticed what Dr. Barnhouse had said to me and how much it had irked me.

By the time we were home from church my pique had passed. Our teenagers, Douglas and Carolyn, sat down with their homework, and Doug and I soon settled into our bedroom, eager to do some reading. We propped ourselves up in bed, spreading around us all our reading materials—issues of Dr. Barnhouse's magazine, a copy of *God's Methods for Holy Living,* and other literature.

Doug opened an old issue of *Eternity* to an article titled "Tomorrow: Current Events in the Light of the Bible." His eyes swept down the page.

"This man is incredible, Marge! He knows something about everything. Listen to this:

" 'First, let me say that I reserve the right to write on any subject in the world that affects the lives of human beings, and that, naturally, covers practically every question under the sun. The field of politics is no exception and it will become increasingly the province of the minister of the Gospel to speak out on political matters, as Rome seeks to control our destinies and we are forced to fight for even the most elementary of our liberties. I do not preach on these matters. When I am before an audience I take the Word of God and give an exposition of a portion of that Divine revelation. I reserve my statements on these other matters for the pages of this magazine.'

"And he goes on to list the voting records of the candidates for United States Senate," Doug said. "Now I didn't think ministers knew anything about politics, and he even knows the candidates' voting records!"

Doug continued reading, this time silently, and I turned my attention to *God's Methods for Holy Living.* Skimming lightly over the Preface, I had barely gotten into the first chapter when the Lord showed me why I had not been able to get my teeth into this book earlier.

"I know," said the text, "that this little book . . . will be read in every part of the world by people in every conceivable state of spiritual advance. You should realize that it takes just as much of the filling of the Spirit of God to receive a message as it does to prepare and give it. Therefore, will you stop a moment and ask the Lord how you are about to receive this message? What is your state of mind and heart? Are you yielding to Him? Perhaps the turning point of your whole spiritual experience would be reached in this moment if you would stop and say, 'Speak, Lord; for Thy servant heareth.'

"Speak, Lord, in the stillness,
While I wait on Thee,
Hushed my heart to listen,
In expectancy."

In shocked stillness I sat listening to the gentle prodding of the Holy Spirit. . . . What *is* the state of your heart, Margaret Bell? Are you truly yielding to Me? In expectancy? What are you "expecting"?

Well, what *was* I expecting? To have my curiosity satisfied? To get new ammunition against the demolition of my long-cherished misconceptions? To find some loophole? Was I indeed wanting to listen *and hear*? Something within me was resisting that word "holiness." Who wants to be "holier than thou"? I sighed and read on.

The second chapter had to do with the sure knowledge of our position in Christ, based on assurance of salvation and leading to "experimental holiness." That word "holiness" no longer carried negative connotations for me. I was ready to discard my preconceived notions and learn what true, biblical holiness was. Here, using the example of the many changes that take place in the life of a newborn babe in the first few seconds of its earthly life, Dr. Barnhouse took me step-by-step through the changes that take place when the life of God enters a heart through the regenerative work of the Holy Spirit.

Dr. Barnhouse proved that, according to the biblical definition, every saved person is a "saint," set apart for His service. God was now at work making me saint*ly*, bringing my unsaintly condition up to my saintly position. No wonder it was such a painful struggle.

Imagine! Me a saint!

THREE

Sunday night the men of the study group had persuaded the minister of our church in Bradenton to go with us to the morning series on Galatians. Still naively supposing that the difference between denominations was one of church government, or of formality versus informality, we had no idea that doctrinal teaching could differ from church to church. Dr. Barnhouse was a Presbyterian; we were Methodists. What difference could it make, if we all knew and loved the Lord Jesus Christ?

Monday morning we were all at the Civic Auditorium early, armed with Bible, notebook, and pen. The meeting started promptly at ten. Without any preliminaries, Dr. Barnhouse was introduced and came to the pulpit. An expectant hush fell on the auditorium.

"Turn with me to the Book of Galatians."

As we opened our Bibles, Dr. Barnhouse said, "In order for you to understand this epistle you must have some background. Let's go back to the beginning of the Christian Church, in Jerusalem. You must understand that it was 100 percent Jewish. No Gentiles were added until the tenth chapter of the Acts. Now, how many people were saved at Pentecost?"

He paused. Several voices from the audience said, "Three thousand."

His voice broke in, "Not one! What happened was that three thousand *saved Jews,* saved under the Old Covenant by believing God's Word, bringing a lamb when they had sinned, and having its blood shed (in recognition that 'the soul that sinneth, it shall die,' meaning that person or the substitute *God* has provided), three thousand saved Jews were 'added to the church.' They heard and believed that Jesus was the promised Messiah, the Lamb of God that taketh away the sins of the world, and so shifted gears out of the Old Testament into the New. Who were they? Mary, Martha, Lazarus, many who had eaten of the loaves and the fishes, many whom Jesus had healed—all Jews. There was as yet no New Testament as we know it: it hadn't been written. For nearly twenty years after Christ's ascension there were no instructions except by word of mouth as the new converts sat under the apostles' teaching. So gradually they went back to doing what came naturally: keeping the Old Testament law as before.

"Now let's look at the Galatians. These were Gentiles, Gauls who had spilled over to Asia Minor from what is now France. They knew their salvation was by God's grace, and not by anything they had done to deserve it. But they were being troubled by some of the Judaizers from Jerusalem who were teaching that after salvation you had to keep on living by the law of Moses. Paul wrote this letter to show them that, having been saved by grace, they were to be kept by grace.

"Now let's read it."

I had been taking notes as fast as I could. If I stopped for more than a second or two to think about what Dr. Barnhouse was saying, I might miss something essential to his next point. I decided to get it all down, and think it through afterward.

Dr. Barnhouse read through the first three verses of Galatians 1, taking time to explain key words and phrases. Then he read verse 4: " 'Our Lord Jesus Christ, who gave himself for our sins, that he might deliver us from Sarasota, Florida. . . .' "

Eyes that had been fastened on his face jerked down to the text: Deliver us from *what?*

"That's what it says: 'From this present evil world'— Sarasota, Florida. And if you don't think 'this present evil world' is Sarasota or Bradenton or New York or Philadelphia or wherever you live, you have not understood the holiness of God."

I felt distinctly uncomfortable. This was bringing it much too close, making it too personal. Sarasota was a *nice* town. So was Bradenton.

He was reading verse 6: " 'I marvel that ye are so soon removed from him that called you into the grace of Christ unto another gospel: which is not another; but there be some that trouble you, and would pervert the gospel of Christ.' What is the 'other gospel'? It is the gospel of legalism; it's the gospel that says you can have a part in your salvation. That is the Devil's gospel. The Devil's gospel is that *you* have something to do with being saved and keeping saved; *God's* gospel is that *He* reaches down and takes you out of the horrible pit, out of the miry clay, and sets your feet upon a Rock. The Devil's gospel then says, 'God is watching you. We have a set of rules a Christian has to follow. If you get too close to the edge, *off to hell with you!*' " With thumb and finger Dr. Barnhouse flicked imaginary sinners off the edge of the podium.

"My dear friends, that's not in the Bible. God calls that a *perversion* of the gospel of Christ."

Dr. Barnhouse then drew a small New Testament out of his inside breast pocket. "Let's let this Testament represent Christ, and this piece of paper, the new convert. When God saves a person He puts him *in* Christ." Dr. Barnhouse placed the paper in the Testament. "Colossians 3:3 tells us, 'Ye are dead [to sin], and your life is hid *with* Christ *in* God.' " He put the Testament, with the edges of the paper showing from within it, into his inside breast pocket again, and closed his coat over it. "Now, when can you get out of Christ? Not until Christ gets out of God, and that's not going to happen. That's grace—saving grace and keeping grace.

"Once we are in Christ, God wants to free us from man-made rules such as 'I don't dance, drink, smoke, go to the movies, or use cosmetics.' Instead, He wants us to live by the Holy Spirit's possessing us, guiding us as to how we live, what we read, what we watch on TV, what we eat or drink.

"Someone once asked me, 'Dr. Barnhouse, can a Christian be a real Christian and still drink a cocktail and smoke cigarettes?' Well, it all depends on who's running your life. If the Holy Spirit indwells you and is in charge of things, don't ask me, ask Him. When something like that comes up in my life I don't worry about it: I simply say, 'Holy Spirit, would You like a slug of liquor? A cancer tube?' "

Shocked silence broke into roars of laughter. Dr. Barnhouse stood there, left hand holding open his suit coat, right hand palm up, proffering to his heart an imaginary tray bearing an imaginary cocktail glass. His face was all wide-eyed innocence. "If He wants one, He can have it. Just be sure it is the Holy Spirit giving you your instructions."

He picked up his Bible. "You see, it isn't what you don't do, but what you *do* do that counts. The average person spends more time on makeup, shaving, TV, funny papers, and self in general than he does on his soul. When is the last time you sat down with this Book and read it, praying 'O God, I want to know Thee. Show me Thyself, and Thy will for my life'?"

Dr. Barnhouse continued preaching through the first chapter of Galatians, commenting at one point on Paul's Damascus Road experience, saying this was not the occasion when Paul was saved ("he was already a saved Jew under the Old Covenant") but that it was here that God "revealed His Son in Paul," who then shifted gears from the Old Testament into the New.

As Dr. Barnhouse spoke, I once again found myself caught up in his simple, illuminating logic and the excitement of watching parts of Scripture fit together—like a jigsaw puzzle you'd once given up on, but which you were suddenly, seemingly without effort, able to assemble. And not only the message, but the man himself was so compelling. When before had I encountered a Christian of such boldness and encyclopedic knowledge? Who else could speak so authoritatively and confidently not only to Christians, but to the world at large?

I was so enthralled that it was a shock when Dr. Barnhouse glanced at his watch and I glanced at mine and we saw that a whole hour had sped by. He looked frustrated.

"Oh, my, it's eleven o'clock, and I've barely gotten through my introduction. We'll take it up from here tomorrow. . . . And, our God and Father, go with us as we go. . . ."

I glanced at our minister, aware of a restlessness there. His face was very red. He was running his finger around his collar, and his brow looked damp. I was alarmed—was he ill? The prayer had ended; people were beginning to move out. I whispered to Doug that I thought we should get our preacher home. He took one look and agreed. As soon as we were out in the air, Doug said to him, "Is something wrong?" He answered in a strangled, furious voice, "He's teaching that damnable doctrine 'license to sin'!"

"That what?"

" 'License to sin.' Once saved, always saved, so you can do as you please!"

Doug and I looked at one another, appalled. To us, these teachings had given no hint of being able to "do as you please." The fact that Jesus Christ loved us with an everlasting love and that nothing we could do could ever take us out of that love had made us more determined than ever to search His Word for His will for our lives, and in His strength, to do that will. License to sin?

We drove the eleven miles back to Bradenton in silence. Our pastor was obviously troubled for us. We were troubled for him. Something very lovely between us had been broken, and we did not know what it was.

Monday night the auditorium was more than half full. Friends had brought friends; excitement crackled in the air. Once again, the meeting started right on the dot. There were no preliminaries: Dr. Barnhouse stepped to the edge of the platform, was handed some questions we had written out, and then walked back behind the podium.

At the Monday morning session he had announced, "Before each of my meetings we will have a question and answer period. I know you have questions: one group I was with was full of them. From now on you can write out your questions, but this morning we'll take them from the floor. Any questions?"

That morning we had stirred restlessly, all a little fearful that we might ask something foolish.

"Questions are like a bottle of olives," Barnhouse had said. "You get the first, and the rest come easily. Usually people have all kinds of questions about the Bible; usually they want to know where Cain got his wife or some such thing. So, how about it? Any questions?"

Still we remained silent. No one wanted to be first. Presently someone blurted out, "Well, where *did* Cain get his wife?" Dr. Barnhouse smiled and nodded. He had gotten his first olive.

He had answered by saying that Cain had undoubtedly married a sister or a niece. "Does that shock you?" he asked. "Don't forget that the human race was still physically pure in those days: sin had just begun its work of pollution. If you had to drink out of the Mississippi River, would you rather drink from it in Minnesota where it is a crystal-clear stream . . . or below New Orleans, where the sewage of a hundred cities is mingled with it? . . . don't forget, Adam married even closer than that—he married his own rib!"

The audience laughed, and more olives began to pop out of the bottle.

By Monday night there was a whole pile of written questions for which people were eagerly awaiting answers. Dr. Barnhouse answered them in the order they were stacked. He hadn't reviewed them beforehand, yet was able to respond to each of them without hesitation.

"First question," he said. " 'What's the difference between the Holy Ghost and the Holy Spirit?'

"William the Conqueror!" he replied quickly. He paused, delighting in the puzzlement that grew on people's faces. Then he explained: "In 1066 William the Conqueror crossed the English Channel from France and conquered England, bringing with him the French language, which, married to Anglo-Saxon, brought forth English. Now English is the only language in the world that has one word for meat on the table and another word for that same meat in the field. The Anglo-Saxon farmer raised a *cu* (cow) in the field, sold it to the French noblemen, who served it for dinner as *boeuf* (beef). In the fields it was *schaffen* (sheep), and on the table, *mouton* (mutton), and so on. When it came to the Bible, from the German, akin to the Anglo-Saxon, came *Heilige Geist* (Holy Ghost), but from the French came *Esprit* (Spirit). As with the words for "meat," these two words became used interchangeably with the one Greek word *pneuma* (breath or wind), from which we get 'pneumonia,' a disease of the breath-box, and 'pneumatic,' a tire with whoosh in it. The Holy Ghost and the Holy Spirit are one and the same, the third person of the Trinity.

"Next question: 'Dr. Barnhouse, don't you believe in religious freedom?'

"My answer is: Certainly! I believe in the right of every man to go to hell in his own way or to heaven in God's way.

"Just as you make the rules as to how a person is to enter your house, by the front door and not by the back window, so God has a right to say how people may come into His heaven. Jesus said, 'I am the door. Any one climbing up by any other way is a thief and a robber.' Jesus did not say, 'I am one of many equally good ways; I am a phase of truth; I am an aspect of life.' He said, 'I am *the* way, *the* truth, and *the* life: no man cometh unto the Father, but by me.' And if Jesus said, 'No man cometh to the Father but by Me,' then *no man cometh to the Father but by Him.*"

"Third question: 'How can you say the God of the Old Testament was a God of love? Look at the horrible things He ordered the Israelites to do to the Canaanites when they took the land, slaughtering everyone, even little innocent children.'

"To understand this you must understand who these people were. *This was the land of Canaan.* Who was Canaan? Go back to Genesis 9. Here we have the story of Noah, after the flood, who planted a vineyard and became drunk on the wine (and incidentally, this finished his witness; this is the last time we hear of him, although he lived 350 more years). Genesis 9 tells us his son, Ham, *the father of Canaan,* saw him exposed in his tent. Verses 24 and 25 say, 'And Noah awoke from his wine, and knew what his younger son *had done to him,* and he said, Cursed be *Canaan....*' Why didn't he say, 'Cursed be Ham'? I believe that Ham caught Canaan doing some sort of perverted sexual act. Turn to Genesis 10:15 and you find that the descendants of Canaan are the Phoenicians, the Hittites, the Jebusites, the Amorites, the Girgasites, the Hivites, the Arkites, the Sinites, the Arvadites, the Zemarites, and the Hamathites. (By the way, these are not Negro peoples. The black race is not under the curse of Canaan, as some have taught.) The Canaanites' worship involved all sorts of sexual perversion, so bad that Sodom and Gomorrah were destroyed by God Himself because of it. These people were demon-possessed and *had* to be wiped out in order to cleanse the land.

"You *must* balance 'God so loved the world' with 'God so hated sin.' More incomprehensible than God's killing wicked people because of their sin is His slaying of His own beloved, sinless Son in order to cleanse *us* from sin...."

For almost ten minutes he stood there, answering with

such sure knowledge I felt secure. When he said, "Thus saith the Lord," you believed it.

After the question and answer period, Dr. Barnhouse launched into his message for the evening, "Where Are the Dead?" Suddenly he was cutting and slashing with the Sword of the Lord. I was horrified. How *could* he? He attacked the Christian Scientists, the Jehovah's Witnesses, the Mormons, the Seventh-Day Adventists, lumping them all together as "cults" and calling what they believed about the hereafter "abominable lies." He waded into the Roman Catholic teaching about purgatory, saying it had been invented five hundred years after Christ's death and resurrection to bring under the power of the Roman Church the invading Huns and Visagoths: they were ancestor worshipers; "Grandpappy wasn't bad enough to go to hell, nor good enough to go to heaven, so they were told he was in an intermediate place and they could get him out for a price." He was sarcastic, almost cruel. I was so angry I was almost in tears. I felt betrayed. Where was the gentle reasonableness of *God's Methods for Holy Living?*

The same woman who before had been on the aisle seat ahead of us was there again, leaning forward with all the battle lust of a ringside spectator at a prizefight. This upset me even more. Where, in this kind of behavior, was Christ's love and compassion?

Doug had been looking puzzled, then thoughtful, and was now nodding in agreement. Apparently that first skirmish was merely leading into what *God* said about the dead, but I was hurting so much I blocked it out, until suddenly Dr. Barnhouse's voice tolled like a bell.

"And the sea gave up the dead—the dead—the dead who died in their sins, who were both physically and spiritually dead. The sea gave up the unsaved dead who were in it, and death and hell delivered up their unsaved dead, and they were judged every man *according to his works,* before the Great White Throne. Now there isn't one person who has perfectly lived up to his own standards, let alone God's, so *by his own standards* he is justly condemned, and sent to the lake of fire.

"But, oh, you don't have to have this judgment of God if you will only receive the grace of God. Receive His Son, the Lord Jesus, and with Him, everlasting life, dwelling forever in His love. Now is the accepted time; behold, now is the day of salvation.

"And our Father and our God, go with us as we go. . . ."

Oh, it is so awful, so awful, I thought. *What he says is so good, and at those times I want everyone in the world to hear him. But why does he have to ruin it by attacking people, the way he did at the beginning? What is it about that man Barnhouse that is at once so wonderful and so maddening?*

Afterward, over ice cream with our gang, I had to ask him, "Dr. Barnhouse, all those cruel things you said tonight at the beginning of your message. Was that necessary? I mean, I thought you were supposed to tell the truth in love!"

"So, you admit it was the truth?"

"I . . . don't know. I never heard it like that before."

"Well, think about it," he said. He turned to someone else, leaving me with his faint tone of condescension ringing in my ears. I felt the blood rush to my face. *That man Barnhouse.*

The following night Dr. Barnhouse explained "the new birth."

"You are an adult audience. You know the process by which you came into being. God uses these same terms to describe the *new* birth. In Ephesians 2:8 He says He has reached down and implanted in the heart the *ova* of saving faith. Then by means of another believer—you, a missionary, a preacher, a tract, the Bible—He sends the Word, which in the Greek of 1 Peter 1:23 He calls by the same name as is used for the male life sperm: "semen," seed. And the semen of the Word penetrates the *ova* of faith, and by this union a new life is born within you, the very life of God placed alongside your own old human nature. Just as you cannot become unborn physically you cannot become unborn spiritually. You have received God's life, and although it *is* possible to fall out of *fellowship* with the Father it is impossible to fall out of *relationship*...."

Afterward I ruminated on some of the fascinating facts I had learned that evening. If God had implanted the faith, and didn't depend on my drumming it up, and if God Himself had supplied the life-giving semen.... I looked up Ephesians 2:8 and 1 Peter 1:23. Saving faith was indeed God's free gift; the new birth was indeed by the seed of the Word.

Underneath my thinking, my subconscious was intruding something foreign that demanded attention. To get it out of the way, I dealt with it directly: *what had he said?* "... the *ova* of saving faith." Oh, no! Surely a man like Dr. Barnhouse would know *ova* was a neuter Latin noun: singular, *ovum,* egg; plural, *ova,* eggs. Yet I was sure *ova* was what he had said, pronouncing it very positively, with great clarity of diction, in an impersonal, scientific tone of voice that made acceptable what in those days delicacy forbade mentioning in the pulpit. Was it possible Dr. Barnhouse could be mistaken?

I talked it over with Doug. We played back the tape: "Ova" was indeed what he had said, not once, which could have been just a slip of the tongue, but twice. This was troubling. If Barnhouse could be wrong on this, he wasn't much of a scholar, and could be wrong on other things.

The next night, when the gang had gathered for the usual after-meeting, I tried to get Doug to mention the problem, but he couldn't bring himself to do it. ("Marge, I'm afraid it's just nit-picking.") Dr. Barnhouse heard us whispering, turned the spotlight of his intense blue eyes full on me, and said, "Got a question, Marge?"

Torn between embarrassment and really wanting to know, I said, "Well, last night you referred to the *ova* of faith. . . ." I left it dangling, hoping fervently he'd correct me.

Instead, he said, "And?"

I continued, miserably, "But, Dr. Barnhouse, you should have said '*ovum.*' '*Ova*' is plural."

Instantly he put back his head and closed his eyes. For a fraction of a second you could almost hear the wheels turning. Then he looked at me again and said, charmingly, "Of course! Of course! Thank you for correcting me," and he smiled reassuringly.

A great gratitude welled up within me. Here was a man who could make a mistake, admit it, and thank you for showing him up! It was impossible to feel triumphant, as I used to do when I got the better of any man. I looked at Doug, who was grinning, and realized that Dr. Barnhouse by his attitude had bested me. *And I was grateful!*

I was beginning to see how the Holy Spirit worked to bind believers together.

FOUR

His voice could thunder, then whisper, then thunder again; while his audience was convulsed with laughter, he'd bring them up short, exposed and shamefaced. Once, when the Word had struck especially hard, he stopped, then said:

"Now I did not write it, dear friends—*I did not write it. This is God speaking,* and if you don't like it, don't hit me: take it up with the Author. All I am is the messenger boy. Suppose you are a boy applying for a job with Western Union Telegraph Company. Do you go to the boss and say, 'I want a job as a telegram deliverer, but I am allergic to grief, so I want to deliver only those messages that say "Happy Birthday" or "Congratulations" or "Will you honor us by...."'? No, you take the message as it is, then deliver it into the hands of the person for whom it is intended. You do not toss it at the door and if it lands in the bushes ignore it and walk away. Nor, if you receive a telegram that says, 'We regret to inform you...,' do you hit the messenger boy.

"This is God's message to you. Only you know what it is saying *to you,* and quite conceivably it is speaking a different message to each of you, although the words are the same. If it makes you angry, *ask yourself why.*"

His radio sermons, read from a script, were superb, but that interplay between speaker and audience, the timing, the reaction, those beautiful, strong hands creating in the air an almost living, visible scene—these had to be experienced to know his full genius. I found myself both hating him and loving him: I hated him for stirring up the still waters of my placid existence and bringing to the surface all the crawly things I hadn't known were lurking down there. I loved him for the outflow of the Holy Spirit through him, binding up, healing where he had wounded so deeply, strengthening, catching me up in an excitement of potential for the Lord that I hadn't dreamed possible. I knew that, for Doug and me, our lives would never again be the same.

Friday afternoon, after I had finished hanging up the wet clothes I had forgotten to take out of the washer the day before, I sat down for a minute to gather my thoughts before it was time to go pick up Carolyn.

Morning after morning we had gone deeply into Galatians; night after night we were challenged and exhorted and torn down, then comforted. By the end of the week my mind was whirling, from so much teaching all at once. Things Dr. Barnhouse had said kept surfacing, to be sorted out and looked at once more, thought about, digested. From notes I had taken while he was speaking I extracted some here, and some there, and wrote down what he had said:

1. In Romans 1:16 Paul declares, "I am not ashamed of the gospel of Christ; for it is the power of God unto salvation to every one that believeth," and that word "power" is from the Greek word dunamis, from which we get "dynamo" and "dynamite." The dynamite of God! If you have a shack sitting on the place where you want to build a skyscraper you must first tear down the shack, then put down foundations that reach the rock underneath, before you can build your skyscraper. If you have built the shack yourself, you are going to resist having it torn down, but believe me, my dear friends, it is necessary. That's what I'm here for: to dynamite the old, self-made shack, then to lay foundations if you have none, or to help you build on good foundations laid by someone else.

(The dynamite had certainly been demolishing my shack!)

2. James 4:7 tells us, "Submit yourselves therefore to God. Resist the devil, and he will flee from you." That's a promise. But don't try the resisting before you've done the submitting!"

3. Some of you have just enough Christianity to be miserable in a nightclub, and not enough to be happy in a prayer meeting.

(After this one I had put three exclamation points!)

4. Too many of you say, "Man is in God's image, therefore God is just like me," so you either worship yourself, or you have a little God in man's *image who is powerless.*

5. God has promised to supply all your need—*not all your* greed.

6. Men are not sinners because they sin: they sin because they are sinners.

And more, and more. I stopped writing. How could I take it all in? I felt as if I were getting spiritual indigestion.

The telephone shrilled. It was Carolyn: "Mother! I thought you were going to pick me up!"

I gathered up my notes and rushed to the car. That man Barnhouse! He certainly was disrupting my household routine.

The following week he was preaching in Tampa, an hour north of us. Eager to learn more, we all trooped up every morning, getting back before the children were home from school; we left them with their homework and returned each evening to Tampa.

The morning series was on the Book of Hebrews. Dr. Barnhouse started each session by having us recite aloud:

The Epistle to the Hebrews
Was written to the Hebrews
In order to show the Hebrews
They had to stop being Hebrews.

It was a catchy little memory peg, but of course he did not mean it literally. He was showing us that God was finished with the Old Covenant. Jesus was the fulfillment of all the promises and prophecies there, so it was complete. God now wanted the Jews to move on into the New Covenant, the New Testament.

"Instead of a lamb, *the* Lamb of God, Christ!" he cried. "Instead of the altar, Christ! Instead of the laver, Christ! Instead of the shewbread, Christ! Instead of the mercy seat, Christ, through the 'veil' of His wounded side, by the pure and precious blood He shed on the cross for us!"

Shock after shock demolished my old, ignorant notions.

" . . . You will not be an angel when you get to heaven." (Shock!) "Hebrews 1:14 tells us that the angels are the domestic servants of heaven, 'sent forth to minister for them who shall be heirs of salvation.' No longer will you be 'a little lower than the angels,' as Psalm 8:5 says we were created; you will be the royal Bride, right there next to Jesus Himself."

" . . . Who are God's chosen people today? Not the Jews. . . ." (Shock!) "The Jews *were* God's chosen people, but 'chosen' for what? Not to be God's little pets, but to be a holy nation through whom the Messiah-Redeemer would come. I believe the Jews will again be God's chosen people during the Great Tribulation to carry the message of redemption to every kindred, tribe, and nation, and as God's earthly rulers during the millennium. But today God's chosen people is the Church, all true believers everywhere, Jew and Gentile alike, all 'one *in* Christ Jesus,' chosen to carry the message of redemption and grace to all the world. Are we doing this?"

Most of the evening messages were about Satan: who he is; what he is trying to do. Dr. Barnhouse took us to Ezekiel 28:11-14, showing that God had created a mighty angel, Lucifer, of the order of cherubim, the wisest and most beautiful of all His creatures, to rule the universe for Him as prophet, priest, and king. As prophet he spoke for God to the universe; as priest he took the worship of the angelic hosts to God; as king he ruled over the universe for God from a magnificent palace on the earth.

"He was perfect in all his ways from the day that he was created until 'iniquity was found' in him. Lucifer must have said to himself, 'I'm so wise, I'm so beautiful, I should get a little credit for myself instead of giving it all to God'—and sin arose by a sort of spontaneous combustion in the heart of Lucifer, through pride.

"And that's the beginning of sin. Until that moment there was only one will in the universe, God's good and perfect and holy will, with the universe in harmony with it. Now there were two wills. Lucifer, created a free moral agent, chose to rebel. He declared (Isaiah 14:14), 'I will be like the most High.'

"Why didn't he say, 'I will be like the Redeemer'? Oh no, that's not what he wanted. Why not 'the Holy One of Israel'? Take a good concordance and look up 'the most high God.' You will find this name first used when Abraham was blessed by Melchizedek who was the priest of 'the most high God, *possessor of heaven and earth.*'

" 'That's it!' said Lucifer. 'That's what I want to be: possessor of heaven and earth!' This was no small rebellion. Lucifer was determined to take over the very throne of God. Well, God allowed him to establish a bridgehead in the lower heavens, but he stripped him of his priestly and prophetic offices, and Lucifer became Satan, the Enemy, forever pitting his will against God's, but able to do only what God allows him to do, as we see in the Book of Job. Apparently he had persuaded a large number of the heavenly host to rebel with him. These are the 'angels that kept not their first estate,' and possibly the demons.

"At this point I believe God challenged Satan.

"Isaiah 45:18 tells us the earth was not created the way we find it in verse 2 of Genesis 1. Now if God did not create the world the way we find it in Genesis, how did it get that way? I believe God said to Satan, 'Oh, so you want to be God. Well, here's a little problem to start with,' and He reached down and scrambled the earth that He had created perfect, long eons before, to be Lucifer's headquarters before he became Satan—and the earth became without form and void, a wreck and a ruin. Imagine Satan's frustration as he tried to put it in order. This could have gone on for long ages. Then, comparatively recently, God said to Satan, 'You've had your chance. Now I'll do it.' All had to do was speak, and order came out of chaos as He reformed and refashioned the earth.

"Then God created the man and the woman, to 'have dominion over the fish of the sea, the fowl of the air, and all living creatures of the earth.' Imagine how Satan must have laughed, 'Do you mean to tell me that that weak thing, *that* is going to take my place?' And he schemed to get them to rebel against God. He deceived the woman, *but Adam was not deceived.* How do we know? First Timothy 2:14 tells us so. Adam knew exactly what he was doing, acting contrary to God's expressed will, but he did it anyway, and sin arose spontaneously within him as it had with Lucifer, and became a part of the human race. The Bible never blames the woman for the Fall: 'In Adam all die'; 'By one man sin entered into the world.'

"Never fool yourself that 'the Devil made me do it.' The Devil can only tempt you to do it. *The choice is yours.* And with most of you *he* doesn't have to work to get you away from God: your own old Adamic nature does the job very well, turning you from God to self.

"If the Devil owned one town completely, ruling everyone from the mayor to the street sweeper, what do you think it would be like? 'Oh,' you say, 'full of gangsters, drunkenness, and depravity of the worst sort.' *Wrong!"* (More shock!) "Satan is not trying to make good men bad and bad men worse. He is trying to make men *good without Christ.* Satan's town would be neat and clean; on Sunday everybody in it would go to a church that denies that Jesus is God the Son. They'd be kind and good and neighborly.

"Satan doesn't run around in long red underwear, with horns, hooves, and a tail. If by such a caricature he can deceive you into thinking he doesn't exist, he can do whatever he wants with you by putting ideas into your mind. Never forget, Satan disguises himself as an angel of light, as we read in 2 Corinthians 11:14. And verse 15 says, 'When you look for the Devil, don't forget to look in the pulpit!' I'll admit that's my translation. The King James says, 'Therefore it is no great thing if his ministers also be transformed as ministers of righteousness. . . .'

"Now, my friends, it is imperative that you realize there is an invisible war going on between God and Satan, and we are called to be soldiers in that war."

Aha! I thought. *The pieces are beginning to fall into place. An invisible war between God and Satan! I've known we were "soldiers of the cross"; I've sung "Onward, Christian Soldiers" almost all my life. But until now I never really thought how real the enemy was. Paradise Lost has always seemed merely fiction.*

At that moment the first faint rumbling of that war came into my consciousness—distant thunder that posed no immediate threat. I had no idea how deeply involved in this invisible war I was destined to become.

Dr. Barnhouse continued: "The Bible calls Satan 'the god of this world,' the god this world worships when it worships anything or anyone other than the God and Father of our Lord Jesus Christ. He is very powerful, but not *all-*powerful: *God* says how far Satan can and can't go. He does manipulate the people on this earth and the beings in the lower heavens who rebelled with him, *when he can,* but he has nothing to do with the running of hell. Oh, get out of your minds Dante's *Inferno,* Goethe's *Faust,* and Milton's *Paradise Lost*—magnificent poetry, devilish theology. Hell was created as a prison for the Devil and his angels, and had to be enlarged to accommodate those rebellious humans who will not come unto the Father by Jesus, and they'll have to stumble over the cross on their way there. There aren't any little imps in hell running around poking people with pitchforks. The Devil has never yet been in hell, has nothing to do with the running of hell, and when he does finally get there he'll be the chief prisoner. The terrible thing about hell is that *God runs it.*

"GOD RUNS HELL!"

I froze in awful comprehension. *Oh, my Jesus! What You have rescued me from! I didn't know—I took You for granted— Oh, my Father, thank You for grace instead of justice!*

On Friday night at our gang's last get-together, Doug said, "Dr. Barnhouse, you'll never know what you've done for me. I sure wish I could have had even one more week of this teaching. . . ."

Dr. Barnhouse said, "Well, why not come along with me for a week or two? I'm traveling alone. There's plenty of room. Can't you arrange your affairs so you can come?"

Doug's eyes lit up. He looked at me questioningly, knowing I might object to his being away.

"Why not?" I said.

"You wouldn't mind?"

"Of course I'll mind. I'll be jealous sick. But I'll manage."

"Well, I don't need to—"

"Don't be silly. Go. You've got to. It's a great opportunity."

Doug turned to the others. "What do you say, gang?"

"Go!" they all said. Someone else went on, "Don't miss it, you lucky bum. What a chance!"

Doug, representing a New York brokerage house, sold municipal bonds to banks along the Florida west coast. He had just made the rounds, visiting his customers as he did once a month; the New York office agreed he could keep in touch by telephone as easily from Alabama or Texas as from Bradenton. He decided to go. We all saw him off at the airport Tuesday, most of us green with envy.

Doug phoned me a couple of nights later with a detailed report of the speaking tour. "Marge, you've just got to hear this preaching!" Doug said that night. "Can't you farm the kids out somewhere and join us?"

"Well," I said, barely containing my excitement, "you'll never believe this, but your parents just arrived this afternoon from Norfolk! If they're willing to take over for me, I'd love it. But how about Dr. Barnhouse?"

"He's right here. He says it's fine. I'll let you speak to him."

The now familiar voice boomed over the wire. "Hello, Marge."

"Dr. Barnhouse, are you sure this is all right?"

"Well, if you can manage with no more than one small suitcase and don't mind riding three in front, fine. The back seat of the car is loaded with boxes of my books that were shipped to me here. Think you can do it?"

"Oh, yes!" Doug's parents urged me to go. It was agreed that I would join Doug and Dr. Barnhouse in Ft. Smith, Arkansas, where Dr. Barnhouse was having his next meetings.

It was night in Ft. Smith when I stepped out of the plane onto the platform at the top of the deplaning stairs. I was greeted with a large snowball that splattered all over me. Startled, I looked down and saw Doug and Dr. Barnhouse at the foot of the stairs, both grinning broadly. An expanse of snow lay everywhere; but Doug had said to bring just the sort of thing I had been wearing in Bradenton! Doug was such a tease: the snowball was the sort of greeting that would delight him. But I hadn't expected Dr. Barnhouse to be grinning approval. What had I gotten myself into?

Hesitantly I descended the stairs, expecting another

snowball. Doug gave me an exuberant hug, Dr. Barnhouse picked up my bag, and they both hustled me off to the car. Barely had we squeezed into the car when Doug enthused, "Marge, I can hardly wait for you to hear the sermon on Christian marriage that Dr. Barnhouse preached!" He then filled me in on all that had been happening.

I glanced at Dr. Barnhouse. While driving, he was listening and practically purring, like a lion proud of his cub.

And thus began a trip that was to last five more weeks and change our lives.

FIVE

By Sunday morning the snow of the day before had disappeared under a warm sun, and my Florida topcoat was indeed adequate. As we emerged from the hotel Dr. Barnhouse was beaming.

" 'This is the day which the *Lord* hath made; we will rejoice and be glad in it,' " he declaimed. "You know, I carry good weather with me. It is as if the Lord had inverted a protective bowl full of sunshine over me wherever I go. It's remarkable."

Dr. Barnhouse's sermon in the First Baptist Church was the same one he had given in Sarasota that first Sunday. Hearing it again I realized how much of it I had missed the first time.

The pastor's wife graciously included us in their invitation to dinner at the manse. Afterward Dr. Barnhouse said, "Now you two run along. I have work I *have* to do. Go on about your business—I'll see you tonight."

Now really! What did he have to do? We were used to evangelists who came with a set of sermons all prepared and were free to socialize. What in the world was there to do?

As we went to our hotel room Doug said enthusiastically, "This would be a great time for you to hear that tape on Christian marriage!"

"Doug!" I begged, "not now! It can wait. I've just got to have a nap. Fatigue has finally caught up with me. . . ."

He looked disappointed as I flopped on the bed and almost instantly fell asleep. When I awoke he was deep in Bible study, making notes and unaware of my gaze. Watching him, I thought, *What a difference the Lord has made in him.* . . .

The outward Doug was still the same. When I first met him he had had a wealth of dark brown curly hair that by now had thinned on top and was beginning to gray at the temples. His eyes—deep, deep brown fringed with thick, straight lashes—could be soft as brown velvet and the next instant flash with anger, an anger that would shoot off like a skyrocket, explode, then fall back to normal—but leave me shattered. When necessary he could be dignified and solemn, drawing himself up to his almost six-foot height and looking as important as the occasion demanded, but normally his was a debonaire, easy manner with everyone from the school janitor to the governor of the state. His flashing smile was irresistible. His Virginia accent was charming. He could insult people and make them like it. In the old days his ready wit would have us doubled up with laughter; yet there was often a hilariously funny barb that left somebody wounded. As the Holy Spirit began to work more deeply within him he recognized this trait as a sort of ego-booster, no longer needed, and began trying to replace it with genuine love. He was still an inveterate tease, but now I could see something else in him, something new, a considerateness that hadn't been there before.

Over supper, I mentioned something in the morning sermon. Doug said, "Explain just what you mean, Sugar," so I launched into my thoughts and theories. Dr. Barnhouse said, "How do you figure that?" Missing the look that went between them, I plunged on, thrilled to have their rapt attention—so I thought. Finally, I paused. Doug, elbow propped on the table and chin resting on his hand, looked straight at me as if absorbed in my exposition. But the corners of his mouth were twitching with amusement, and suddenly I was aware I was being baited.

Aghast, I looked at Dr. Barnhouse: deep masculine dimples appeared and vanished as he tried to suppress his laughter. Those rascals had been leading me into a discussion where I was in way over my head and trying to fake it. I had expected an uplifting atmosphere, yet here they were, aiding and abetting one another as my brothers used to do. I looked from one to the other, realized the trap I was in, and decided, "If you can't lick 'em, join 'em."

"You win! You win!" I said, laughing.

They both exploded into uproarious laughter. Doug patted my hand appreciatively. "You're OK, Sugar!" he said, and went into another paroxysm of laughter, in which I joined wholeheartedly.

From then on there was an easy camaraderie between us. I found myself being able to say, "I don't know," without feeling embarrassed to admit it.

On the way to the church Doug said to Dr. Barnhouse, "I've been into the Bible all afternoon, putting together some lessons for my class. I can see how the Old Testament foreshadows the New; I can see God laying the groundwork of His 'eternal principles,' as you call them, all through the Old Testament, but what possible use is there in the 'begats'? Who cares who begat whom?"

"I'll preach on that tomorrow night," said our mentor. "You'll see."

Monday night the pages of our Bibles rustled as Dr. Barnhouse said, "Tonight I want you to turn with me to the little Book of Jude, verse 14."

The New Testament! But the begats were in the Old Testament! Doug looked at me, disappointed, then snapped to full attention as Dr. Barnhouse read: " 'And Enoch, also, the seventh from Adam, prophesied . . . to convince all that are ungodly among them of all their ungodly deeds which they have ungodly committed, and of all their hard speeches which ungodly sinners have spoken against him.'

"Who is this Enoch? To find out, go back to the Old Testament, to the Book of Genesis, to Adam.

"Genesis 4:1: 'And Adam knew Eve his wife; and she conceived, and bare Cain.' (And she didn't know she was holding in her arms a little murderer.) Verse 17: 'And Cain knew his wife; and she conceived, and bare Enoch.' *Enoch!* But Jude speaks of 'Enoch the *seventh* from Adam,' and this is only the *third* generation: Adam, Cain, and Enoch! 'That's right,' says God. 'Don't let My Enoch get mixed up with the Devil's Enoch. This is the Devil's Enoch.'

"Now, verse 25: 'And Adam knew his wife again; and she bore a son, and called his name Seth.' Verse 26: 'And to Seth, to him also there was born a son; and he called his name Enos: then began men to call upon the name of the Lord.' So we have here the beginning of the godly line.

"Now we go to chapter 5, which traces 'the generations of Adam' through this godly line. It starts by saying that when God created man, He created him in His own image. Verse 3: 'And Adam... begat a son in his own likeness, after his image; and called his name Seth.'

"Why doesn't it say Adam's son was in the image of God, if Adam was created in the image of God? Because Adam was no longer in the image of God. After the Fall, Adam was in the *broken* image of God, and Adam's sons and his sons' sons and all of his progeny down to you and me are in the image of *Adam,,* not in the image of God. Romans 8:29 tells us that what God is doing today is re-forming and refashioning His image in us who have believed.

"All right. Adam is one. And if we count down from Adam, through Seth, we find the Enoch who is the *seventh* from Adam. Verse 18: 'And Jared... begat Enoch.' 'That's *My* Enoch!' says God.

"Do you see how important the so-called 'begats' are?"

Doug let out a long, low "Phewww," and, raising his

eyebrows, looked at me out of the corner of his eye. I grinned.

Dr. Barnhouse continued. "Now there's no word in the Book of Genesis about Enoch doing any preaching. But those two verses in Jude tell us, 'Enoch, the seventh from Adam, prophesied,' and Enoch's sermon follows. In these few lines in Jude 14 and 15 you can see what kind of a preacher he was.

"Now turn to Hebrews 11:5 where God the Holy Spirit has recorded this about Enoch: 'By faith Enoch was translated that he should not see death; and was not found, because God had translated him [or, 'God took him']; for before his translation he had this testimony, that he pleased God.' Why did he please God? Because he was willing to stand up and say that most of the Hollywood starlets are *harlots*—" (Doug and I sat up straight, eyes wide with shock.) "—and that the selling of automobiles by the exhibiting of half-naked women beside them is a sin for which God will *rot* America. And to say to people that this is *ungodliness* in the things we do and the way we live, tossing God a tip of our time and money in passing. America spends twice as much on its complexion as it does on its soul. *Ungodly.*

"Of course Enoch did not face quite that type of thing, but let's find out what *was* happening at the time Enoch walked with God and preached about ungodliness. He was talking about his cousin."

Dr. Barnhouse took us back to Genesis 4 and showed us that this cousin, the seventh from Adam in the line of Cain, was Lamech.

"What was this cousin like? The Bible says that Lamech took two wives. Here's the beginning of all the flaunting of sex. We know from Malachi and other Scriptures that God says a man should have one wife. But Lamech took two wives, and their names were Adah and Zillah. 'Adah' means 'beauty,' and 'Zillah' means 'adornment.' So the emphasis is now upon a feminine civilization. To these are born sons who introduce music and art and sculpture and culture, and a high level of civilization, but all centered on man. And over there on the corner is Enoch, holding a street meeting and crying, 'Ungodly!'

"Now don't misunderstand: in themselves art and music are good. If God has given you this gift, use it, for the honor and glory of God—but be sure you don't put it *in place of* God. We have many thousands of people in these United States who have art and music and culture but leave Christ out. This is the thing that God curses: that men should take His gifts and reject His Son.

"Now back to Genesis 5:24: 'Enoch walked with God: and he was not; for God took him.' In the New Testament we find what this means. Hebrews says, 'Enoch was translated that he should not see death; and he was not found, because God had translated him. . . .' I'll bet there was a big search. But Enoch walked with God, and one night they walked, and they walked, and they walked, and finally God said, 'Enoch, you're tired. You don't have to go all that way back. Come home with Me.' And He took him bodily to heaven.

"What did they talk about as they walked? They talked about his cousins. The New Testament says, 'Before his translation he had this testimony, that he pleased God.' The Lord was pleased that Enoch said, 'Ungodly.' The Lord was pleased that Enoch called sin by its right name. The Lord was pleased that Enoch did not compromise. He probably didn't get an invitation to the unveiling of Tubal-Cain's statue or to hear the first presentation of Jubal's Symphony in F. 'Oh,' said someone, 'I saw the most disgusting scene as I was coming to the theatre: old Enoch was on a soapbox at the corner, crying, "Ungodly! Ungodly!" ' 'Yes, my dear, there are people like that in the world: fanatics.'

" '*But he had this testimony, that he pleased God.*'

"Earlier, God had said to Enoch, 'I'm going to destroy this civilization. Call that little baby your wife is expecting

"Methuselah," which means, "When he is gone, it will come." ' "

The sermon went on, dramatically describing how Methuselah was born, grew up, and had a grandson named Noah, who built an ark and proclaimed the coming of a flood. Then the passage of 120 more years with Methuselah still living, longer than anyone else had ever lived. " 'Oh,' says God, 'will they repent?' "

"Then at age 969, Methuselah died. The ark was completed, and when Noah and his family and all the animals were safe inside, it started to rain. And all of the murderous, lustful, feminine, idolatrous, artistic civilization of Lamech went down before the flooding rush of the judgment of God, as God will one day destroy the American Way of Life—not by a flood, but by fire. Utterly, absolutely, completely. Unless we repent, 'But he that doeth the will of God abideth forever.' "

The closing prayer was a heart cry for repentance. We were tremendously moved.

Afterward Doug said, "Dr. Barnhouse, you sure hit between the eyes tonight. After this you can never say you don't preach against worldly behavior!"

"Doug, I *must* preach against what God says He will judge us for. I *must* preach against immoral behavior. And all this emphasis on sexual lust is immoral. As to the 'I don't dance, drink, smoke, go to the movies, or use cosmetics' routine: the *motivation* is what's important—*why* you do or don't do these things and whether or not the Holy Spirit is running your life—not the behavior in itself. That's why I don't preach against those things. But the Holy Spirit is the *Holy* Spirit. Just as He cannot condone the blatant sexuality coming out of Hollywood, He cannot tolerate the subtle iniquity of ordinary people who think themselves good and decent, but who are caught up in the American lifestyle. These, who are self-centered and who deny God, I must expose for what they are."

One night over ice cream, Doug asked, "How do you have time to dig out all this stuff? Don't your people take a lot of your time? Our pastor is run ragged all the time."

"When I first took the pastorate at Tenth Presbyterian Church," Dr. Barnhouse replied, "I told my people they would get *one* pastoral call. After that, if they saw me coming to their door they could be sure either the sheriff or the undertaker was right behind me. I have an assistant pastor, who is a real *pastor*. He and the deacons take care of the needs of the congregation. I am a Bible teacher. I could not do the kind of research I must do if I had full pastoral duties. My congregation knows this and is willing to give me this freedom. I live in a eighteenth-century farmhouse just outside of Doylestown, an hour north of Philadelphia, where I have an excellent research library. I do most of my work there. People *can't* just 'drop in' to see me: they must have an appointment."

As we learned more and more about both the ministry of Dr. Barnhouse's church and the Evangelical Foundation, I wondered if there might not be some conflict between the two. He had told us that the Evangelical Foundation was started originally as a vehicle for the Bible Study Hour, although the charter was broad enough to carry anything. It now included Dr. Barnhouse's wider ministry: Portable Church Services, the conference ministry, the projected film ministry, and of course *Eternity* magazine. Originally its base of operations was Tenth Presbyterian Church. They used the church offices and Sunday school rooms to get out the magazine, and the basement of the church for the recording studio.

"Every week everything had to be shoved out of the way so Sunday school could be held Sunday morning," he told us. "Then Monday it all had to be dragged out again. I was editor, author, voice, the works, with Paul Hopkins as recording engineer and business manager, and a couple of secretaries as assistants, and I was going in all directions at once. Then a member of my church, a man I had led to

Christ, said, 'Look, Dr. Barnhouse, this is too big for the church,' and—how the Lord provides!—he bought one of the brownstone mansions four doors from the church to be used as our headquarters.

"My original board consisted of Cliff Harrington, of the Philadelphia School of the Bible, Bob Grasberger, a Philadelphia lawyer, and me. Since then Winfield Scott, the real estate man who gave us the building, and Bill Thorn, another attorney, have been added.

"Paul Hopkins is business manager. He's a wonderful fellow, utterly dedicated to the Lord. You'd like him. He was a young executive at Sun Oil, on his way up, but chose to throw in his lot with us and work for the Lord, with no guaranteed future except in heaven. When we moved over to 1716 Spruce Street we added others in various secretarial and gal Friday capacities. Recently, Ralph Keiper, a Baptist minister who teaches at the Philadelphia School of the Bible, has joined us as a contributing editor and researcher. He's a little fellow, almost blind, with a wonderful personality and a keen mind, and he really loves the Lord. Dr. Mary Bennett, who helped me get *Eternity* started, is managing editor; our circulation manager is Lucille Martin. There are others who come part time as the need arises, and every one of them clear down to the man who does the janitorial work is a born-again Christian totally dedicated to the work.

"Why on earth did you call it a foundation?" Doug asked. "No capital, no financial backing—"

"I know. I'm beginning to realize it was a mistake. Originally it was meant to convey the idea that the world's 'foundations' are repositories of great wealth to be distributed, but that *our* 'Foundation' is the Lord Jesus and *we* are distributing 'the unsearchable riches of Christ.' Someone even suggested it should be called 'How Firma'!"

"Oh, no!"

"Not seriously, of course. But it *is* a handicap to be misunderstood, because if thousands of people did not send in each week their two or three or more dollars, we'd fold tomorrow. We run that close to the ragged edge. If any of the Bible Study Hour programs on any of our coast-to-coast stations doesn't pay for itself within a year, we give it up and try another. I firmly believe we *must* reach out, and if the Lord wants us there He'll make the money come in; if He has other plans, the money doesn't come and we withdraw. It is a glorious experience to give yourself to Him completely and let Him lead. It's how I have lived all my life. When I was a young man living in France, my wife and I would plan what we could spend, and if there was a sudden emergency we calmly went ahead as if everything was normal, depending on the Lord to supply our need. He never failed to do so, though very frequently at the last possible minute! It's an exciting way to live."

Doug kept probing. "But how does your church function, with you away so much of the time?"

"Doug, it's a funny thing. I offered to resign several years ago, because I felt they needed a full-time pastor, not an itinerant preacher with others filling his pulpit during his absence, and I felt God had called me to my conference ministry. But they wouldn't hear of it. So when I'm away I see to it that some of today's greatest preachers fill my pulpit, and my people are really *fed*.

"I live and work at the Farm, and just go in on Sundays to preach, and during the week to keep appointments and record the radio messages. At the Foundation, we have a fantastic engineer who has the highest standards of broadcast quality, Don Wetzell. He records me and takes out the 'fluffs' and smooths the whole thing out. So I try to tape as many programs as I can with him, rather than in studios in other cities.

"My own secretary, Naomi Veit, lives at the Farm. Now *there's* a twenty-four-hour Christian. Talk about your gal Friday! Someone asked her how she put up with Dr. Barnhouse, and she retorted that she wasn't working for Dr. Barnhouse, she was working for the Lord, and *He* had given her this work to do, so, of course, she is doing it as unto Him! Why, one Saturday night I arrived in Harrisburg at midnight to preach Sunday morning and discovered I had only the brown brogues I was wearing. My good black shoes had been left at the Farm; where could I borrow any big enough? Do you know, that girl drove all night so I'd have those shoes to wear into the pulpit Sunday morning. She pays the household bills and keeps my books straight; she sees that the house is kept in repair and that the house-keeper functions as she should; on Sunday mornings she has the car packed with whatever I'll need in town that day (because I frequently tape my messages then), and it's filled with gasoline and waiting at the door for me so all I need do is step into it. What a capable woman!"

Doug said, "She sure sounds like a prize. Marge, when we get home I'll expect you to start doing that for *me!*" I made a face at him.

Dr. Barnhouse laughed, then continued, "The Lord has surrounded me with a lot of terrific people to support me in my work, which is certainly branching out. For instance, these movies I'm making are really pilot films. What I really want to do is have a television program. *That* is the coming thing, mark my words. There will be refinements that will bring down the cost, and everyone who now has a radio will have a television set in his parlor. The garbage that people will be looking at *must* be offset with God's Word, presented in inescapable clarity. There are all sorts of ways to go about it, with good taste and dignity and yet with lively interest.

"My Portable Church Services have proved this— through them many people who haven't been exposed to the cultural things of life are introduced to really fine preaching and the great hymns and the finest of organ and instrumental music."

I thought of the night in Sarasota when Dr. Barnhouse had told his audience about these Portable Church Services. In an era when most recording was still being done on phonograph records, he had been experimenting with tape recordings: first on wire tape, and then with a plastic tape. He had produced a tape recorded framework for a church service built around a rousing sermon written by the illustrious preachers of the past: Luther, Wesley, Spurgeon, and others. The tape was wound on a seven-inch reel, and played reel-to-reel on a portable machine not much larger than a portable phonograph. (How ponderous those machines seem, now that cassette recorders have been invented! But at the time we thought they were wonderful.)

There was a printed order of service, and the audience participated just as in a regular church service. Hospitals were using it, and prisons, and scattered small churches without a regular pastor, wherever there was a 110-volt circuit to plug into and a devoted layman to get the people, few or many, together.

This unique brainchild of Dr. Barnhouse's had been written up in *Time* magazine. Doug had been intrigued with the idea. What a wonderful tool for his men's group! He thought of migrant workers, of isolated forestry stations, of ships at sea. Where people couldn't get to church, he could get the church to them!

Now Doug was leaning forward eagerly as Dr. Barnhouse continued with his ideas on using the newer medium of television to spread the gospel: "It's a matter of exposure and absorption. The world is geared to feed the flesh; I am called to feed the soul and spirit and help strengthen and train these so the Enemy can be flouted. First John 2:16 speaks of 'the lust of the flesh, and the lust of the eyes, and the pride of life,' and the whole entertainment world is calculated to feed these. Psalm 34:8 says, 'O taste and see that the Lord is good.'

"If only I could give them a really good taste, who knows how many who otherwise wouldn't get even a taste will start hungering and thirsting after righteousness?"

I watched Doug's face as he listened. I could sense his imagination being caught up in Dr. Barnhouse's vision for the work.

Then, impulsively, Dr. Barnhouse asked, "Doug, would you consider coming on the board of the Foundation?"

The question took Doug completely by surprise.

"We certainly could use you."

I could tell by the sparkle in Doug's eyes how much he would love to say yes, but his natural practicality prevailed. "I'll need some time to think about it. And pray about it."

What an exciting proposition! It seemed that Doug and I were being drawn deeper and deeper into the life and work of Donald Grey Barnhouse.

Tuesday morning we stepped out of the hotel into pouring rain. I retreated to the shelter of the portico.

"Oh, Dr. Barnhouse!" I mourned, "what happened to your protecting bowl of fair weather?"

"*This* is the day that the Lord hath made," he said, sternly. "We *will* rejoice and be glad in it!"

After the Bible study that morning we took Dr. Barnhouse to lunch. I was looking forward to it. Doug and I felt free to discuss anything with this man, not knowing that he was held somewhat in awe in evangelical circles and that few people would have dared to disagree with him to his face. In retrospect, I am aghast at some of the areas in which I challenged him, but I am glad I did. The friends he valued most were the ones who had the courage to stand up to him.

During our conversation at lunch, I brought up something that had really bothered Doug and me: in the pulpit he would often drop big names or mention some sort of special social privilege that he had had. This somehow seemed a lack of Christian humility, and it also cluttered his messages.

So I plunged in: "Dr. Barnhouse, wouldn't that illustration about the Panama Canal be better if you got right to the point and left out all that about the high Army official who made it possible for you to be right there on the bridge with the Captain?"

He looked astonished. "But a story lives by its details!"

"It dies by them, too," I said grimly. "You lost me completely when I first heard it. I was fascinated by the story, but had lost the thread of the sermon itself by the time you got to the point. And do those big names really matter?"

He turned this over in his mind for a moment, then said firmly, "A story *lives* by its details," so I dropped it, discouraged.

To my surprise he used that illustration that very night. A small smile caught the corners of his mouth as he glanced briefly at us, then said, "Once in the Canal Zone, I had the privilege of going through the Canal on the bridge of one of the ships. . . ." Then he launched briskly into the main point of the illustration, which was indeed clarified by the pruning he had done.

I began to understand the technique of coping with such a person as Dr. Barnhouse: Drop the seed and go away; let the Lord give the increase!

SIX

"Doug, I know you two had planned to go home at the end of the week, but I have a proposition for you." The three of us were sitting down to lunch at a nearby restaurant. Dr. Barnhouse was unveiling another of his surprises. Part of what made the man Barnhouse so exciting was that he was full of ideas—not just theological ideas, but everyday ideas and innovations, some practical and some not so practical.

"As you know, I fly to California at the end of the week to make some pilot films for my series. I need someone to drive my car to Houston so it'll be there when I conduct meetings there in two weeks. Now, I know you have other commitments, but I'd like you and Marge to do this for me, if you're able, and then to stay on there for the meetings."

Temptation! "I don't know," Doug said after a moment. "Of course, we'd love to, but we'll have to check with home."

The waitress came to take our order. Doug and I ordered, then Dr. Barnhouse said, "I'm hungry for seafood. I think I'll have the swordfish." I wondered about his choice: Didn't he know it was risky to order fish this far from the ocean? It was probably shipped frozen, but even so, this was a small restaurant. You never knew about such places.

The waitress dumped the plates down in front of us un-ceremoniously. Dr. Barnhouse looked annoyed. She brought the coffee, sloshing some of it onto the saucer, which irritated him further.

"Where's the tartar sauce?" he barked.

I stared at him. Even if the service wasn't the best, there was no reason for him to act rudely.

The waitress retreated to the kitchen. We could see some sort of consultation going on, then much activity, while Dr. Barnhouse's fingers drummed on the table and his fish got cold. She finally emerged with a sauce dish full of mayonnaise with large chunks of onion mixed into it and set it down in front of him. He took one look.

"You call that tartar sauce? Take it away!" She picked it up, burst into tears, and fled to the kitchen. I couldn't believe it, yet I had seen and heard it.

Doug said, "Oh, come on, Dr. Barnhouse! This isn't exactly the Waldorf! What did you expect?" and he laughed his infectious laugh. Dr. Barnhouse relaxed, said ruefully, "I suppose it was stupid of me. But I did have my mouth all set for fish with tartar sauce. Well, thank you, Lord, for cold fish. I suppose it's better than nothing. But not much better." And he began to eat, obviously not enjoying it.

Later I said to Doug, "What came over him? I've never seen him like this. Doesn't he believe what he preaches?"

"Look Marge, the man is human. This just isn't one of his days. It'd be awfully easy to think a man like that was practically God, and the Lord had to show us he isn't."

"But doesn't it shake you?"

"No, Sugar. You see, in this race I'm betting on the Horse. Barnhouse just happens to be the rider at the moment."

That night after the meeting Dr. Barnhouse put on his coat without his usual buoyancy. "You and Marge go on and get some ice cream. I'm going back to the hotel. I feel rotten." Alarmed, we looked at him. His face was flushed and his eyes looked feverish. Doug took his arm and said, "We're going with you." Out we went, Doug greeting people as we pushed through the departing crowd, Dr. Barnhouse gruff and irritable. When we got to our floor, Doug said, "I'm going to see that he gets right to bed," and disappeared with him into his room. I went to our room, took off my coat and hat, and sat down, helpless. Surely God wouldn't let anything happen to Dr. Barnhouse!

Doug poked his head into our room. "Go sit with him, Marge, while I try to locate a doctor. He's really sick."

I opened the door of Dr. Barnhouse's room and tiptoed in. He lay so still. He looked so defenseless, eyes closed, hair rumpled. I laid my cool hand on his burning forehead as I used to with my children when they were ill, and as with them so long ago I could almost feel my strength flow into him. A large bright tear squeezed out from under his closed eyes and coursed unheeded down his cheek. Incredible! Was this the great, the invincible Dr. Barnhouse?

Doug came in, followed by the minister of the church and a doctor. I slipped out and went back to our room, but couldn't settle down. It wasn't long before Doug returned, obviously relieved.

"Well, it's not food poisoning. It looks like it's just one of those twenty-four hour flu bugs that are making the rounds. The doctor has given him some medicine and says he'll be all right in the morning.

"Strange how the Lord works things out. It's a good thing we were here with him. It must be terrible for a man like that to be sick and alone."

He hung his overcoat in the closet, put his hat on the shelf, then turned with a look of decision in his dark eyes. "You know, Marge, I believe I *will* go on his board of directors. I can see how his kind of ministry needs a team behind it and I'd like to be part of the team. And who knows? Maybe someday, when our kids are grown and gone and don't need us and he is old, we can take care of him, *unless*—Marge, what that man needs is a wife! It is all very well to be 'totally dependent on God,' but God Himself said it is not good for a man to be alone, and if ever a man needed 'a help suitable for him,' Dr. Barnhouse does. But when would he have time to find one? Now, let's see. . . ."

And we began casting about in our minds for a suitable person, naming several people we knew. We knew that Dr. Barnhouse had been married before; his wife, Ruth, had died of cancer some years earlier. By now he was used to living and traveling alone, yet we could sense his desire for companionship.

Two days later we were driving a fully recovered Dr. Barnhouse back to the hotel. He had just consumed with great relish a delicious luncheon at the home of new-found, eager young friends whom his messages had inspired that week. He was silent until we had swung out into traffic. Then he exploded at us.

"I know what you two are up to, and you might as well stop it right now!"

(How did he know? We had so cleverly maneuvered him into a seat next to a charming lady who had no idea what we had in mind. What made him suspect . . . ?)

"Look. People are always trying to match-make. I know the symptoms, so stop trying to sit me next to eligible widows or I'll embarrass you."

Doug and I looked at one another, abashed.

"I'll tell you what I did one time. It was cruel, but obviously necessary. They gave me for a dinner partner a lovely woman—attractive, mature, and by the look in her eyes, willing. The way our hostess introduced us I knew what was cooking. I seated her, sat down, unfolded my napkin, and said, 'Delightful gathering, isn't it—uh—what is your name?' She murmured her name. I smiled impersonally and turned to the lady on the other side of me. After some brief conversation I turned back to my dinner partner and said,

'Are you enjoying the meetings, Mrs., uh. . . .' She murmured her name again, and I completed my sentence, using her name. She said, 'Oh, yes! I. . . .' I cut her off with 'I'm so glad,' and, turning back to the other lady, got involved in a long theological question. By this time I could feel the resentment building up in my dinner partner, so silently asking the Lord to suture the wound, I made the final severing cut. I turned back to her and said, 'Forgive me. I'm afraid I am neglecting you, Mrs., uh, what *is* your name?'

"She said her name once again, this time clearly, distinctly, acidly. 'And really, Dr. Barnhouse,' she said, 'you needn't bother to make the effort.' Then *she* turned away from *me* this time, to the man on the other side."

"Dr. Barnhouse!" I cried. "You *didn't!* You *couldn't!*"

"I could," he said, "and I did. And I would do it again."

Doug and I had wrestled with the idea of driving Dr. Barnhouse's car to Houston. It was a great excuse for going on with this wonderful cross-country adventure, one in which every mile driven in the car seemed to be another leg in the journey of the soul. But should we? We called home and talked it over with the children and Doug's parents. All was well; they urged us to go on with it; and so we agreed to take Dr. Barnhouse up on his proposition. We would drive his car on to Houston.

Saturday morning found Doug and me heading south after leaving Dr. Barnhouse at the airport. As the big black Buick rolled off the miles Doug kept shaking his head.

"Marge, this is fantastic. Why, four weeks ago he didn't even know us. I'm sure he hasn't had us checked out, yet he has entrusted this car, all those books, his equipment, and *all that money* to two total strangers! For all he knows we could keep on going and disappear forever in Mexico!"

I looked at Doug, so weighted down with the responsibility of it all as he drove along, and thought how a man's integrity is almost tangible. Doug's word *was* his bond, and anyone could tell it.

That money! In my mind's eye I could still see the deacons in the back office after the final meeting as, without even checking it, they had poured the "love offering" out of the offering plates into a big brown grocery bag. I could see us back at the hotel, dumping it out on a table and counting it (more than $2000!). I could hear Dr. Barnhouse's "Thank You, Lord!" as he scooped it back into the sack which he then rolled closed.

"This is a big help," he said. "As you know I have to earn on these trips enough to carry me through the rest of the year, pay my secretary and household expenses, and finance the Evangelical Foundation (except, of course, what comes in directly to us through the mail). It's a funny thing how people don't mind paying a lecturer, a writer, or a radio personality. In fact, they'll even buy tickets and pay large sums cheerfully—unless he happens to be a preacher, in which case they often feel a tip is enough! I know these people have given cheerfully and sacrificially. Lord, bless them 'exceedingly abundantly'!"

I could sense Doug's uneasiness; undoubtedly he was thinking about the enormous amount we had spent on the Sarasota publicity and the Civic Auditorium, and the resultant small love-gift left over for Dr. Barnhouse. Yet Dr. Barnhouse had accepted that graciously, with no hint that it was even less than a "tip"!

I remembered that morning before we left for the airport, how Dr. Barnhouse fished a handful of bills out of the money sack, counted them, stuffed them into his pocket, then stowed the sack in the trunk of the car as if it had been a sack of potatoes.

No wonder Doug was shaking his head. That man Barnhouse!

After making our way south to Houston, visiting friends en route, we met Dr. Barnhouse's plane from California. With great relief Doug returned the car keys to him.

"Dr. Barnhouse, it's all yours. When we get to the hotel we'll help you recount the money. By the way, how come you trusted us with it when you hardly know us?"

Dr. Barnhouse looked at him, an affectionate twinkle in his eye.

"I wasn't trusting *you*, Doug. I was trusting the Lord!"

Once more we were on the road, Houston behind us.

"Tell me, Dr. Barnhouse, what is the secret of your phenomenal memory recall?" Doug had been impressed. "When that woman came up to you last night, you said, 'Oh, yes, you were sitting in the third row in the balcony on the left, with the lady in the pink coat. . . .' How do you do that?"

"You may have noticed that I look my audience over very carefully before I speak. God is going to give each person there something from His Word, and I like to get the picture of what each one looks like. There isn't any secret to it, really. When I was a child there wasn't any radio or television or all these passive things that children waste time on today. A friend and I played a game where we'd stand in front of the Variety Store window and look into it for X number of minutes (we shortened the time as we got better at it) and we'd turn our backs and write down everything we could remember seeing. Then we'd check, and the one who had the most items won. Great training. It's a matter of looking and *registering what you see*. Same thing in spiritual matters. . . . . 'They have eyes but they see not. . . .' It takes practice."

We drove a while in companionable silence. Eventually Doug spoke his thoughts aloud.

"I still don't understand predestination. If everything is already planned for us by God, doesn't that mean we can't do anything about it? Do we just sit back and let it happen? Isn't that fatalism?"

"No, not at all," Dr. Barnhouse replied. "Fatalism is the Mohammedan doctrine that all things come by blind chance. Predestination is the Christian doctrine that everything comes from the plan of a loving, all-wise Father. The Greek word is a combination of 'pro,' meaning 'beforehand,' and the word for horizon: God limits our horizons in advance. Break the English word into its components and we have 'pre-destination.' As with the Greek 'pro,' the Latin 'pre' indicates that God has determined our destination beforehand. Marge, you have your Bible there. Turn to Romans 8 and read verses 28 and 29."

Dr. Barnhouse was driving. I was sitting in the middle. Scrunching over toward Doug to give myself enough room to open my Bible, I read, "And we know that all things work together for good to them that love God, to them who are the called according to his purpose. For whom he did foreknow, he also did predestinate to be conformed to the image of his Son, that—"

"Stop there. What does it say is our predestination?"

" 'To be conformed to the image of his Son!' "

"And that is what He is doing in every circumstance of our lives. Remember, when I preached on Enoch we saw that we are no longer in the image of God but in the *broken* image of God: children of Adam. But God is *recreating* His image, the image of His Son, in those who believe. Whether we submit willingly to this, or whether we rebel, He *is* going to accomplish this, for His Word tells us that 'when he shall appear, we shall be like him.' Our horizon, our destination, determined beforehand, is heaven, in the likeness of His Son.

"Hebrews 12:1 tells us He has marked out the course we are to follow, 'the race that *is set before us,*' just as surely as our roadmap has marked out the course that will take us to our destination. *So we had better follow it.*"

Doug let out a long breath. "Sure is serious, isn't it?"

"Yes, but that passage goes on to say, 'For the *joy* that was set before him [He] endured the cross,' He came that His joy might remain in us, and that our joy might be *full*— John 15:11. The chief end of man, according to the old Scottish Catechism, is to glorify God and *enjoy* Him forever. So let's rejoice!" Dr. Barnhouse broke into the hymn "Rejoice, Ye Pure in Heart." It was infectious: smiling, we hummed along the verse with him, not yet knowing the

words to all the great old hymns, but at the chorus we were
with him: "Rejoice! Rejoice! Rejoice, give thanks and sing!"

It wasn't long after our singing had subsided that Doug
was once again deep in thought, his one-track mind back in
the groove. "Dr. Barnhouse," he said, "I think I have it
straight on predestination, but that brings up something
else. If God has already decided who is to be saved, why
bother to evangelize?"

"Two reasons: first, Jesus told us to do it. Second, *we
don't know who they are.* So we cry out, 'Whosoever will
may come!' Someone says, 'I will!' and we say, 'Praise God!
This one is in the elect, and God has just reached down and
jiggled his willer!' "

Doug whipped notebook and pen out of his pocket.
"That's great! Just great! Now could you repeat that exactly
as you just said it? Then I can give it to my class straight."

Dr. Barnhouse groaned, "Oh, Doug, *don't* give them
warmed-over Barnhouse. The same Holy Spirit who
taught me can teach you. You have the gist of it; now you
go to the Bible and dig for yourself, and you'll come up
with something fresh and good and *your own.* Then your
authority will be the Word of God, not the words of a man.
Just remember that of his own volition man never would
have come to God. He is spiritually *dead.* I use the illustration of the Bavarian wood carver who came into the kitchen
with a sack of newly threshed wheat. In the top of the sack
was a small twig just the color of the wheat. While waiting
for dinner he took out his knife and from the twig carved a
handful of wheat kernels that looked absolutely real. His
wife called him; he rose, leaving the carved wheat in a little
pile at the edge of the table.

"When he came back the carvings were gone. His small
son, when questioned, replied, 'I put them in the sack. I
help Papa!' The man looked into the sack. The false were
indistinguishable from the real. Now, how would you find
out which was which?"

Doug shook his head. "Beats me!"

"Suppose he planted all of them, and watered them, and let the sun shine on them. Which would sprout?"

"The real, of course."

"Why?"

"Well . . . because they have life in them."

"Exactly! So we go into all the world, and water people with the Word, and shine the warmth of God's love on them, and the ones *in whom God has already put His life,* conceived but not yet born again, start to grow. And God brings them to new birth and gives the increase."

As we approached Alexandria, Dr. Barnhouse said, "We have plenty of time for a good dinner before the evening meeting. Since you two will be flying back to Bradenton tomorrow, let me treat you to a farewell dinner. I know a really good restaurant here."

We accepted with pleasure. I even had time to set my hair and fix it properly.

As I stepped out of the car at the restaurant, the wind caught me, wrecking my careful hairdo. As we entered the lobby, I saw my reflection in the door and was horrified. "Wait for me here, it won't take a minute," I said, leaving them and rushing into the ladies' room to repair the damage. In record time I emerged, but the men had disappeared. Figuring they had gone in to get a table, I put my hand out to open the dining room doors. Suddenly both doors were yanked open from within, and I almost fell into the room. Doug was on one side, Dr. Barnhouse on the other, both simultaneously proclaiming loudly, "Ta-TA!"

Every head in the dining room swiveled toward me; every eye was riveted upon me. The floor did not open to swallow me, despite my fervent prayers, so summoning what dignity I could, I entered, took each proffered arm and was escorted across the room to our table. Doug bowed in mock deference; Dr. Barnhouse seated me ceremoniously, then leaned down and whispered, "After all, you *are* a daughter of *the King!*" before taking his seat.

My baleful glance went from one to the other of my tormenters, sitting there scanning their menu as if this were normal behavior. Which one dreamed it up? I'd get even!

The next day Doug was taking his turn driving the car. As he cautiously rounded a curve on a narrow mountain road the right rear wheel edged off the shoulder and got stuck. This delayed us, and we missed our flight back home; we decided to continue with Dr. Barnhouse to Atlanta, where we'd pick up another flight home. But once there, Doug hinted that we just might be able to stay over a few days.

"Oh, no you don't!" Dr. Barnhouse said. "My correspondence is in a horrible predicament. I'm behind in my editorials and my radio scripts, and about everything else. I told you I phoned my office in Philadelphia to have my secretary drive down here to dig me out. Well, she has arrived and is staying with the preacher's family, and expects me to be ready to start work tomorrow afternoon— so I'm saying good night to you right now. You can meet me here at five tomorrow afternoon and we'll have our very last farewell dinner, and then Monday I'm packing you two off to Bradenton so I can get to work."

Walking toward his motel room shortly before five Sunday afternoon, I was keenly aware of the finality of this farewell dinner and a bit envious of Doug who would be with him again in Philadelphia in three or four weeks to meet the board of the Evangelical Foundation.

As we knocked we could hear Dr. Barnhouse's voice booming in dictation, then his rapid footsteps as he came to open the door. Behind him, both beds were piled with neatly stacked papers; on the dresser all his reference books were lined up in orderly array. How different from the way his room usually looked!

"Come in and meet my secretary," he said, beaming.

A tall young woman, pad and pencil in hand, arose with queenly dignity and turned to greet us.

"Mr. and Mrs. Bell, this is my secretary, Miss Veit."

I don't know what I had expected—flat heels and a

middle-aged, tweedy look and a no-nonsense attitude, perhaps—but not this. Dark hair curled around a beautiful young face. Her dark, intelligent, gold-flecked eyes had that special radiance I had come to recognize in true believers. Her greeting was alive with genuine interest. I liked her instantly. She stood quietly as Dr. Barnhouse asked me to glance at a manuscript we had discussed the day before; I suggested a few changes; he accepted them and handed the manuscript to Miss Veit. It was a disappointment to hear his brisk, "That's all for now, Miss Veit. Thanks for extricating me. I'll see you later," as he ushered us out the door and closed it behind him.

"Couldn't Miss Veit join us?" asked Doug.

"I never eat with my secretaries. They need a rest from me!" He took my arm on one side and Doug's on the other and swept us off to the car.

Dinner was hilarious. Through Miss Veit's miracles of organization, the most urgent of Dr. Barnhouse's chaotic affairs had already been dealt with. Pressures off, he and Doug were once more teasing and baiting me. Even though this was fun, I felt cheated. This, instead of the riches of God's Word?

I chided, "What would your audiences think if they could see the great Dr. Barnhouse out of his pulpit, exchanging uproarious witticisms instead of thundering, 'Thus saith the Lord'?"

"They'd probably wish they could join us! And I'm sure the Lord Himself is enjoying it with us: He is here, you know, where two or three are gathered in His name. He loved sociability. *Thus* saith the Lord, 'He giveth us richly all things to *enjoy.*' Thank You, Lord, for food and fellowship! And for Thyself."

And then we were airborne, with the earth dropping away beneath us as we headed home. The fantastic adventure was over. Doug had already opened his briefcase and was busily working up a report for the gang. Tucked into his suitcase was a taped greeting for them from Dr. Barnhouse, made Saturday night, giving the highlights of the trip, and including remarks by Doug and me.

I wondered if I would ever see Dr. Barnhouse again. How my feelings toward him had changed in a few short weeks! From a name on a book he had become a voice on the airwaves; then a towering figure behind the pulpit; then an instructor who was both stimulating and annoying; then the "DGB" of *Eternity* who had opened for us a window on the world; then a friend, delightful at times, impossible at others; then almost an older brother in the obvious affection he had for Doug and me. Who would have dreamed, in the beginning, that we could accept him, and he us, so comfortably, just as we were!

Thank You, Lord, I thought. *You are what has made the difference. We needed to grow in You before we could really understand what it means to be Your child and part of Your family, with Your love binding us all together.*

I thought of how when Dr. Barnhouse preached his voice boomed through his entire body, imparting to everything he said a vigor that communicated a literal physical strength to the hearers. We would go out of those meetings strong in the Lord and the power of His might. What *joy* he radiated! When one *knows* what salvation is all about how could anyone be a long-faced Christian? And we were beginning to know, now, what salvation was all about. The rest of our lives would be spent growing in that knowledge, exalting the Lord Jesus Christ, delighting in His love and grace.

And all because of that man Barnhouse.

II

My Heart an Altar, and Thy Love the Flame

SEVEN

Home again, a new urgency impelled Doug and the men of his group, a new energy empowered them as they lived out the teachings they had received through that drenching in God's Word, first through those weeks of Dr. Barnhouse's teaching, then in their own digging into the Word, using his methods. Their outreach was fantastic: not only were alcoholics, drug users, and convicted criminals transformed, but also "nice people," who like us had thought they were "all right." Like those early disciples, they were turning the world of Bradenton-Sarasota upside down; how far beyond the ripples were felt we'll never know. Of course, we thought we were unique, but through the years I have seen this same pattern emerge from the teaching of Donald Grey Barnhouse, as groups like ours have become irradiated by the Holy Spirit through the *dunamis* of the gospel he preached and have reacted in exactly the same way.

The March and April issues of our new subscription to *Eternity* magazine had arrived during our absence. Doug whistled in astonishment as he read the March "Window on the World."

"What?... What?" I cried, scrambling to look over his shoulder.

"Read this on school prayer!" he said, handing me the magazine.

It was entitled "Non-sectarian Prayer," something we had endorsed enthusiastically, thinking it would at least get prayer back into the schools. It read:

There has been much discussion in New York State concerning the proposal to open each day's session of the public schools with a non-sectarian prayer. There have been those who oppose it on the grounds that it violates the principle of separation of church and state. We have not been surprised to see associations of Hebrews and free thinkers oppose the prayer, but we have been surprised that some Protestant groups have been in favor of it.

What right does any Christian have to offer a non-sectarian prayer? Christ our Lord has said, 'No man cometh unto the Father, but by me' (John 14:6), which means, if it has any meaning at all, that God Almighty has never heard a non-sectarian prayer. We must not forget that the one true God is the God and Father of our Lord Jesus Christ, and that any attempt to approach Him without coming through Christ is an attempt that is garnered by Satan.

In order of goodness and evil we must rank these things as follows: A prayer in the name of Christ offered by a believer in Christ. This alone is truly acceptable. Then the following are evil: (1) no prayer at all; (2) more evil, a prayer in the name of Christ offered by an unbeliever; (3) still more evil, a non-sectarian prayer offered by unbelievers; (4) most evil of all, a non-sectarian prayer offered by a believer in Christ.

Shocked and sobered, I handed the magazine back to Doug. "We sure do have a lot to learn!" I said.

(Now, thirty years later, the issue of prayer in schools is still being argued. I wonder what DGB would have thought about the right of students to truly voluntary prayer in groups not led by unbelievers and which did not require the school's endorsement or sponsorship.)

Several days after our return I finally heard the tape on Christian marriage, and could understand why Doug had been wanting me to hear it. I could also understand why the Lord had kept me from hearing it until then: I needed first the preparation of that trip and the humbling self-discovery that invariably followed each magnificent exposition of God's Word. Now, on this tape, God again raised His mirror, and I came face to face with myself and was ashamed.

Doug set up the tape recorder, flipped on the switch, and settled in his chair to enjoy "Christian Marriage." With some trepidation I listened that first time, afraid he and Dr. Barnhouse might be conspirators, scheming to knock me off my high horse. Instead, God the Holy Spirit began speaking to me, as He had when I had read *God's Methods for Holy Living*.

Dr. Barnhouse started by saying that everything God created was designed to illustrate spiritual truth. He said the greatest of all the illustrations in the Bible was that of marriage. The relationship between a husband and wife was a picture of Christ in relation to the Church. That was why faithfulness in marriage was so important: "For God says, 'I created the human race in the way I did to show that when I was joined to a person in salvation, I was joined to him forever.' " Dr. Barnhouse then quoted from Ephesians 5: " 'This is a great mystery: but I speak concerning Christ and the Church.' "

So far, so good. I began to relax.

He then told how he enjoyed performing the wedding ceremony for a couple who really loved the Lord: such a contrast to the weddings in the movies, where it all seemed so unspiritual. ("Particularly," he said, "when you know the Hollywood 'bride' is working on her fifth husband.")

"But I get a couple in front of me—John and Mary—and there comes a time in the ceremony when I join their hands, look at the groom, and say, 'I, John, take thee, Mary,' and he repeats, 'I, John, take thee, Mary' (and, you know, I can tell by the way his muscles tense just what kind of husband he's going to be!). 'To be my wedded wife,' I say, and the groom echoes, 'To be my wedded wife.'

"And so the ceremony continues: 'And I do promise and covenant before God and these witnesses, to be thy loving and faithful husband, in sickness and in health, in plenty and in want, in joy and in sorrow, as long as we both shall live.'

"And when the groom finishes, I repeat the same words for the bride. At the wedding rehearsal, the bride will look at me at this point and say, 'I, Mary, take thee, John,' and I say, 'No, my name is Donald. Look at *John*—you're taking *him*. Even if you have to make a quarter turn to the right and turn your back on your bridesmaids, look at him!' "

(In the background of the tape I could hear the audience's amused reaction.)

"And then, looking at him in a way that no Hollywood producer could ever capture, she repeats after me, 'I, Mary, take thee, John, to be my wedded husband; and I do promise and covenant before God and these witnesses, to be thy loving and faithful wife, in sickness and in health, in plenty and in want, in joy and in sorrow, as long as we both shall live.'

"Now in the course of the ceremony I speak to them about the nature of Christian marriage. The audience is seated after the bride has come in. After they have exchanged rings and before I pronounce them man and wife, I say, 'Mary, *God* says you are to obey your husband. . . .' "

(*Uh-oh! Here it comes!* I thought.)

He repeated Ephesians 5:22-24: " 'Wives, submit yourselves unto your own husbands, as unto the Lord. For the husband is the head of the wife, even as Christ is the head of the church; and he is the savior of the body. Therefore, as the church is subject unto Christ, so let the wives be to their own husbands in every thing.'

"Mary, this is God speaking. *God* says the woman is to obey her husband. Any woman who does not is getting cheated in marriage. Every *good* woman wants a husband who can manage her. This is an instinct in the heart of the woman. If you don't believe it, go to any block in town, and if there is one house where the woman really runs the man, listen to how the other women talk about him: 'Is he a man or a mouse? Why does he let her run him around her little finger? Why doesn't he stand up to her? Why doesn't he show her he's a man?' In Eden, in the third chapter of Genesis, God said to the woman when pronouncing the curse, 'Thy desire shall be to thy husband, and he shall rule over thee.' This is a fact of life, a fact of psychology.... So Mary, the highest ideal of *your* love is the highest human love in this world.

"But John, God has not given you a slave. God has not even given you a servant. For John, if the Bible says a word to the wife that seems incredible, it says a much more severe thing to the man. For it says, 'Husbands, love your wives even as Christ also loved the church, and gave himself for it.' If the ideal of the woman's love is the highest human love, the ideal of the husband's love is *divine* love. And no woman in this world is going to have any trouble obeying a man who is willing to be crucified for her. Every woman knows that."

I glanced at Doug. He looked uncomfortable.

Dr. Barnhouse warned, "Because this is a symbol of Christ's relationship to the Church, John must never make any jokes about marriage, such as 'Come on in and meet the Ball-and-Chain.' Can you imagine Christ saying that about His Church?"

He pointed out that a marriage that disintegrates into separation and divorce did not have in the beginning the realization of what true Christian marriage is: "Man is a trinity of body, soul, and spirit. This carnation that you see here has a body, but no soul and spirit. You cut it, and it dies. An animal has a body and a soul. In the Old Testament the Hebrew word, *nephesh,* soul, is used both of man and of animals: *self*-consciousness. That is why Jesus said that the foxes have *their* holes, and the birds of the air have *their* nests, to which they return. But man has body, soul, and *spirit: God*-consciousness."

He spoke of those who marry "body to body": she's blonde; he's tall, tan, and terrific. They meet and marry, but soon the glamour wears off and they're in the divorce courts. In marriage there has to be more than physical attraction. Then there are those with mutual interests, who marry "body to body, mind to mind." These last a little longer, especially if they are cemented together with children. But the true Christian marriage is the union of body, soul, and spirit.

"When I speak about marriage to the young people in my church I tell them, 'Friendship is the prelude to courtship; courtship is the prelude to marriage. Now someplace along the line you must find the spiritual status of the mate. If you can't pray on your date there's something wrong with your date. You should be able to pray, "Lord, keep our friendship pure and clean in Thee, and may all that we do be to Thy honor and glory." Every marriage is a triangle: the man, the woman, and the Lord. And if the Lord is not in His proper place in that triangle, anyone can move in.'

"Before the young couple is married, I tell the bride and groom that the man must be in authority. I say to the bride, 'Mary, do you love him enough to obey him?' 'Yes, I do.' Then, to the groom, 'John, do you love her enough never to command her?' That's the acid test.

"If you can't agree on something that can wait, put off the decision until you can reach an agreement. But in any immediate decision the man must make the choice and the wife must not question it. Why? BECAUSE GOD ALMIGHTY SAYS SO, THAT'S WHY." His voice thundered over the tape, making me jump. He continued, "Furthermore, any *good* woman wants it that way."

I sat there in a state of shock, realizing that for me this was true. I had fought against the idea of the ultimate authority of the man, but I would not have wanted a wishy-washy husband.

"When my younger daughter was about five she came to me saying, 'Daddy, I have a riddle. What's most like half of the moon?' Well, I had heard that one when I was about her age, but it is the duty of a father never to know the answer to a riddle. So I named everything round and orange that I could think of, and finally said, 'I give up. You tell me.' She answered, 'The other half of the moon!'

"Well, what's most like a woman in this world? A man. What's most like a man? A woman. Now everyone knows a man is *infinitely* superior to a woman—at being a man. And a woman is infinitely superior to a man at being a woman. But if a man is feminine or a woman is masculine, there's something wrong and everyone knows it. But as long as a woman says, 'I'm a woman and I'm going to be a success at being a woman,' God has nothing finer. Oh, what a job a mother has, to bring up sons and daughters of *character,* to lead them to Christ and cause them to grow in the nurture and admonition of the Lord!

"Now a word to the husband. 'John,' I say, '*you* are the high priest of the household. The *father* is the one who is to ask the grace at table.' " (Doug was suddenly sitting up, leaning slightly toward the machine, listening as if he had not heard this before.) "*The father* is the one who in the morning is to gather the family, open the Bible, read a few verses, and pray briefly. But I tell you this, men—I tell you this in the name of the Lord God Almighty—and don't try to get out of it: if you do not have family worship, your home is not a Christian home. It's a caricature of a Christian home. . . . You are responsible for the religious life of your home, and you are responsible for the character and lives of your children. The law of this city and of this state and of the United States holds a man responsible for his minor child. If he takes your car and hits somebody, they can sue *you.* The law holds *you* responsible. *So does God.* That's why there must be discipline."

He told of traveling with his wife and four children. They carried with them a small bag they called "the family worship bag." It contained a Bible, a hymnbook, and a Ping-Pong paddle (this was in the days when such a paddle was smooth wood on both sides). "Any man who does not discipline his child is unworthy to be a father," he declared. "You see, a child from the beginning respects law and order. If you want your child to respect you, you must discipline him or her in a prayerful way. Teaching Junior to obey you teaches Junior how to obey God. To allow Junior to get away with anything in parental discipline will ultimately make it more difficult for him to believe and obey God. . . . 'Well,' you say, 'I'm giving my child liberty. I'm not teaching him religion. I want him to grow up and make all his own choices.' Well, then, do the same thing about brushing his teeth: wait until he's grown up and can make his own choice—when he has no teeth! Some of you say the reason you don't go to church is because you were *made* to go when you were young. Is that why you've stopped taking baths? 'But I haven't stopped taking baths!' you say. Well weren't you *made* to take them when you were little, and didn't you yell about it? In other words, you lie. You're putting out an excuse. You are in sin and you want to live that way. John 3:19 says, 'This is the condemnation, that light is come into the world, and men loved darkness rather than light, because their deeds were evil.' So if you're not yielded to the Lord, it's because you're doing something deep in your heart or back in your life someplace that you're ashamed to have the Lord bring out into the open."

He castigated his hearers for not calling the extramarital affairs of certain movie stars by their right name—harlotry —and for letting *them* rule our morality and forge our standards instead of the Word of God. He said these are "like lightning when it strikes." Some other women he likened to a little brush fire, trying to emulate the lightning. But, oh, the others who are willing to stay home and be a hearth fire, as God intended, where a man can warm himself before going out into the dog-eat-dog world where he works!

We had discussed this to some extent on the trip. He had

pointed out that in 1 Corinthians 11:9 God tells us, "Neither was the man created for the woman; but the woman for the man." Then he took us to Genesis 2:18 which quotes the Lord God as saying, "It is not good that the man should be alone; I will make him a help meet [that is, a helper suitable] for him." He had become practically livid over the metamorphosis of the two words "help" and "meet" into "helpmeet" or "helpmate," thus obscuring God's purpose: that she should be suited to her husband's needs. No two men have identical needs, so whereas one might need a clinging vine, another might need a strong, outgoing wife. He had no objection to a woman's doing things outside the home if first she had taken care of her husband, her children, and her home. But we hadn't discussed the *husband's* responsibilities, which was why I had been a bit nervous about what he might say on this tape. If only husbands would be the way he said God intended them to be!

His voice went on: "But men, in passing let me say this: there is one thing in which *you* must obey your wife implicitly, and that is in anything she ever tells you about any other woman. . . . God gave you your wife as a red flag to warn you against predatory females!

"Now another word for men—and this is very important: a woman has to be told that she is loved. Say it with valentines on Valentine's Day [the day on which this sermon was preached], with candy and with flowers occasionally, and sometimes with the dishrag, but above all, *say it with words*. A man doesn't have to be told his wife loves him. He knows that she does. Fact of life: the sun rises in the east and sets in the west; my wife loves me. But a woman has to be *told*, early and often.

"And men, do you know there is a flat statement in the Bible that says God won't answer the prayers of a man who's fool enough not to understand his wife? First Peter 3:7 flatly states that God is not going to answer the prayers of a man who is a megalomaniac around the house: 'I'm the man; *I* earn the money. Do it this way! Do it that way!' "

Dr. Barnhouse's voice was rough and autocratic. He went on, "A man's a *fool* who tries to order his wife around. 'But,' you say, 'you just said he was to command!' But it's to be done as it says of Jesus: 'He drew me with the cords of *love,* and thus He bound me to Him.' "

He told of a couple who had come for counseling. "The husband was distraught: 'But I've given you this, this, and this—I don't know what more you want!' Through tears she said, 'John, you have given me everything in the world, except yourself.' I think there are people to whom the Lord Jesus Christ would say the same thing. You sing, 'I Surrender All,' but you give up *things* instead of yourself."

(Startled, I heard the clock strike. The sermon had been going on for more than an hour! Yet it seemed only minutes.)

There followed a sobering treatment of marriage and divorce, according to the Bible, based on the Book of Hosea. Through the story of this prophet, Hosea, Dr. Barnhouse demonstrated the never-failing love and faithfulness of God toward those of us who have believed in Him, even when we are running away. He went on: "What does the commandment mean that says, 'The Lord will not hold him guiltless that taketh His name in vain'? 'Oh,' you say, 'that's swearing.' No, that's faithlessness. I'll show you this by means of a story that was in the papers several years ago, about a young major in the army who married a socialite in a fancy wedding, then flew immediately, without any honeymoon, to Europe to be on the commanding general's staff. It wasn't long before the gossip columnists were reporting that the bride was going first with this man, then with that one. When the bridegroom returned a year later he had the marriage annulled on the grounds of 'common fame.' What had happened? She had taken his name, but she had taken it in vain.

"Now there came a day when you were saved. What happened when you believed in Jesus Christ? From heaven the Lord Jesus Christ said, 'I, Jesus, take thee, sinner, to be My Bride. And I do promise and covenant before God and these witnesses to be thy loving and faithful Savior and Bridegroom; in sickness and in health, in plenty and in want, in joy and in sorrow, in faithfulness and in waywardness, for time and for eternity.' And you looked up to Him and said, 'I, sinner, take Thee, Jesus, to be my Savior and my Lord. And I do promise and covenant before God and these witnesses to be Thy loving and faithful Bride; in sickness and in health, in plenty and in want, in joy and in sorrow, for time and for eternity.' And you came in Miss Sinner, but you go out Mrs. Christian—*Christ*ian. You now bear His name, and if you flirt with the world, if you live in adultery with the world, if you want what the world wants in society, in 'appearances,' in emulation, in following earthly standards, in failing to put the Lord first, then I tell you in the name of *God* you have taken His name, but you have taken it in vain. And *'the Lord will not hold him guiltless who taketh his name in vain.'*

"Now we're going to pronounce the benediction. There are two or three conclusions to be drawn: Maybe some of you husbands need to go home and put your arms around your wife and say, 'Dear, I've mistreated you and neglected you, but I do love you.' Maybe some of you fathers need to gather your children around you tomorrow morning, open your Bible, and say, 'Your father hasn't been a proper father. From now on we're going to have family worship, and I am going to take my proper place as the head of this household.' Maybe someone here needs to say, 'Lord Jesus, I joined the church, and then I went out and lived with the civilization that is our civilization, and I gave Thee a tip on Sunday morning—sixty minutes and a few dollars—and I thought I was doing something. But I realize now I've been faithless to Thee. From now on I want to look up into Thy face and say, "Lord Jesus, I love Thee, and I will be Thy faithful Bride." '

"Let us bow in prayer."

We bowed. Doug put his face in his hands. My own heart was overwhelmed.

Lord, I love Thee!

When the tape was over and the others who had shared it with us had gone home, Doug said, "Sugar, I guess I have a long way to go to be the kind of husband the Lord wants me to be. Funny, I didn't hear that part of it so much when he was preaching it. But it sure hit me tonight." Doug paused, and then his voice became filled with emotion. "Be patient with me, Sugar. He's really working on me!" At this, a rush of remorse swept over me about my own failings. My heart filled with tenderness toward this proud husband of mine who had been willing thus to humble himself before his Lord—and me.

The marriage tape created real difficulties for the others. Each spouse had heard only what was meant for the other. They had gone home and fussed: "So! Did you hear what he said? Why don't *you* act that way?" "He did not say that!" "Yes he did!" So it wasn't long before people phoned, asking, "May we hear it over again?" Then, on the second hearing, the Holy Spirit revealed to them what had first been perceived darkly; the mirror reflected the truth and the Word shafted home to the heart.

(Several years later Dr. Barnhouse preached this same sermon in Oklahoma City. Afterward he stood down front as usual, greeting people and answering questions, but the pastor went back to the narthex to speak to people as they left. One of his parishioners stomped up the aisle, slamming her hat on as she came muttering, "Men! Men! Men!" The pastor put his hand on her arm to detain her, saying, "Just a minute. Did he say anything that wasn't in the Bible?" She pulled away, giving him a baleful glare. "And who wrote the Bible?" she asked. "Men! Men! *Men!*" And she swept out into the night.)

But I knew beyond question that Almighty God, not

men, had authored the Bible, so the words smote me with conviction. More and more clearly I was seeing how my generation of women was distorting our God-given role. It was during the 1920s when I was growing up that women in the United States won the right to vote, cut their hair, used lipstick, rouge, and eye makeup unashamedly, wore slacks, smoked publicly, and drank in "speakeasies" during Prohibition. Marriage was considered a fifty-fifty proposition instead of a hundred-hundred proposition, and most of us would have died before going one fraction of an inch farther than our 50 percent of giving in our marriage. But Dr. Barnhouse's sermon made me uneasy. Was it possible that what we thought to be "liberation" was really a degradation, a "license to sin"?

EIGHT

The board of the Evangelical Foundation voted Doug a member, and he made several trips to Philadelphia. He was impressed by the caliber of the men surrounding DGB, but began to be uneasy about some of the things he was learning about the human side of his hero. Doug was a practical-minded businessman, as were so many of those connected with the work of the Evangelical Foundation. DGB seemed impractical and often naive. Until Doug understood him better he thought his methods seemed outlandish. What DGB, leaping with enthusiastic abandon into this movie venture, called "faith" Doug suspected was "tempting the Lord" in the wrong way. Didn't the Bible say in Luke 14:28 that a man intending to build a tower should first count the cost? Yet here was DGB, with no experience whatsoever in "show business," plunging on a grand scale into the making of motion pictures to illustrate the gospel, expecting the money to come from somewhere. He was confident that churches everywhere would be eager to show the finished product, and was even talking as though a studio and personnel for showing the films were already hired, sound and projection equipment had been purchased (plus a station wagon to transport them), and an itinerary for the showings had all been worked out. Yet actually it was all still in the idea stage! Crazy. Unbusiness-like. And Doug began to go through what some have called "Barnhousitis," an affliction that invariably hit earnest Christians, particularly new believers, at the outset of close association with DGB. If they weathered this period they were forever stronger, having learned that despite all DGB's human failings his was a sovereign God whose Word could be trusted implicitly and who did rule DGB's life. This confident faith enabled him to expect great things from his God and prepare for them, but relinquish them if it appeared that God had other plans for him.

"You can't help loving the guy," Doug told us after one of those trips. "He'll fight you down to the last ditch; then, if you really are right, he'll give in, follow your advice, and thank you for it. He's amazing. Sure, he rubs me the wrong way lots of times, but what the Lord is accomplishing through him is really something. And you know, it's great to be part of it all, and to know that a guy like that isn't all-sufficient, but really does count on the rest of us to channel him."

Doug's men's class at our church doubled, and doubled again. The men responded warmly to his positive, explosive, action-packed teaching. He had brought back from our trip innumerable illustrations and attention-grabbers to make the gospel vividly alive. The sovereignty of God and our eternal security in Him were the heart of his teaching.

One day Doug came home looking very burdened. He reported that he had had another long session with our pastor, who had been trying to point out to him what he considered the fallacy of these doctrines. Doug had tried to show him how biblical it was, and had stood his ground on its being God's truth. The pastor had finally said that he guessed Doug was not basically a Methodist, that he could not continue to teach this doctrine in a Methodist church, and that perhaps he would be happier elsewhere.

"Elsewhere?"

"That's what he said."

"But—your class!"

"They'll manage. The fellows who have been teaching when I've been away do a great job, and it shouldn't make any difference in the Friday night group. The Lord will work it out."

Bits of objections we had heard when we first brought Dr. Barnhouse to Sarasota surfaced in my memory: "Barnhouse is a troublemaker"; "Barnhouse is divisive." I knew Jesus had said, *"Not peace, but a sword."* I was beginning to understand that perhaps it wasn't Dr. Barnhouse, but the gospel that was divisive.

Sick at heart, we quietly began looking for a church that would meet our needs.

During this period, our subscription to *Eternity* magazine was proving to be a new channel for spiritual growth. Dr. Barnhouse's editorials were eye-openers. His "Window on the World," putting the news into biblical perspective, was fascinating. The articles and Bible study helps by various gifted writers were feeding our hungry minds. Often there were statements about which I would have challenged Dr. Barnhouse. I longed for the days of our trip when, trapped in the car, he was there to answer our questions. I envied Doug, who was seeing him frequently. When he returned home I would quiz him about DGB's opinions on various subjects, and couldn't quite believe him when he said there never was time for any of "that sort of question and answer."

Then came the October *Eternity*, commemorating Dr. Barnhouse's twenty-fifth anniversary as pastor of Tenth Presbyterian Church in Philadelphia. Doug was already in Philadelphia, helping with some of the planning for the anniversary mass meeting at the town hall on October 2, so I had the magazine all to myself. I was curious to see the contents. The June issue had printed a brief notice that the entire October issue would contain articles by men who had been blessed by Dr. Barnhouse's exposition of the Word of God; it also invited brief testimonies from readers. It stated that "the purpose of this issue is to glorify the Lord, not man; if testimonies are not written to the glory of God, they will not be usable."

The opening article, by "R. L. K.," the "Ralph L. Keiper, Contributing Editor" of the masthead, stated that this issue recognized the ministry as unique: twenty-five years of exalting the Word of God "with clarity in exposition, with precision in presentation . . . in convicting, cleansing, saving power."

There followed article after article, each an exposition of biblical truth, accompanied by a brief testimony, by prestigious men of the evangelical world.

One testified how Dr. Barnhouse's mission to the great Cambridge University in England had literally turned the students' thinking around. Another told of the far-reaching effect of DGB's loving and joyful ministry in war-torn Belgium and France as a young man, right after World War I. Still another sketched the forceful impact of his ministry at the English Keswick Convention.

All emphasized Dr. Barnhouse's gift of being able to meet lofty liberal theologians on their own ground, yet be intelligible to the simplest minds. "The gospel in mighty power but in great love" echoed through the testimonies. "He not only defends the faith but exults and revels in it. He has that quality . . . of laughing in the adversary's face and always finding unexpected treasures which he brings forth to the dismay and discomfiture of all gainsayers."

The more I read, the more appalled I became at my naiveté on that trip, how with my little pea-sized brain I had dared to say some of the things I had said to this man. But with all his mighty intellect he had been so *human.* I thought of some of the outrageous baiting he and Doug had subjected me to, putting my own wit to the test, presenting an entertaining and never-ending challenge. I decided he had deserved anything I had said. But I also recognized that I had not really appreciated the full stature of the man and his ministry. How gracious of the Lord to have allowed

Doug and me to have the mind and heart of that man at our disposal long enough to ground us in the faith. It was already producing fruit a hundredfold in our Bible classes, our personal ministry, and in our gang.

Doug returned from Philadelphia awed by all he had experienced. He brought back a calendar of events, a commemorative booklet giving Tenth's history, and a wealth of stories of people he had met and things that had happened. Our gang rejoiced with him, and our women's Bible and prayer group redoubled our prayers for Dr. Barnhouse. We decided that what he most needed was a wife, and asked the Lord to give him, not the one he might choose, not the one we might choose, but the one the Lord Himself knew was the right one for him.

At Christmastime I was to meet two of the Evangelical Foundation staff. Nan Michaelson and Ralph Keiper were married in December, and we had invited them to use our guest house for their honeymoon.

They were a delightful couple, Ralph was small and slightly rotund, with a mischievous sense of humor. He was almost blind, but somehow this did not seem a handicap.

Together we searched for and cut down our Christmas tree and decorated the house for the holidays. Ralph mimicked Dr. Barnhouse in a way that was outrageous. But despite all the iconoclastic fun-poking, Ralph really loved this man who had brought him to the Lord and whose gifts he both appreciated and respected.

"You see, B's purpose isn't just to teach us to master the Word," Ralph told us, "but to make the Word master us. He teaches not only *what* to believe, to be a true Christian, but *why* to believe it, to become a mature Christian. And the remarkable thing is that he uses every means of communication to do this."

"That's for sure," Doug said, thinking of his own involvement in the work.

"What you may not know is what he does when he is off on his summer trips," Ralph said. "He visits mission stations and recharges the missionaries. One of them told me it is so easy for them to get stale on the field, and so refreshing to hear that kind of doctrinal teaching. This is one of his greatest works."

Curious, I asked, "Ralph, you're a 'research consultant.' What do you do?"

He smiled impishly. "That means I do whatever no one else wants to do! Actually, what led me to the work was B's deep interest in the university world, and the fact that he gives answers, not retorts. Part of my job is digging out the material he needs for those answers: Greek, Hebrew, obscure references—things he could do himself but hasn't the time. And of course my own mental furnishings profit by all this, too. I've learned that B's great strength is his unshakable belief in the absolute sovereignty of God and the absolute authority of the Scriptures."

With all the holiday activities, the Keipers' visit, and our friends' and the children's comings and goings, it was a busy, happy time. We were sorry when Nan and Ralph had to leave.

Toward the end of December Doug came in with the mail, calling, "The January *Eternity*'s here, and it has a new cover."

I joined him on the porch. He held the magazine up for me to see. Concentric circles against a cloud-flecked blue sky replaced the 1952 design depicting a veil-like curtain hanging in folds against the sky. I didn't like this one as well.

Doug opened the magazine and exclaimed, "What's this?"

"What?" I echoed, going over to see. I settled myself beside him on the couch, and together we shared something remarkable.

On the inside of the cover, instead of the usual ad there

was an article by Dr. Barnhouse called "New Year's Resolution." It continued to the inside of the back cover, en-
wrapping the magazine. It began:

"I have never made any resolutions at the New Year since
I was a child, for I soon learned that they were in the same
category as vows—there is no strength in man to keep
them. But for some weeks I have been thinking over a
course of action that would be different from previous.
courses of action, and thought that it might be well to tell
the *Eternity* family about it."

He then told about a conversation with a member of his
Twenty-fifth Anniversary Celebration committee, shortly
before the event. Speaking of the men who had worked on
the preparations, this man had remarked, "Those fellows
certainly love you."

He went on: "I was stunned for a moment. He left my
home shortly thereafter, and I walked out under the trees
thinking about that statement. I knew that I loved many
people, and loved many of them very dearly, but I had
never thought about their loving me. My family, yes; but
others . . . I remembered when I was a small boy and came
to my first day in school. They kept me in the first grade
for about two hours and then I was marched into the second
grade. That year the first-graders hated me because I was
the smart kid that had gone ahead, and the second-graders
hated me because I was the first-grader that had come in to
show them up by my being there. At least, I thought they
hated me; and to think such a thing conditions one as much
as though it were a fact. So I developed the practice of doing
my work in an attitude of not caring what anybody in the
world might think. And I rather carried that attitude
through my life.

"But that night, listening to the kind things that were
being said, hearing the testimonies of those who have been
saved through my ministry, and remembering the words
that had been spoken to me, 'Those fellows certainly love

you,' I began to think that perhaps a whole lot of people did love me, and suddenly I saw that this was going to make a big difference in a lot of things. . . .

"Early in my ministry I conceived the idea that I must strike out against all error wherever I saw it. I used only one kind of ammunition. I hit an error wherever I saw it. If it was in Christian Science, Unitarianism, or in Romanism, I swung hard. If it was in some fundamental leader with whom I was in 95 percent agreement, I swung hard at the 5 percent. From now on I am going to use two kinds of ammunition, and I believe that there are many cases in the latter [5 percent] class that I will just let go unnoticed. Perhaps they do not like the 5 percent difference in me, either! . . .

"I want to have Christian fellowship with a much wider circle of people. . . . I want to make my circle of Christian fellowship on the basis of the fact that a man is going to be in heaven with me. If he is, then why not get a little closer together here and now? Give him the benefit of the doubt on the things we do not agree upon as soon as we find that we agree upon man's complete ruin in sin and God's perfect remedy in Christ. . . .

"Within my own denomination there are men with whom I have not had much fellowship because of ecclesiastical differences. Without in anywise changing my theological outlook, and without lowering my right to unveil, editorially, specific heresy when I find it in print, I want to move closer to many men who are undoubtedly going to be with me in heaven, but with whom I have disagreed on denominational emphasis. . . ." He pointed out that a report he had read of a meeting in the ecumenical field sounded exactly like what happened in a meeting of fundamentalists he had attended: "They had come together, read reports, argued, and disbanded without doing anything. . . . And I thought of the need of more unity among believers in this world today. Sometimes I think, 'Don't men realize that this is 1953 and the H-bomb has been perfected?' "

I interrupted, "Wait a minute! Wait just a minute! Is he saying fundamentalists should be fellowshiping with the ecumenical people?"

"That's *not* what he says, Marge. He is saying that there ought to be more unity among *believers,* no matter what camp they're in. There *are* some believers in the ecumenical camp, you know. Look at us, before we had good teaching!"

We read on. Dr. Barnhouse told of meeting a Christian in China who was affiliated through his missionary with a denomination that had split. In America the two groups would not take communion together. In China, should a Chinese who had been led to the Lord by missionaries of the other side of the split be forbidden communion with that other believer? It did seem ridiculous.

"Hoo, boy, this will raise some fundamentalist hackles!" cried Doug, as we read the next paragraph:

"And I would be dishonest if I did not recognize that some of the things that have been accomplished by the National and World Councils are truly magnificent achievements for the Lord Jesus Christ. Take for example the work that has been done among the hundreds of thousands of refugees. . . . More than cups of cold water have been given in the name of the Lord Jesus, and in this, every believer who feels himself loved by the Lord Jesus Christ must rejoice.

"I could go on for several pages more, and may at some future time. There may be a few of my readers who will not like what I have written. I assure them that there is no deviation whatsoever in what I have written here from all that I have written through the years. In fact, I believe that the love of Jesus Christ must mellow a man, that the Holy Spirit who dwells in me is the same Holy Spirit who dwells in all who have been born again, and that He must move to draw us all toward the Lord Jesus. It is my prayer that I may humbly follow His leading and put no barriers that He has not placed Himself. . . .

"I am trying to think ahead. Is it possible that a few Russian bombs may drop on one of our great cities in the next few years? If so, working side by side in the rubble, I shall hope to call out on a Sunday morning, 'Let all who believe in the Lord Jesus come here... I have a loaf of bread, and I am going to tear off a small piece and remember Him.' I will pass this loaf around the crowd, and let all who will take his portion, so long as he knows his portion is Christ. And it would be good if we didn't have to wait until the bombs fall...."

Doug looked up from the ending of the resolution. "It takes a great man to humble himself like that," he said. "Watching him at the twenty-fifth anniversary, I knew something big was happening deep inside. He sure has put himself out on a limb."

In the back of my mind stirred something I had read in the second of Dr. Barnhouse's booklets on Romans, which came monthly to those of us who gave regularly to the Bible Study Hour. I found it in his fascinating study of Romans 1:8, 9. As Dr. Barnhouse pointed out, verse 9 shows that the Apostle Paul "had a universal yearning for all men, and a universal love toward all those who had believed in the Lord Jesus Christ," but "... to me it is very revealing that Paul had to call God as his witness that he was praying for them... there seems to be every indication in the epistles that Paul knew he was considered hard by those to whom he preached. Alone in his own heart he must have longed for the softness of the nature of the beloved disciple, John, whom Jesus loved, and who leaned upon our Lord's bosom the night of the Last Supper. When John told Christians that he loved them, they all answered warmly to his personality and felt themselves beloved of John.... We know from his second epistle to the Corinthians that some people did not like [Paul]. He hit too hard. Some people thought him dogmatic, didactic.... His blows were sledgehammer blows.... There may well have been those who came to him and said, 'Paul, show a little more love....' Temperamentally and psychologically, he was unable to show it."

I checked for the date the booklet was written: 1949—
four years earlier.

"Doug," I said, "listen to this," and I read him the next
paragraph:

"And may I, the writer, say this, if a candle can compare
itself to the sun: that I understand the heart of Paul in this
cry to God for witness of his love. For all my life I have
faced this same psychological dilemma. When God established the genes and chromosomes of my makeup, there
was not put into the mixture anything of effervescence. It
is impossible for me to wear my heart on my sleeve. There
is a little of John in me, and much more of Paul. There may
be many Christians who have been accused of pride, or
arrogance, or dogmatism, who know deep down in their
hearts that they are seeking by every way possible to have
the Lord Jesus Christ magnified in their being. They love
with an intensity that hurts and which manifests itself in a
hardness of outward attitude, though at the same time, like
Paul, they may say, 'I love . . . I pray without ceasing for
you . . .' and feel it necessary to add, 'God is my witness. . . .'"

Doug took the booklet and reread those pages.

"He's sure going to need a lot of prayer," he said.

After the holidays we took up our search for a church home
again. Because Doug was in and out of town so much, his
absence from our Methodist church was not noticed at first.
For our children's sake I stayed on for a while, and no mention of leaving was made to me. Our daughter, Carolyn,
was in the class I taught. I decided to keep away from doctrinal differences and emphasize a joyful Christian walk.
The older group that our son Douglas was in, taught by one
of our gang, was Christ-centered and jumping with activities. It would be hard for them to change.

Doug visited other churches of other denominations. For
a while I went with him to a small, independent Bible
church, but we didn't feel quite comfortable there.

We were at this stage in our search when, in February of

1953, Paul Hopkins, the business manager of the Evangelical Foundation, brought his family to Florida for a month's vacation in our guest cottage. Paul and Doug had become close friends. After our experience with the Keipers, I was anticipating with joy this visit from another of DGB's staff.

Paul was a perfect foil for DGB: a tall, quiet, gentle man in his mid-thirties, with tremendous strength beneath the gentleness. His wife, Jeanne, was also still water running deep: a statuesque ash-blonde young woman with an arresting, quiet beauty, soft-spoken and a joy to be with. They made me aware of my own overly kinetic energy. I found myself slowing to a better, less anxious pace when with them. David and Sydney, their little son and daughter, were a delight. Paul's mother, a gracious, white-haired lady who loved to make delectable goodies, kept our kitchen redolent with cookies and cakes and pies during their entire visit.

Through Paul I could better understand some of Doug's perplexities about DGB. I began to see that working with DGB could be as exhilarating as managing a thoroughbred horse: properly handled, he ran a magnificent course—but you had to understand him. Doug had once said, "I'm betting on the horse: Barnhouse just happens to be the rider at the moment." Now I saw the picture reversed: Dr. Barnhouse was the steed and the *Lord* was the rider, in complete control of DGB and every situation. As long as DGB submitted his will to God's greater will, God could accomplish great things through him, but would allow him his head if he stubbornly insisted on his own way.

Paul, with his more mature knowledge of such things, was helpful in guiding us in our search for a church home where we could worship and serve without any reservations. Eventually we affiliated with Bradenton's First Baptist Church where we found solid teaching of the sovereignty of God, emphasis on the security of the believer, Jesus Christ magnified as God the Son as well as Son of God, Savior and Lord, and a congregation for the most part actively witnessing and reaching out to others with loving concern.

All this time our Sarasota Bible class, so ably taught by Mrs. Northen, had been flourishing. On some Friday nights as many as 150 people would gather to hear the Scriptures taught. Afterward, over cookies and coffee, animated discussions would fly. Back in September of 1952 a new translation of the Bible had been the topic of the day. With the stamp of approval of the liberal National Council of Churches and a translation committee mostly made up of modernists, we had been sure it would twist the Scriptures. We had also been suspicious of the well-financed publicity campaign that was launching it. September 13, 1952, was the scheduled publication date of this new *Revised Standard Version* of the Bible.

This had been planned to be the first serious challenge to the *King James Version,* the beloved English translation that had been in use since 1611. Now, to a generation that has available so many translations and paraphrased versions of the original Hebrew and Greek Scriptures, the initial furor over the RSV must seem ridiculous. But at that time it was serious. Any version of the written Word that did not glorify the Lord Jesus Christ, the Living Word, was anathema to the evangelical or the fundamentalist. Unfortunately, we were more emotional than technical in our appraisal of how this glorifying was being done.

As soon as we could, our gang examined this new translation, looking at texts that were key passages. Various fundamentalists who had seen advance copies had been screaming what they thought was wrong with it. In the first thing we checked they were right: the prophecy in Isaiah 7:14 of the virgin birth of Christ, was distorted: they had translated the Hebrew word *almah* as "young woman" instead of "virgin" (although in the New Testament quotation of this verse in Matthew 1:23 they did use the word "virgin"). Without reading any further and without checking the actual Hebrew (which we later found does indeed say "young woman," but does not imply by that term "non-virgin"), we had been quick to condemn the new version. We had decided we would stay with the KJV's beautiful cadences and its now-familiar, albeit archaic wording. An article in the November 1952 *Eternity* had confirmed our good judgment. Dr. O. T. Allis, Dr. Barnhouse's first professor of Hebrew, had given a scholarly review, showing the weaknesses of the translation and its obvious bias. We learned that Dr. Barnhouse himself had written a scathing denunciation of the New Testament portion when it was published in 1946, although he did admit that some passages were considerably clarified by the RSV.

Imagine our shock when seven months later the June 1953 *Eternity* carried a major article by Dr. Barnhouse entitled "I Have Read the RSV," which called the RSV a "useful tool"!

As Doug and I sat on the porch to read it, I said, "This is carrying that New Year's Resolution a little too far!"

We read the opening paragraph:

"I have heard a great deal about the new *Revised Standard Version* of the Bible during the past months and have found some people who are fanatically against it, and some people who are fanatically for it. I have put a very telling question to many of them. 'Have you read it completely?' In no case did I receive an affirmative answer. In all the history of biblical literature I do not know of any book that has had so much a priori judgment, both adverse and favorable. I have now completed the reading of the RSV Bible."

We looked at one another guiltily. We had judged it without reading more than one passage in Isaiah and its corresponding New Testament passage.

"I am concerned with but one question, which may be broken down into subdivisions later. My question concerns the content of the RSV, and whether it is an accurate translation of the Hebrew and Greek of the Old and New Testaments, and whether its mistakes and errors are such that it is untrustworthy for an individual to read."

He summed up the heated controversy, then said, "Now that some of the smoke has cleared away, let us make a calmer appraisal of the volume and see its merits and its demerits, and its value for various classes of people."

He told of his method of explaining the archaic words of the KJV as he taught. (For us this had been one of the best aspects of his teaching.) He had been doing his own translation of the Psalms, using the Hebrew, the Septuagint (Greek), the Latin, and many other translations. He discovered that it so very closely paralleled the new translation, he need not make any more translations of his own. He reported that fundamentalist translators on the mission field had found the RSV exceptionally helpful.

Speaking of Dr. Allis's review, he reiterated that it was true the translators do not believe the doctrine of inspiration: "The Bible is, to them, a purely human document, written by men who were setting down their groping search for religious truth. . . . But in spite of this, the *Revised Standard Version* is one of the best translations ever made of either the Old or the New Testaments. If it were put into the hands of an unsaved man, he could easily be led to a knowledge of Christ through its reading. If a man had no other translation and started to write a biblical theology, he would come, with no other tool, to the doctrines of the Trinity, the virgin birth of our Lord, the person and work of the Savior, and the inspiration of the Bible. In spite of the bias of the translators, their own work teaches all of these doctrines and more. . . .

"If some critic says that I have fully approved the RSV, and that I have become a modernist by so doing, you may classify him as someone who had read my words and twisted them to his own ends in order that he may attack me for those ends. All I am saying is that we have a new and very useful tool *if we accept it with its limitations,* neither abhorring it nor accepting it as final.

"And if you hear such criticism, ask the critic if he has read the RSV—every line and note of it. And does he know

Greek and Hebrew? And does he recognize the hundreds and hundreds of simplifications and clarifications in the RSV? And are the blatant biased passages sufficient to condemn the whole thing as a tool to be used to increase our knowledge of the Word of God? . . . It is a tool, and many of its edges are sharp, some of its edges are dull, and a few of its edges are chipped and broken. But on the whole it can be a very useful tool."

"Well!" I said. "What do you think?"

"I think," Doug replied, "we'd better read the RSV."

Early in 1953, on one of his trips to Philadelphia, Doug met the executive director of the North Africa Mission, whose offices were in the Evangelical Foundation building at that time. This mission needed someone to coordinate the monetary systems of the various North African countries it served, for more efficient distribution of supplies. Doug was asked to go to Tangiers to set this up and administer it until a trained missionary could take over. If when he got there it looked like a job of more than three or four months, Carolyn and I would join him in Tangiers. Carolyn would attend the University of Rome in the fall. (Our son, Douglas, was now a Naval Air Cadet; he would stay behind.) It was all very exciting.

Doug applied for passport and visas. He haunted the mailbox waiting for them to come. He packed his woodworking tools and other hobby equipment for long-term storage. In case it would be a briefer absence and I stayed home, he explained to me details of income and other taxes, as well as various business affairs I would have to attend to. Carolyn's graduation from high school on June 3 culminated a time of eager anticipation.

But that very night Doug suffered a massive heart attack.

He was rushed to Bradenton's small emergency hospital, which was the nearest. Treatment to dissolve the clot that partially blocked the heart was begun.

By the next afternoon there was enough improvement for our doctor to be cautiously optimistic. Doug lay there, revising his plans. At one point he lifted up on one elbow, and said, "Sugar, if anything happens to me, be sure to call Dr. Barnhouse. He'll know what to do."

"Oh, Doug, please lie still! Nothing's going to happen. Doug, the whole gang will be at prayer meeting tonight, and I know God will *have* to hear our prayers—"

"*Marge!*" The vehemence of his voice stopped me short. *"Don't you dare pray for God to keep me in this world.* Don't you *dare* mix your human will with His will. Ask that *His* will be done, and that we'll be willing to accept it, whatever it is. But don't you tell Him what to do! If He's ready to take me to heaven, I'm ready—and I'm eager! And I know He'll take care of you. But if He isn't ready to take me, *do you think anything could?*"

My spirit soared. Of course! *Nothing* could! I went happily to prayer meeting that evening, where we praised God for all He was doing and all He was about to do. At home I went promptly to sleep, convinced Doug would be well in no time.

God had other plans. I was awakened by a two A.M. call from the hospital. The clot had suddenly shifted and was blocking the heart. I rushed to the hospital. There I saw a flurry of doctors and nurses around Doug; oxygen and emergency equipment were set up around his bed. He cried a low cry, "I'm so cold! So cold!" and hot water bottles were packed around him immediately. I whispered, "The Lord is here, Doug. Hang on!" He winced once in pain and in a sharp cry of panic said, "I'm afraid!" I held his hand and recited Psalm 23.

Then the rising sun reached out a finger of light and touched Doug's face; his eyes opened wide and he looked out, out, beyond, with surprise, joy, and longing, it seemed. Then quietly he was gone.

My heart went with him. Not grief, but joy filled me— joy which was almost envy. How could death be like this?

The open door, the sunlit garden beyond that Dr. Barnhouse had once likened it to. Yes.

In this strange mood I moved through the inevitable "arrangements," then went home to the terrible task of telephoning the relatives.

At last Doug's words of the day before filtered up into my consciousness. "Be sure to call Dr. Barnhouse." I hesitated. It was still so early. But Paul Hopkins would be at the Evangelical Foundation. I'd call him and he could tell Dr. Barnhouse.

Once he was on the line, I said, "Paul, do you really believe Romans 8:28?"

"Of course, Marge."

"Well, so do I . . . I don't know how the Lord will do it, but I'm hanging on to it hard. Paul . . . Doug had a heart attack night before last. And Paul—he's gone."

There was utter silence at the other end. Then he said, "Marge, are *you* all right? Yes, you *are* all right, I can tell. Thanks for letting me know. I don't know what to say. I'm shocked. . . ."

"Yesterday Doug said if anything happened to be sure to call Dr. Barnhouse. Will you tell him?"

"Certainly. Marge, this *is* a shock. Can we do anything?"

"Everything has been arranged. Everyone has been wonderful. Three years ago I couldn't have taken it, but . . . I can't tell you . . . the peace that passeth understanding . . . and as long as I keep my eyes up it keeps my chin up."

"Staff prayer meeting is about to begin. You will be held up mightily, Marge, and I'll call back later. I'll tell Dr. Barnhouse. Bless you."

I hung up slowly. Dr. Barnhouse called minutes later. His voice boomed over the line: "Marge! Paul just told me! Why didn't you call me direct?"

"I thought it was too early."

"Paul says you're all right—that the Lord is upholding."

"I guess I'm still in shock. But I never knew death could be like this." I told him what Doug had said ("Do you think anything could take me?") so I *had* to know this was God's will even if it didn't make sense. I told him about the shaft of sunlight, about how Doug had looked, about what he had said. "He wanted me to be sure I called you."

Dr. Barnhouse seemed frustrated. "I cannot possibly come . . . I'm preaching the baccalaureate at Barnard and then flying immediately to Europe, and I won't be back until the end of July. This grieves me. I wish I could be there. You know my prayers will be with you, even if I can't. If there is anything at all that I can do, please don't hesitate to call. Lord bless you, Marge."

The possibility that he might come had not occurred to me. In a way I was glad he couldn't. His teaching had undergirded us, but this was a personal "family" affair for our Florida group, and Dr. Barnhouse would have been an outsider.

Our minister's car, bringing Carolyn in from her senior houseparty at the beach, stopped outside and Carolyn ran up the path. She clung to me tightly for a moment, then drew back and looked into my face.

"It's all right, Mommy," she said. "Daddy was going on a journey, and he's just gone on a longer one. We had planned to join him . . . and we will, someday!"

NINE

It was strange to know that Doug would not be coming back from that journey. I had to adjust to making my own plans and taking care of my own affairs. Shortly after the funeral I had come to Proverbs 3:5, 6 in my Bible reading, and decided that these verses would be my "life text"; "Trust in the Lord with all thine heart; and lean not unto thine own understanding. In all thy ways acknowledge him, and he shall direct thy paths."

In Him I felt secure: He *would* direct my paths.

Douglas had returned to Pensacola and the Navy. Carolyn and I decided to take a trip to Albany, New York, to see my mother. We planned to be in New York City on the way back, on a Monday night when Dr. Barnhouse would be preaching at his New York Bible class, so I wrote Paul Hopkins for his schedule. I wanted my brother Wally to go with us to the class and share some of that great teaching.

As we pulled up in front of our New York City hotel that last Monday in July I was astonished to see Dr. Barnhouse bound out of the restaurant across the street where apparently he had been keeping watch. How dear of him! He took charge immediately, as in the old days of our trip with him. He saw that the car was taken care of, the luggage taken up to the room, and even came up with us to be sure our room was all right. In the elevator he looked hard at me, like a doctor figuring a diagnosis: "How *is* everything, Marge?"

"Well, frankly, I am just coming out of the numb stage. It's an odd feeling, being a widow. When we went with Mother to the club for dinner yesterday, one of my oldest friends, recently a widower, saw me, and with *that look* in his eyes sat up and straightened his tie, and suddenly I realized I *am* a widow, and had better be on my guard."

He gave me an odd look, shook his head slightly, and ushered us off the elevator.

"Tell me about your brother Wally." As we followed the bellboy to the room I explained that because Doug and I had grown so under his preaching I wanted Wally to hear it too; Carolyn and I were having dinner with Wally and Carolyn's date, but we would be at the meeting before it began.

"How about some ice cream afterward? Then if he has questions we can discuss them."

Bless him! *Of course....*

When the class was over, Dr. Barnhouse didn't wait to greet people down front as usual. Instead he took my arm and all five of us started down the steps of the church together. At that hour the sidewalks were crowded with people; somehow Dr. Barnhouse and I were separated from Wally, Carolyn, and her date, who went forging on ahead across Times Square.

His voice drew my attention.

"Do you believe in predestination?"

Intense blue eyes looked down into mine with a look that started an old-fashioned blush creeping up to the roots of my hair. We were flowing across Times Square with the flood of pedestrians; his guiding hand on my elbow tightened with a sort of urgency and pressed my arm against him. He *knew* I believed in predestination.

"What do you mean?" I countered, forcing myself to

look right back at him, as if I didn't know exactly what—
to my astonishment—he meant. All the time my heart was
beating wildly and crying silently, "Oh, no, Lord—not I!
I'm not the type! I'm not the one—not *I, Lord!*"

He stepped up onto the curb and he never took his eyes
from me. It is a good thing we had been cushioned and
borne along by all the hurrying people because we might
as well have been in the middle of the Sahara for all the
notice he had been taking of the dangers of traffic. His eyes
were at once bold and shy and, yes, *scared.*

"If you don't know what I mean, I'll never mention it
again, because I don't want my feelings hurt. But if you *do*
know what I mean . . . well, later on—at a more appropriate time—we'll discuss it further."

Well! My husband had been dead barely two months.
This was really too much! I bristled, desperately trying to
keep things on an even keel. The blush was clear to the
crown of my head. His touch, instead of the familiar, kind-
ly guidance of the great Bible teacher, was charged with
electricity.

"I think you're terrible!" was all I could manage to say.
He whooped like a young boy, gave my elbow a squeeze,
and cried, "That's all I wanted to know!" (What did he
think I had told him?) He then stepped out at such a brisk
and buoyant pace that even my long legs had trouble
keeping up with him.

Baffled, I looked at his handsome head thrown back, his
strong profile above me. Could it be that I was called to
answer my own prayer for a wife for this man? When Doug
died, I had told the Lord with all the sincerity of a heart as
yielded as I knew how to make it, "I'll go where You want
me to go, do what You want me to do, be what You want
me to be," but—*this?* I knew how Moses must have felt
when from the burning bush the Lord had informed him
He was about to liberate the children of Israel from Egypt:
"Very interesting, Lord. Great!" *And Moses, you're the one
who's to do it.* "I? Oh, no, Lord, not I! I can think of all sorts

of reasons why I'm not the one. . . ." *But, Moses, I have chosen you.*

My heart cried, "Lord, show me! Open the door if it is to be opened. Shut it if it is to be shut. . . ."

By this time we had caught up with the others. Soon we were laughing and talking over ice cream and coffee, and I wondered if I had imagined it. Afterward, Dr. Barnhouse escorted us back to our hotel.

"Stay over at least through Friday, Marge, and go with me to the Coatesville meetings. I'm speaking on the subject of 'Where are the Dead?' and I think you should hear this."

"But, my Bible class!"

"You'll have more to give them after this. You will be called upon many times to comfort those who have lost loved ones, now that you yourself have been through it and know what they are up against. This will give you something that will put them firmly on the Rock, with joy. 'Sorrowful, yet always rejoicing. . . .' "

I should get back, I thought. *And yet . . . and yet. . . .*

I stayed. Tuesday morning, Carolyn flew back to Bradenton for a wedding, while I drove to Wayne, just west of Philadelphia, to spend the rest of the week with Jeanne and Paul Hopkins, who welcomed me warmly. Paul suggested that I go in to the Evangelical Foundation with him Wednesday morning, attend a staff meeting, and meet the people Doug had talked about so enthusiastically.

That evening Dr. Barnhouse picked me up for the half-hour or so drive to Coatesville. It was like the "old times" of our trip back in the beginning, although it seemed strange not to have Doug there too. Once or twice I thought I saw "that look" in Dr. Barnhouse's eyes, and put up my guard, but mostly he maintained an attitude of relaxed friendship, reminiscing about that other trip, letting me see how much he had valued Doug's friendship and advice. And the sermon—oh, the sermon! Part of this I had heard in Sarasota all those months ago. But this time Dr. Barnhouse's tone was different. There was no lashing out.

Next morning, Paul and I took the Paoli Local to Philadelphia. As the train stopped at Bryn Mawr I thought how often I had waited on that platform for that train back in my college days.

In about half an hour we were in Philadelphia. We made our way down Seventeenth Street and my attention was drawn to the building ahead of us on the corner of Spruce Street.

"Paul! Isn't that Tenth Presbyterian Church?"

"That's Tenth," said Paul. "Haven't you seen it before?"

"Never! I saw the pictures of it in the booklet Doug brought back from the twenty–fifth anniversary celebration, but that's all. So that's Tenth!"

We had turned onto Spruce Street and were passing it now. I looked at the weathered old bricks, the truncated towers, one on the left and a smaller one on the right, that had once borne soaring steeples, long since removed because age was crumbling them. Across the front, at the top of some steps, beautifully wrought iron gates closed off the entrance. It looked serene, aloof. I wished I could see it when the gates were open, with people crowding in.

Then we were four doors beyond the church, climbing the steps of the old townhouse that was headquarters for the Evangelical Foundation. Paul introduced me to the various staff workers. I was glad there was time before the meeting to speak to Nan and Ralph Keiper, and to meet the newest member of the staff, Russell Hitt, who would be managing Dr. Barnhouse's conference ministry.

The staff meeting was held in Dr. Barnhouse's office, a large room on the second floor that had an elegant fireplace faced with jade green tiling, a large desk, several nondescript armchairs, and a hide-a-bed couch where he could spend the night when he had early morning appointments in town. Folding chairs had been set up for the staff.

The format of the meeting was probably standard for most religious organizations, but for me it was brand new and impressive. It began with a time of individual prayer, followed by prayer for the requests sent in by radio listeners. Paul reported both the progress and the needs of the work for that week, then gave a devotional message, closing with a prayer of praise and thanksgiving. I was overwhelmed by the whole tone of the meeting: here were people who really believed in what they were doing, and I sensed that even the humblest job was being done to the glory of God. What a backup team for DGB!

Afterward, Paul took me through the building. On the way to his office, which apparently had been the library of the old house, we passed through what had at one time been a living room, now converted into a general office. Over the beautiful fireplace mantle the staff had inscribed the motto they had chosen for the work:

And whatever ye do, do it heartily, as to the Lord, and not unto men . . . for ye serve the Lord Christ.   Col. 3:23, 24

We visited the various departments. Throughout, I marveled at the way the rooms had so easily been adapted to office space while still preserving the old fireplaces and beautiful ceilings.

Paul took me up Seventeenth Street to the Warwick Hotel for an elegant lunch. There, in an offhand way, he began to tell me what a really terrific person Dr. Barnhouse was. I couldn't believe my ears: it sounded just like Doug and me, matchmaking, on that trip! *Lord, are You trying to tell me something? Paul obviously doesn't know that Dr. Barnhouse is already way ahead of him, yet here he is with apparently the same idea. . . . "If two of you shall agree on earth as touching anything that they shall ask. . . ." Lord, are You, through Paul, telling me this really is Your idea?*

When Dr. Barnhouse picked me up for the Wednesday night meeting in Coatesville I saw "that look" in his eyes again, unmistakably, but he quickly masked it and asked what I had been doing all day. When I told him of my visit to the Foundation he said, "Why didn't you let me know? I'd have come in from the Farm and escorted you around myself!"

I laughed. "Doug and I disrupted your work enough, on that trip! I hadn't realized how much until I saw the magnitude of the ministry. I am impressed with your Evangelical Foundation staff, Dr. Barnhouse."

For the rest of the trip he filled me in on the various secretaries and other workers, giving me their backgrounds and how they happened to come to work for him.

The sermons in Coatesville all that week were tremendous. How little the average Christian really knows of his position in Christ! How little *I* knew of what God wants us to know about the joy of eternal life with Him after death, or the dreadfulness of eternal existence without Him. Questions I hadn't known I had (because my conscious mind had avoided them) were answered so simply from God's Word.

"I am often asked, 'Dr. Barnhouse, do you believe the fires of Hell are literal?' I am forced to answer that if you have trampled the blood of Christ underfoot, and *will not* 'come unto God by Him,' then I hope for your sake that they *are* literal. Because if they are not, they are so much worse they cannot be described in human speech. Words are for conveying ideas: if literal, this is strange 'fire,' for it is described as 'outer darkness' where 'their worm dieth not, and the fire is not quenched.' And if you go there, you will stumble over the cross of Christ as you go.

"Every once in a while you hear someone joke, 'Ha! *I* don't want to go to heaven! I'd rather go to hell and be where all my friends are!' But you won't see your friends. God says, in 1 Samuel 2:9, 'The wicked shall be silent in darkness,' and in Psalm 31:17, 'Let them be silent in the grave,' never knowing the touch of another hand or hearing another voice, with no companion but memory churning in endless frustration: 'He did *that* to me'; 'I wanted that and never got it'; 'She said *that* about me and I never had a chance to get back at her.' How much worse it is than literal flames if the worm of conscience never dies and the fire of memory is never quenched.

"However, you must understand that before the Resurrection the place of *all* the dead, saved or unsaved, was, in Hebrew, 'sheol'; in Greek, 'hades'; in English, 'hell.' Before Christ died this was divided into two places (call it East Hell and West Hell, if it will help you to see the difference), and between the two there was a great gulf fixed. On one side was torment in hell, and on the other side was paradise in hell, referred to also as 'Abraham's Bosom.' Jesus, as He hung on the cross, said to the repentant thief hanging beside Him, 'Today you shall be with me in paradise,' and when He died His soul and spirit *descended into hell,* the *paradise* side of hell. Here were all who before the cross had believed God's Word and obeyed it, saved by bringing a lamb and having its blood shed for their sins.

"The Book of Hebrews tells us that the life-blood of those sacrifices covered their sins but did not *pay* for them. But when Jesus, 'the Lamb of God *that taketh away* the sin of the world,' hung on that cross, all of those Old Testament sins were uncovered and placed upon the sinless Son of God. When He died, those sins were *paid for,* along with the sins of the whole world to the end of time. Oh, can you imagine the high joy of those in the paradise side of hell when Jesus appeared to them and announced that their long wait was over, that their sins had been paid for forever, and that He had come to 'take captivity captive,' empty paradise in hell, and take them, cleansed by His blood, into the very presence of the heavenly Father? And when He rose again on the third day, He did just that, and from then on paradise has been in heaven, with God Himself. So now, when a believer dies, to be absent from the body is to be present with the Lord, as we read in 2 Corinthians 5:8.

"But for the unbeliever *nothing has changed.* When he dies his soul and spirit go to the torment side of hell, there to await the final judgment, becoming more hard and bitter as the years roll on. . . ."

At the end of that sermon he reminded the unbelievers that the cross *was* there, blocking their way to hell, and he implored them not to bypass it and go unheeding into that dreadful, eternal outer darkness. "Claim the redemption Christ has bought for you, and enter instead into the joy of eternal life!"

The following night this question was in his question box: "My sister was raised a Christian, along with the rest of us, knew the Bible stories, and learned many Bible verses when she was little, but when she was older she turned hard and bitter against the Lord. She has recently died. She was such a good person, humanly speaking, I can't bear the thought that she might be in hell. Is there a chance that the Lord might have relented a little and let her into heaven?"

Dr. Barnhouse's answer: "God's holiness demands that anything or anybody entering His presence must be cleansed by the shed blood of the Lord Jesus Christ—and that includes our prayers. So there is no chance that the Lord might 'relent' in His entrance requirements for heaven. But there is every chance that your sister may have repented. None of us can know the state of a person's heart at the moment of death: a seemingly 'lost' person may repent at the last moment and be just as saved as the repentant thief on the cross. Let me illustrate:

"In England at the turn of the century a young mother, knowing she was dying of tuberculosis, concentrated on teaching her little son to memorize as many Bible verses as possible, whether or not he understood them. By the time he was five years old he knew more than five hundred verses. The mother died, and the child was sent to her brother, a worldly man who was determined the child was not to be a 'sissy.'

"At the age of nineteen or so this young man was put in charge of training the cadets in Queen Victoria's navy. What a change! It was said he could swear for two hours without repeating himself, and he bragged that he didn't need God and was going to make his young cadets as tough as he was.

"One day on maneuvers he was in the crow's nest shouting instructions laced with blasphemies. The cadets climbed the rigging, set or furled the sails, leaped to battle stations, did his bidding. The sea was totally calm under a clear sky. Suddenly the young man shouted through his megaphone, 'Look at me, you blankety-blank-blank cadets!'

"Every cadet froze in position; every eye turned to him as he stood there in the crow's nest, a commanding figure. He flung his arms wide and cried, *"If there is a God in heaven, why doesn't he strike me dead?"* Scarcely were the words out of his mouth when a giant ocean swell rose out of nowhere and pitched the ship violently; to the horror of the cadets the young man tumbled headlong into the ocean.

"If that had been the end of the story any one of them could have said, 'I just saw a man go straight to hell!' But they grabbed a boathook and fished him out, and as they pumped the seawater out of his lungs they heard him mumbling something and thought he was still blaspheming. Instead he was saying, 'Jesus! Jesus! Oh, praise God for saving my soul!' In those brief moments from the time he toppled from the crow's nest to the time he hit the water all the Bible verses his mother had taught him had come rushing back through his mind. He realized the horror of what he had been and said and done, asked the Lord to forgive him, and was saved. Shortly thereafter he left the navy and became one of England's noted street preachers.

"In this same way the Bible verses could have come back to your sister with convicting power, and she could well be in heaven."

That night his sermon was on heaven. "Don't think for a minute that all you'll do is sit on a cloud, strum a harp, and polish your crown. These things are symbols: the harp signifies ecstacy, as music does; the crown signifies rule.

"Imagine being at the peak of perfect health and vitality. Imagine never getting tired, and having all of eternity to do to the glory of God the things He has given you gifts for. Are you a botanist? I can imagine God creating a new planet for you, teeming with wildflowers and new species of plant life, then saying, 'Go there and classify them for Me!' " Dr. Barnhouse began naming other interests and showing how God could use us to glorify Him in them. His audience leaned forward, new joy on their faces.

"Once after I had preached this sermon a man came to me and said, 'Dr. Barnhouse, until now I haven't really looked forward to heaven. I thought I'd be bored. But now—!' and he wrung my hand.

"What will heaven itself be like? Well, for one thing, you won't have a mansion. *'What?'* you say. 'I won't have a mansion? But I've looked forward to my mansion, and Jesus Himself promises me one, in John 14:2.' Now do you really want to be stuck off by yourself in a big, ostentatious mansion anxiously watching to be sure no one else has a bigger or grander one? No, no! The *Revised Standard Version* correctly translates John 14:2 this way, 'In my Father's house are many *rooms.'* You will be in your heavenly Father's own house, and Jesus Himself has prepared the room that will be exclusively, uniquely yours. You know how it is when you expect guests: you consider their likes and dislikes, their needs, little things that will delight them, and you prepare the room. The Greek word means 'abodes.' Your abiding place will be in the Father's house; you will be an intimate part of the family, as David tells us in Psalm 23, *dwelling in the house of the Lord for ever."*

Night after night I listened as the great doctrines of the Bible were unfolded and made plain: death, burial, resurrection, the afterlife, the second coming of Christ, and it was more and more glorious. Then on the final night he talked about what happens to the believer at the actual moment of death, as he goes to meet his Beloved at last.

"And what is more, if Jesus is truly your Savior, you

will not pass across the threshold of death alone. Let me illustrate.

"Suppose a mother has a son in the service. She doesn't know when he'll be home, but she goes about saying, 'When John comes home, he'll dig the garden.' 'When John comes home, he'll fix the windowshade.' 'When John comes home, he. . . .' 'When John comes home, he. . . .' Then one day there is the sound of a step on the stair, the door is flung open, she looks up and cries, 'John! *You!*' Now, why did she change from 'John, he. . .' to 'John, you. . .'? *Because John had come in the door.* Now listen: 'The Lord is my shepherd; I shall not want, *he* maketh me to lie down in green pastures; *he* leadeth me beside the still waters. *He* restoreth my soul: *he* leadeth me in the paths of righteousness for his name's sake.' But [and at this point Dr. Barnhouse leaned forward over the pulpit] 'Yea, though I walk through the valley of the shadow of death, I will fear no evil: for—' " He stopped, and without a break *"Thou!"* breathed up from the audience like a prayer. He echoed softly, "Thou! *'Thou art with me.'* Thou hast come for me, oh, my Savior. I do not walk the valley of the shadow of death alone. Jesus Christ comes into the room as a real presence at the moment of death to enfold me in His arms and take me as His own to the Father's house."

Faces all around me were radiant, although eyes—including mine—were blurred with tears.

Doug had cried out, "I'm afraid!" but at the moment of his death I knew he was afraid no longer, and now I knew why: *"Thou!"*

TEN

The last night of the Coatesville meetings, Dr. Barnhouse took me back to the Hopkins's; once again I felt his hand at my elbow, guiding me up the porch steps to the front door. Putting his hand under my chin, he turned my face up to the light. His eyes traveled over my face, my hair, then my face again, with a look of deep tenderness.

"Marge," he said, "before that trip with you and Doug was over I knew I was falling in love with you. I determined not to let it happen. I figured that with so many people trying to marry me off, maybe that was what I needed, and I'd marry the first eligible woman I met. But it just didn't work . . . and now the Lord has made *this* possible. . . ."

Gently I took his hand down from my chin, opening the front door with my other hand. So I *hadn't* imagined it on Monday night; I needed time. . . .

"Good night, Dr. Barnhouse," I said softly.

He had not let go the hand that had touched his. He lifted it to his lips, kissed it gently, and said, "Good night, Marge." Then he turned and went quickly to the car.

I went in, closed the door, and leaned against it. In some strange way it was as if I were closing the covers of a book in which I had been totally absorbed, that I had now finished: my twenty-two years with Doug Bell as my husband. I would enjoy going back, leafing through the pages, remembering our sometimes stormy but nevertheless wonderful marriage, but the reality was no longer there. Love, gratitude, regrets, joy—yes, but as if it had all happened to a different me. After glimpsing all week through those sermons the glories of heaven I couldn't wish Doug back. . . .

My feelings toward Dr. Barnhouse were all mixed up. Doug and I had really loved him as a friend, as a person. Now there was a whole new dimension of feeling, a different kind of love, welling underneath the other. I couldn't cope with it—not yet.

That night I drifted off to sleep with Proverbs 3:5, 6 running through my mind: *Lord, I do trust You. Lord Jesus, in all my ways I do acknowledge You. Direct my paths!*

Saturday morning, with my bags all packed for the drive to Baltimore that afternoon, the first leg of my journey home to Florida, I was having a leisurely breakfast with Jeanne and Paul and the children when Dr. Barnhouse called. He had a few words with Paul, then asked to speak to me.

"My son David and his wife are here for the weekend. I'd love to have them meet you. Can't you swing by the Farm for lunch? Baltimore is only a couple of hours from here and I can put you on the turnpike at a nearby interchange in plenty of time for you to be there for dinner. . . ."

I hesitated. I wasn't sure I was quite ready to see him again so soon. But I wasn't expected in Baltimore until afternoon . . . and I did want to see the famous Farm . . . and it would be nice to meet his children. . . .

"Well—yes, I'd like that."

"Paul can tell you how to get here. I'll see you shortly!"

I put down the receiver. "Shortly!" But I had planned to spend the morning with the Hopkinses!

Paul heard me hang up, and called, "Your coffee's getting cold!" I went back to the dining room. He said, "DGB told me he wants you to meet David and Mary Alice. Great idea! You'll like them. When you've finished your coffee, I'll put your bags in the car and give you directions. It's a beautiful day for the Farm!"

Jeanne smiled a somehow conspiratorial smile and said, "I'm so glad you'll get to see it!" *(Jeanne, too,* I thought. *Everyone seems to be throwing Dr. Barnhouse and me together.)*

Within half an hour I was on my way.

Paul's instructions took me in less than an hour into Doylestown, then down Pebble Hill Road. As I reached the lane leading to the house, I saw Dr. Barnhouse coming eagerly out to meet me. He jumped into the right front seat as I slowed for the turn. Joyous vitality radiated from him.

"Drive right on past the house and park at the circle," he said, looking at me fondly.

Great maples arched over the lane; a split rail fence on the right was abloom with scarlet roses; beyond it was a sun-drenched meadow fragrant with new-mown hay, and beyond that a small lake. On the left the pillars of the porch shone white in the cool shadows of the maples as we passed the house. I pulled up at the turnabout beyond the house, parking in the shade of an enormous maple tree.

Dr. Barnhouse leaped out of the car, walked swiftly around, and opened my door. One hand on the door handle, the other on the door jamb, he blocked my way, looking teasingly at me. The only way for me to get out was into his arms! I slid across the seat and got out the other side. Laughing, he came around, took my hand, and said, "Come, meet David and Mary Alice!"

Instead of leading me back to the steps that went up to the porch and the front door he turned up a small path to what looked like a wing on the main house. (Later I was to learn that this was actually the original house, built in 1720. The "main house" had been added in 1780.) We climbed three stone steps, crossed a worn old doorstep, and stepped into an enchanting large room, obviously the dining room. On three sides it was half-paneled in wood that was painted colonial blue, one of my favorite colors. Windows recessed in eighteen-inch-thick fieldstone walls let in the sunlight. In the floor-to-ceiling paneling of the fourth wall was a huge walk-in fireplace, with an old copper kettle hanging there on a crane. A door in that wall opened, and in came David, followed by Mary Alice.

David looked as his father must have looked at that age. Preparatory to going as a missionary to India he was a medical student at Columbia University in New York. Mary Alice was charming. They seemed a happy pair, obviously soon to become parents.

Introductions over, Mary Alice opened the door through which they had just come. "We're putting some lunch together," she said. "Want to come join us in the kitchen?"

We followed her into a big, modern kitchen, where vegetables fresh from the garden were heaped on the counter by the sink. "Let me help!" I cried, picking up a paring knife.

Dr. Barnhouse and David sat down at the big center table and were given corn to shuck. After an hour of happy conversation and agreeable work, lunch was ready. We decided to eat right there in the cheerful kitchen, where we could keep the muffins hot in the oven and the corn steaming, ready for second—and third!—helpings.

As we were finishing our dessert, I was suddenly aware that the cuckoo, which had been popping out of the clock on the wall every half hour, had sounded three o'clock.

"It can't be!" I cried. "It's awful to eat and run, but I'm afraid I've got to run." I rose from the table.

Dr. Barnhouse put a restraining hand on my arm. "But you can't go yet—I haven't shown you the house! And the garden! And—"

"Dr. Barnhouse, that will have to wait until next time. I *must* go."

As I said "until next time" his eyes lit up. I realized there undoubtedly would be a "next time."

"I'll take my car and lead you over the shortcut to the

road that will take you to the turnpike," he said. As he put me into my car, he laid his hand softly for a moment on my cheek. David and Mary Alice stood behind him, calling out their good-byes. His lips soundlessly formed the words, "I love you." Then with a cheery "Follow me!" he went to his car.

All the way to Baltimore I was in turmoil. I said nothing of this to my relatives. We were so busy catching up on family news that no one asked me what I had been doing in Philadelphia. Sunday I continued on my way, stopping in Norfolk to see Doug's parents.

As we sat at dinner that night the telephone rang, and Doug's father answered it. "It's for you, Marge," he said. "Dr. Barnhouse."

With some trepidation I answered. Dr. Barnhouse said Paul had told him where I'd be. He just wanted to be sure I had arrived all right; he wondered where my next stop would be and when I'd be home. When I returned to the table Doug's father asked, "What's with Dr. Barnhouse?"

I looked from one to the other of those dear faces. *Lord, I prayed, guide me. I wouldn't hurt these two for anything in the world. Crossing Times Square that night I asked You to open the door if it is to be opened, and shut it if it is to be shut. If this door closes, then that's my answer.* "I'm afraid he's falling in love with me."

Doug's father paused, fork halfway to his mouth.

"Is that *bad?*" he asked.

Astonished, I looked at Doug's mother. She put down her knife and fork, and leaned toward me earnestly.

"Now Marge," she said, "there's no point in your sitting home alone grieving your heart out. Dr. Barnhouse is a good man. Now, don't *en*courage him—but don't *dis*courage him, either."

The door had fallen flat off its hinges. *(Lord, what are You trying to tell me?)*

In the long stretches of driving after I left Norfolk I argued with the Lord, pushing aside my emotions, telling

Him Dr. Barnhouse was fourteen years older than I; I was not the right type; I didn't know enough; it was too soon.

The Lord just seemed to smile, not saying a word.

Home again, I plunged once more into Child Evangelism and my Bible classes and the prayer group. I decided not to say anything to my friends yet: I had to get my own feelings straightened out first.

Then letters began coming from Dr. Barnhouse. He wrote me of his doings, sharing his thoughts, disclosing his innermost self to me like a friend, but with opening and closing endearments that made my heart pound like a schoolgirl's and turned the letters into love letters:

The Lord gave me a wonderful sermon for today. My introduction told of finding an article in Fowler's English Usage *entitled "Love of the Long Word" which pointed out traps people who use too many long words get themselves into. . . . He then spoke of great prose in simple words and quoted a paragraph with 101 words, 89 of which were words of one syllable. Then I outlined my sermon in words of one syllable:*

> I *All have sinned* Rom. 3:23
>
> II *The Son of God loved me* Gal. 2:20
>
> III *He died for all* 2 Cor. 5:15
>
> IV *Come to me and I will give you rest* Matt. 11:28
>
> V *We shall be like him for we shall see him as he is* 1 Jn. 3:2
>
> VI *Go and sin no more* Jn. 8:11

Many people were greatly blessed and as the faucet gets cold from the water flowing through so I was refreshed. And writing to you here refreshes my heart.

I could imagine how he might have fleshed out that outline, and was wishing I could have heard it. I loved his sharing of this in a letter. The trouble was, it began, "Dear

Darling dear," and ended, "Your own love, Donald," taking for granted that everything between us was settled.

What do you do with a man like that? I felt trapped. I had always been sure I could control my own destiny and make my own decisions. I was a living example of the little plaque one sees, "Lord, there is no situation that You *and I* together cannot handle." Apparently a sovereign God had already decided, without my help. Yet all the while through my annoyance there kept sounding softly, "Dear Darling dear... Your own love, Donald... Dear Darling dear...."

When the October issue of *Eternity* arrived, I saved it until the busyness of the day was over and I could curl up in bed, and read what I had looked forward to since it was announced in the September issue: *The Invisible War.*

The Invisible War! From the first time I had heard Dr. Barnhouse mention it, as he preached in Tampa on "Satan: Who He Really Is: What He Is Trying to Do," I had been interested in knowing more about it. Dr. Barnhouse had said he was in the midst of writing a book about it; now it was appearing in serial form, in *Eternity,* beginning with the October 1953 issue. According to the Bible, every believer is a soldier in that war. I wanted to learn how to use "the whole armor of God" of Ephesians 6:10-18.

An editorial in the September issue had announced that these installments of the book would cover "the whole plan of God from the time of the creation of Lucifer down through the fall of Lucifer and the consequent steps which God took in the light of the entrance of sin into the universe. The story of this invisible war is then traced through man's creation, the entrance of sin into the human race, and the conflict of the ages, the triumph of the cross of Christ and the ultimate manifestation of God's final victory."

With great anticipation I opened the October issue to the first installment, and was plunged immediately into one of his great illustrations explaining the "gap theory," which he had touched on lightly in Tampa. As with so many of his books, I had heard him preach on much of the material, but it was good to see it in print and have time to re-read and digest it. This began with Genesis 1:1 and the gap theory, then launched into how to study your Bible to get from it the message God wants you to hear.

The ending of this installment whetted my appetite for more:

"Some time ago, I took my family. . . . to see [the Grand Canyon], certainly among the greatest of all the scenic wonders of this earth's surface. We arrived at our cabins just as darkness was falling, and it was night before we were able to go to the rim of the canyon. At our feet lay a blackness as deep as the night above. My children stood beside me as I told them what lay at their feet. I described the vast chaos that was between us and the pinpoints of lights, fifteen miles away on the southern rim. It could not be seen in the darkness of the night, and all that I had told them had to be taken on faith. But next morning we returned for the sunrise. First of all we could see the outline of far peaks, towering high above the canyon. They were visible while the pit beneath was still in darkness. As the moments passed, we began to see the rough outlines of the canyon rim, though the bottom still lay invisible in the darkness. It was only when the sun had lighted the peaks fully and the canyon's rim was bathed in light that the scene below became visible. So it is with the study of the Word of God.

"The light of God comes to the human heart progressively. 'He that cometh to God must believe that He is, and that He is a rewarder of them that diligently seek Him' (Heb. 11:6). Then the peaks light up. We see Sinai and tremble at the law, realizing our death in sin. Then Mt. Calvary shines forth and we see the Saviour dying in our stead. We believe and are saved. Then light grows clearer, and we begin to know more about ourselves and our daily walk. Then we begin to see the light of God fall into the great deeps of His eternal plan; only then can we hope to have the answer to the great questions of the past and the future which rise out of the fact that there is an invisible war which is being fought furiously and in which we have a greater strategic role than we might imagine."

I glanced back at what had preceded that closing passage. It was all so simple, yet so profound. *(Lord, who am I, to be a "help suitable" to a man who knows so much and can express it like this?)*

I decided I'd like to have Mother meet Dr. Barnhouse. I wrote and told her I wanted to see the fall foliage. I could drive up to Kentucky to visit Dad's sisters; she could fly out and meet me there, and we could drive the Pennsylvania Turnpike together when the color was at its height. Dr. Barnhouse had invited us to stop in Doylestown en route. "He knows you love old china; he has a collection of eighteenth-century teacups he thinks you might enjoy seeing. How about it?"

So it was arranged. Dr. Barnhouse telephoned me immediately upon receiving my letter accepting his invitation.

"Marge, this is marvelous! When? When?"

"Well, we can fit the date into your schedule."

"Tomorrow!"

"Silly! Seriously, when in October would it suit you for us to come?"

"How about Saturday the tenth? I'll be preaching in Kansas City that week and flying home Friday night. You and your mother could come in to Tenth Church on Sunday and hear me preach, then stay on—"

"Wait a minute. Let me look at our schedule. No, we'd have to drive on to Albany Sunday because Mother has an appointment there on Monday. But we could arrive in the late afternoon on Saturday the tenth and spend Saturday night at your Farm."

As we drove on the turnpike through glorious color a few weeks later, Mother was asking all sorts of questions about the Farm. I told her what Dr. Barnhouse had told Doug and me: for years he and his family had lived in a house directly behind Tenth Church, with nothing but sidewalk around it. The children had to be taken five blocks to a park for green grass to play on. He and his wife had dreamed of retiring to the country someday, where they could grow their own fruits and vegetables and have eggs fresh from their own chickens and milk fresh from their own cow. Then, at forty-two, his wife developed cancer. Knowing she might not have long to live, Dr. Barnhouse determined that she should have her dream farm. While he was off on his conference tours, she and little Dorothy would drive through the countryside around Philadelphia, looking. One day they crested a small rise in the road, near Doylestown, and his wife cried, "There it is!" There was no "For Sale" sign on it, but she felt certain that was "it."

When Dr. Barnhouse came back home he investigated. In the providence of the Lord it had been put on the market just that morning. A wealthy friend offered the down payment, and his church agreed to continue the manse rent allowance they had been paying over the years, which would cover the monthly mortgage payments.

The place was overgrown with weeds; poison ivy tangled the hedgerows and choked the trees. But the seventeenth-century field stone house was sound. The topsoil in the fields was twelve to sixteen inches deep; he and his two boys and Uncle Toby (his wife's brother) cleared and plowed and harrowed and sowed, little by little reclaiming the land and restoring the beauty of the house. He had an apartment built over the garage, where for a while Toby and his wife, Gertrude, lived. They oversaw the Farm when he was away. He placed it in irrevocable trust for his children and named it "Barchdale," Barnhouse Children's Dale. When his wife died he continued to live there, bringing in a Latvian family, displaced by World War II, to do the farming.

Dr. Barnhouse had written me that the chrysanthemums he had planted that spring were just coming into bloom, and the place was beautiful.

Mother and I approached Barchdale, and I pulled to the side of the road and stopped for a moment. A quarter of a mile away the maple trees that lined the lane leading to the house blazed with color. Long afternoon shadows lay across the lawns. The white columns of the porch shone in slanting sunbeams. No wonder his wife had fallen in love with it!

We started again, and turned into the lane. Dr. Barnhouse came striding out to meet us. My heart leapt when I saw him. I was afraid he was going to hug me, but he restrained himself.

We were escorted to our room and left to freshen up. Dr. Barnhouse was waiting at the foot of the stairs when we came back down.

"Come walk with me and see how the new chrysanthemums are doing," he said, holding out a hand to each of us. Mother begged off, saying she really was tired and wanted to rest before dinner. Dr. Barnhouse and I wandered off across the lawn. He walked along the flower border, shedding an almost palpable love upon each riotous pile of blossoms lifting to greet him. We crossed slowly to the lane of glowing maples that lined the driveway, looked back at the chrysanthemums, then made a full circle. There was beauty, beauty in every direction. I was glad he had such a place to come to after the kind of pressured existence Doug and I had experienced with him, which, repeated at intervals over and over, was his life. I found myself feeling very tender toward him.

"These chrysanthemums were a gift," he said. "My, the things people have given me. Just wait until Christmastime. A lady in our church always gives me an enormous box of cookies; a couple in Ohio sends me fruitcake; a friend in Oregon always provides me with a box of the most delicious pears."

My tenderness vanished in irritation at what seemed such egotism. He went on and on.

"I receive this . . . and this . . . and that. . . ."

"Receive, receive," I said. "Always receive! What do we *give?*"

He looked at me reproachfully. "But Marge, I have *already* given. Don't you see? These are love-gifts from full hearts that have been blessed and want to bless me in return. *Marge!*" His mind seemed suddenly to shift gears. He grasped my shoulders with delight. "Do you realize what you just said?"

I looked at him blankly. "What did I just say?"

"You said *we*. 'What do *we* give?' So your heart knows you are mine even if you don't want to admit it!" His eyes held mine, searching, sure and yet unsure. Then his great arms were around me, his lips against my hair. The tenderness began to engulf me again, drowning my shame at my lack of understanding, rising in great waves. This time I didn't try to fight it. I lifted my lips to his.

A car turned into the lane. Donald Barnhouse, Jr., a tall, studious-looking young man, was arriving for the weekend. He had brought with him an attractive young woman named Katherine Hamilton. Both were students at Princeton Seminary. They accompanied Dr. Barnhouse, Mother, and me to dinner at one of Doylestown's famous old inns.

After an excellent meal we went back to the Farm, where Dr. Barnhouse showed us his teacup collection, each cup with a fascinating story behind it. He was charming, solicitous, entertaining. Mother was captivated.

Next morning as he and I went out to put the bags in my car, he whispered confidentially, "Donnie and Kathy told me last night that they are engaged to be married."

"Oh, that's *nice,*" I beamed. "I'm so happy for them!"

I glanced up to the porch, where they were standing talking to Mother.

He leaned toward me eagerly and whispered, "And how about us?"

I had struggled all night with that. It did seem so right—and yet. . . .

Watching my eyes, he didn't wait for an answer. "Stop back on your way home from Albany," he said urgently. "We'll talk about it then."

On the road again, Mother said, "He's in love with you, isn't he."

"I'm afraid so," I answered.

"Well, he certainly is a charmer. How do you feel about him?"

"I don't know. It's so soon. . . . I just don't know. But I keep having the strangest feeling that Doug sort of bequeathed me to him. He was so urgent about my getting in touch with Dr. Barnhouse because 'he'd know what to do.' I think I could love this man very deeply if I let myself."

During my visit at Mother's in Albany I was invited to tea by Mrs. Clarence Traver, wife of a well-known Albany surgeon. Dr. Barnhouse often stayed at their home when having Bible conferences in the vicinity. She said "Barney," as she called him, had told her I was in town and thought we would enjoy knowing one another.

I went with a great deal of curiosity. Her home, formerly the governor's mansion on Willett Street facing Washington Park, was elegant. Mrs. Traver was an attractive Bostonian who for years had taught women's Bible classes in and around Albany.

After exploring various fields of mutual interest, Mrs. Traver said casually, "Barney tells me you two are going to be married."

My mouth dropped open. "But *I* haven't told *him* that yet! He certainly is taking a lot for granted!"

She laughed. "That's Barney for you! I can see why he would want to marry you. Just be sure you know what you're getting into!"

(I was glad for the trip Doug and I had made with him. How well we had come to know him, the human side as well as the man in the pulpit!)

That night Dr. Barnhouse called. "When are you coming back down? I've been able to secure six good seats for one of the hit Broadway shows, for Thursday night. Donnie, Kathy, David, and Mary Alice are going with me, and we'd love to have you join us."

This rather shocked me. "I thought you didn't go to the theater!" I said.

"Oh, Marge, you know I'm not a don't–do–this, don't–do–that legalist!" he laughed. "That is as ridiculous as saying, 'I thought you didn't read books.' I don't read trashy books or filthy books, and I'm just as selective about the shows I see because wherever I go the Holy Spirit indwelling me must go too. The reviews of this show are good. 'He giveth us richly all things to enjoy.' I expect to enjoy it, and I know you will too."

(My relief at having it put thus into proper perspective made me realize that since my total commitment to Christ, because of the fundamentalist circles I had been moving in, I had been harboring some inner guilt over having always loved the theater and having engaged in amateur dramatics in my younger days. How subtly "legalism" can creep into one's thinking!)

"You can come straight to the Farm," he went on. "Then you and I will drive over to New York, picking up Donnie and Kathy in Princeton on the way. Mary Alice and David will join us at the theater. Unless, of course, you'd rather not come with us," he teased.

I had another idea. "Let's go over early, and you can all be my guests for dinner before the show!"

"Terrific! But that's cutting it pretty close for you to get down here Thursday. If you'd come Wednesday, you'd be here for the installation of Dwight Small, my new assistant pastor, at Tenth that evening. You could sit with Miss Veit during the installation, then come back here with us for the night. That would give me Thursday to show you around the place, before we have to leave for dinner and the theater. How about it?"

My conversation with Mrs. Traver flashed across my

mind. With a start I realized I had said, "But I haven't told him that—*yet." Did that "yet" mean "yes"? I know I have to make a decision, so I might as well go on down there a day early and face it, yes or no. Lord, guide me!*

"I'll be there!"

Late Wednesday afternoon I pulled into the lane. Coming toward me from the house, Dr. Barnhouse appeared joyous but controlled. He opened the car door for me, but this time he wasn't playing any games. He stood back for me to get out. He didn't touch me—except with his eyes, which enfolded me with such depths of love it scared me. It was as if he had accepted our eventual marriage as foreordained of God, and had already given himself to me completely. I found myself leaning toward him, wishing he would put his arms around me. Then, looking over his shoulder, I saw Miss Veit moving about in the kitchen, and was glad he hadn't.

"I thought you'd never get here." His voice clasped me to him, although he still had not so much as touched my hand. He shook his head slightly, a gesture I was to recognize later as his will pulling his mind into action. He held out his hand. "Let me have the trunk keys, and I'll take your bags up to the guest room. Miss Veit has fixed a bite of supper. As soon as you've freshened up we'll eat, and drive on in to Tenth."

Naomi Veit greeted me as I entered the house. I thought, *Oh, I'd like you for a friend!* As in Atlanta when I first met her there was that instant binding of our spirits, in spite of her being so much younger.

Within an hour we had finished our supper and were on our way. The drive to Philadelphia was an educational tour. Dr. Barnhouse seemed to know something interesting about everything. "This is the Naval Air Station. Those are captured Japanese and German planes there behind that wire fence. . . . This is the Quaker Meeting House where William Penn used to attend. And there behind it are the original stalls where the horses and buggies were left during the meeting. Look across the road: see the graveyard behind that low brick wall? Notice that every gravestone is identical, and the same height from the ground. Know why? The Quakers believe that in death all men are equal." A bit further on we passed a large, high-walled cemetery, with monuments higher than the wall, and through the wrought-iron gates glimpsed ornate grave markers and fenced lots. "This is how the rest of the world does it," he said.

As we drove down Seventeenth Street I could see Tenth Church, with gates open and people mounting the steps. Dr. Barnhouse turned onto Spruce Street and pulled into an alley that ran between the church and the building next to it. He let Miss Veit and me out at the front of the church, then, pulling farther into the alley to park, he went into the church by a side door.

I felt a tug of excitement as Miss Veit and I climbed the front steps. At last I was entering this church about which I had heard so much. We were escorted down one of the side aisles and seated fairly close to the front. I looked around as discreetly as I could, curious to see this place but not wanting to be obvious.

A large white pulpit in three curved sections dominated the front of a platform that was perhaps three feet high, with a large communion table before it. Behind the pulpit was a small table flanked by two chairs; behind that, against the wall, a semicircle of carved armchairs was built into an elaborate dado half as tall as the curved ceiling above it. That ceiling! Gold leaf and green fresco combined to make such a beautiful geometric design! My gaze traveled from the vaulted ceiling there to the enormous brown marble columns that supported the main ceiling, each with its own individual intricately designed capital. A gallery of polished wood with a carved top rail above which was an iron guardrail extended around the two sides and the back of the church. The seats up there and the pews around us were filling rapidly. My attention was drawn back to the platform, where a door in the back had opened and Dr. Barnhouse and a group of men had started to file in.

The installation was impressive. I was glad I had come. Afterward, at a reception in a large upstairs room behind the pulpit, meeting Dwight and Ruth Small was a happy experience. As I watched Dwight moving affably among the people I thought how his gift of shepherding would complement Dr. Barnhouse's gift of preaching.

We didn't stay long. As I stood enjoying a conversation with some people who had met Doug, Dr. Barnhouse came looking for me, with Miss Veit in tow. He apologized for rushing me off, saying he had work to do and had to leave.

On the way home he explained who various people were and how Dwight's coming would take considerable responsibility off his shoulders. (*If I marry this man,* I thought, *I'll be a minister's wife. A* minister's wife! *I'm not sure I'm equipped for that. . . . What in the world is required of a minister's wife?*)

Back at the Farm, Dr. Barnhouse stopped the car at the little path leading to the dining room, apparently the entrance most used. He opened my door, helped me out, said, "Miss Veit, would you put the car away, please?" and gave her a fatherly smile. Then he took my elbow and we went into the house. He hung my coat with his in the coat closet, then ushered me into the living room. Once more that cherishing love was flowing from him.

The furniture had been rearranged since Mother's and my visit. The couch was now facing the fireplace, where a fire had been laid. After seating me on the couch, he went over and lit a match to the fire. When he was sure it had caught, he turned and watched me for a moment, as if he couldn't quite believe I was there. Then he put a stack of records on the record player, and my heart lifted with joy as the opening strains of Beethoven's Seventh Symphony swelled into the room.

He sat down beside me on the couch. Putting his arm around me he drew me to him, laying his cheek on my hair. We sat thus for a long time in utter contentment,

Beethoven's glorious music swirling around us as we watched the little flames leaping. It was as if I belonged there.

"Marge, tomorrow night may I tell my children that we are going to be married?"

I put my head back on his shoulder and looked full into his eyes, into incredible depths of love. *Lord, You'll just have to equip me!*

"You may tell them," I said.

ELEVEN

Early next morning I found Naomi Veit already in the kitchen when I went downstairs. Dr. Barnhouse had not yet come down. The night before when the symphony ended, he had sent me up to the guest room to bed, telling me that he really did have work to do, that after he'd gotten some books from the downstairs library he'd be working late and hoped his typing wouldn't disturb me. Rousing around two A.M., I could hear his typewriter, faintly, from down the hallway, so I rightly assumed he would not be rising very early.

Miss Veit and I sat talking over steaming cups of coffee, waiting for him to come down. This amazing young woman was indeed everything Dr. Barnhouse had told Doug and me, and more. I learned that she loved to cook, so in addition to her secretarial duties she prepared most of the meals, although Mrs. Balodis washed the dishes and cleaned the house. I knew that Miss Veit liked me. With difficulty I repressed the urge to tell her about our engagement, which Dr. Barnhouse and I had decided had better be kept secret for a while, only revealed to our children.

In about an hour he came bounding down the stairs. At breakfast he attacked his food with gusto, beaming at me so fondly I was sure Miss Veit would guess what was behind it all. Breakfast over, he told her he'd need her in an hour or so, then took me on a guided tour of the house. In every room were treasures: gifts from people blessed by his ministry, or things brought back from far places. Each had an intriguing story, as did the house itself. Finally he left me to browse in the downstairs library, a converted sun porch off the living room, while he went upstairs to his study to work with Miss Veit.

That night, at dinner before the show, his children didn't seem surprised in the least at our "news." (I wondered how many others had been told, before I had even said yes. That rascal!) I wasn't sure my own children were ready for this yet, so I begged the Barnhouse clan not to spread it abroad until I could get my own used to the idea. In any event the marriage would not take place until the following summer.

The play was a light-hearted comedy. Afterward we said good night to David and Mary Alice, not knowing that they would be going from the theater directly to the maternity floor of Presbyterian Hospital, where Katherine Ann was born that night.

Dr. Barnhouse took Friday and Saturday off to show me around his eighty-two acres of fields, meadows, and woods; there was even a little lake with a tiny island. He loved every part of it and wanted me to love it too. He delighted in little surprises that would give me pleasure. For instance, as the car swept up a tree-shaded hill, he said, "Cover your eyes until I tell you to look!" Entering into the game, I covered my eyes obediently. I could feel the car turn and bump along a farm road. "Keep them covered!" *(What fun! I thought. How young at heart he is!)* He stopped the car, came around to my side, and opened the door. "Keep them covered!" he said and helped me out. We walked perhaps ten steps over meadow grass. "Look!" he said grandly.

I looked and gasped at the beauty of the rolling sweep of Pennsylvania terrain below us, the bronze foliage of oaks, the thick dark of evergreens, the splashes of gold and flame where other trees still held some of their leaves, the meadows, the fields with their brown shocks of corn. He stood behind me, hugging me tightly and saying, "I knew you would love it! I *knew* you would!" Then, with a sweep of his arm, he pointed out the property. "The Farm boundaries start down there where the thick woods are, and go there . . . then there . . . then there . . . then there. . . . Come on, Marge! Oh, there is so much to show you!" Taking my hand he rushed me back to the car. As I climbed in, feeling such a closeness of spirit to this man, there flashed across my mind the "perfect wife" Doug and I had picked out for him. *(Oh, no, Lord! Wonderful as she was in many ways, she would have frowned on all this "nonsense," or laughed at his little games and stifled his exuberance. Thank You for choosing me! I do love it!)*

There were rare trees and shrubs to show me, most of which he had planted and lovingly pruned. He had all sorts of ideas for future plantings. I listened with enthusiasm: this was one of my hobbies too. He pointed out the wild geese on the lake, and showed me the wood ducks in one of the inlets. I had always been an avid bird-watcher: imagine his being one too!

Saturday night when he reluctantly left me to go to his study and put the finishing touches on his Sunday sermons, I sat down and wrote Mother a long letter about my decision, knowing I could count on her to keep it a secret. Putting it on paper somehow sealed the reality of it.

Sunday morning at Tenth Presbyterian Church, Miss Veit and I sat near the back so she could slip out immediately after the service, stand near Dr. Barnhouse in the narthex, and take notes on any matters that came up as he greeted people at the door.

Everything proceeded like most Sunday morning services in any Protestant church—that is, until the Scripture reading. As Dr. Barnhouse came to the pulpit, Naomi Veit leaned over and whispered, "We call this the sermon before the sermon." Indeed, it was. He read the morning Scripture passage and spent ten minutes analyzing, unfolding, and explaining it to the congregation.

Later, when it was time to take the offering, Dr. Barnhouse said, "If you are not a Christian, you are not invited to give. The offering is like the communion table: it is for believers only. . . ."

Throughout the congregation, I saw startled newcomers pausing, with purse partly open or the hand on the way to the pocket, in an agony of indecision. One man chewed his thumbnail for a moment, then put back into his pocket the folded bill he had previously taken out.

That morning, Dr. Barnhouse's sermon was "Walking with God," from Micah 6:8. The text flowed majestically from his lips, "He has showed you, O man, what is good; and what does the Lord require of you but to do justice, to love kindness, and to walk humbly with your God?"

I had heard this text preached before by others, but with the emphasis on man's works: doing justice, loving mercy, and walking humbly. But the way Dr. Barnhouse expounded it changed the whole concept. God had become greater and greater, and His desire to walk with me was almost incomprehensible. But instead of making me feel insignificant, it made me secure. I could trust my life and all of me to a God like that, who didn't expect me to be anything but myself, and would supply all the strength I needed to walk with Him.

As Dr. Barnhouse preached I wondered if perhaps the Lord had been speaking first to him, then through him to us, and therein lay the power. With so much natural vigor and knowledge and magnetism—both physical and intellectual—Donald Grey Barnhouse would of necessity have to humble himself moment by moment before his Lord if they were to walk together.

The final hymn burst from hearts full to overflowing: "My hope is built on nothing less than Jesus' blood and righteousness." Such singing! But when they came to the second line of the last verse, Dr. Barnhouse stopped them. After some confusion and quieting down, he said, "In the hymnal I know that reads, 'When He shall come with trumpet sound, Oh, may I then in Him be found....' If your hope truly is built on Jesus' blood and righteousness alone, then you should *know* you *shall* be found in Him at the last trump! So let's not have any little wishy-washy 'Oh, *may* I then.' Proclaim it! 'Oh, then I *shall* in Him be found! *Sing it!*"

The organ led off, and those voices reverberated to the very throne of God, I'm sure: "Oh, then I *shall* in Him be found; dressed in His righteousness alone, faultless to stand before the throne. On Christ the solid Rock, I stand; all other ground is sinking sand."

Late Monday afternoon Dr. Barnhouse and I started out for his Monday night Bible class in New York, taking a short-cut through the rolling countryside. As soon as we were out of sight of the house he pulled the car off the road, kissed me, and said, "What's my name?"

Puzzled, I said, "Dr. Barnhouse, of course."

" 'Dr. Barnhouse,' " he mimicked. "We're going to be married, and you're still calling me 'Dr. Barnhouse.' You've been doing it all week! You sound like something out of a Charles Dickens novel. Now, dear, my name is 'Donald.' Say it." Playfully, he flicked the tip of my nose with his finger.

"Oh... how can I?"

"Say it!"

"Donald." My voice was very small.

"Now say, 'Donald, I love you.' "

I didn't have any trouble with that.

He pulled the car back onto the road again. All the way to New York he made me practice calling him Donald.

As we crossed from Pennsylvania into New Jersey he took my hand, lifted it, and intoned solemnly and totally out of context, "I have learned in whatsoever state I am therewith to be content."

I laughed and said, "Oh, Dr. Barnhouse!"

He said, "Oh, *what?*"

I corrected myself: "Oh, Donald!"

In the middle of the tunnel under the Hudson River, as we crossed from New Jersey into New York, he quoted Philippians 4:11 again, anouncing that in *that* State he had learned to be content. *Oh, Donald.*

The New York Bible class was held in St. Luke's Lutheran Church on 46th Street just off Broadway. Little groups of people, faces shining with expectancy, eagerness in their step, were streaming into the church as we entered. Here, he was again "Dr. Barnhouse," the eagerly awaited Bible teacher. In this place how could I call him "Donald?" Again I became the pupil as I was seated and watched him go to the platform, take a stack of written questions one of the ushers handed him, and start looking through them.

I looked around. This New York Bible class was a true cross section of that great melting pot of Americans and foreigners, educated upper class, simple lower class, and those in between. Many had driven in from suburbs an hour away.

DGB had bragged to Doug and me that his class had had "the longest run on Broadway, longer even than the well-known musical, *Abie's Irish Rose!*" He told us that one night he had asked the audience to recite John 3:16, each in his or her native tongue. Thirty-eight languages or dialects were represented. Yet his diction was so precise that each could understand him perfectly, and some even attended for the purpose of improving their English.

At a reception the class had for us after we were married one middle-aged woman said shyly to me, "Mrs. Barnhouse—I shook hands with him tonight! I've been coming to this class for fifteen years and this is the first time I've had the nerve to shake his hand!" I smiled, remembering my feelings about calling him by his first name. I wondered how many others were so in awe of that towering figure in the pulpit with his thundering voice that they didn't realize he was an ordinary (well, maybe a *little* extraordinary!) human being named Donald.

The next morning I started back home to Florida, promising to call "Donald" each evening from wherever I stopped for the night.

When Carolyn and Douglas were home for Christmas, I broached the subject of my marrying DGB. At this time I had thought that after we were married I would be in Doylestown when Donald was there, and in Florida with Douglas and Carolyn when he was traveling. Naturally they had ambivalent feelings, but it seemed to me that on the whole they were relieved. After all my years of worrying about them the tables were turned: they had been worrying about me being at home alone!

It was decided that the engagement would be announced officially in March, when a week of meetings was scheduled for Donald in Bradenton. In connection with this I received a letter from Dwight Small, Donald's new associate pastor at Tenth. He said he had talked to Paul Hopkins about announcing it there, and had suggested that a special insert be printed for the Sunday Calendar. This separate sheet would contain our pictures and an announcement of relevant facts, and would give Dwight something to take with him to give out at the New York class on Monday night. Then in his next paragraph he put his finger on one of my worries.

"When we came, Ruth and I wondered what reception we would have from the people of Tenth Church, and I can imagine that you have some of the same thoughts about now. Well, we have been very happy to feel their warm affection and I have no hesitancy in saying that you will share this experience."

Reassured, I tucked the letter away for future reference.

In Bradenton the formal announcement appeared in the

papers Sunday morning. Donald's first meeting was Sunday night, so that morning we attended my church, for the first time sitting together in the pews. As we entered the church, many friends surrounded us, wishing us joy. We barely got to our seats in time.

To my embarrassment, during the sermon Donald sat with head down and eyes closed, for all the world as if he were going to sleep. How could he! I poked him. Immediately his head came up, eyes open and alert. Rather than whisper, I wrote a quick note imploring him to remember he was in the public eye, and must look interested even if he wasn't. He looked at me reproachfully, but dutifully glued his eyes to my pastor for the rest of the sermon.

Afterward he said, "Marge, I really wanted to hear what the man was actually *saying*. I always close my eyes when I want to listen intently without distractions!"

"Donald," I said firmly, "there are times when you just cannot do what *you* want to do. Everyone is going to be watching you very closely, ready to pounce on anything the slightest bit amiss. For our Lord's sake, as His witness, you *must* behave in a way that will not bring criticism on you or your ministry. You wouldn't like it if my pastor sat in *your* audience, looking as if he were going to sleep! Besides—oh, Donald—I was *embarrassed!*"

"I am an oogid glyph!" he declared, the picture of contrition. It was the first time I had heard that appellation, but I would hear it often in the future whenever Donald was disgusted with himself. Apparently it was a term he made up on the spur of the moment. Intrigued, I was unprepared to hear him cry out almost desperately, "Marge, it's not too late to back out! Are you sure you want to marry me?"

If I ever had any doubts, they were all swept away in that moment. A glad yes! rose from the depths of me, "Oh, *yes!*" He gave me a bear hug. The enormous orchid he had sent me to celebrate the announcement of our engagement was spared annihilation only because it had fallen off before he could crush it.

That night, orchid back in place, I settled myself to hear him preach.

As usual, he began his week of meetings by explaining how the offerings would be used, then launched into the questions that had been written by audience members after the morning session. After answering several challenging and interesting questions, he picked up the last one, glanced at it, looked out over his audience and made a helpless, how-do-you-answer-something-like-this gesture. Then he read the question aloud:

"How do you have the nerve to ask for money for your organization when your fiancée is sporting that big orchid? I'd like to give my wife an orchid, but I can't afford it. Why should I pay for yours?"

Into the shocked stillness his answer came:

"The Bible says the workman is worthy of his hire. If you brought some secular lecturer here and paid five dollars or more for tickets, you wouldn't question what he did with the money. I have earned every penny that goes into the offering, working sometimes sixteen hours a day to prepare these messages. However, I prefer to think people give out of love for the Lord, for blessings received, and not to pay my hire. As for me, I work as unto the Lord, out of love for Him and concern for you and for your Christian growth, not for the money that comes in, necessary though that is for the work. I don't splurge very often, but this is a very special occasion. If you do not want to have a share in my joy, by all means do not give—your share would perhaps be one penny. But I'll still give of myself to you, and hope you'll be blessed."

He sat down, the offering was taken, then he stood to preach.

The sermon was "Words of One Syllable," the outline of which had so intrigued me. Now I heard it in full, and all of us were blessed by it. It was over two years since he had exploded in our midst the dynamite of the gospel. Some of those who had heard it had gathered up the pieces of their demolished self-built shack and rebuilt it, but the majority of his hearers had expanded into new dimensions of spiritual growth. I had been listening to his radio program every week, but hearing him again in person after so long a time was electrifying.

The week of meetings flew by. The after-meetings disturbed me: no longer was there the eager search for new truth among our gang, but rather a critical spirit of dissension and division. The Lord had surely directed Donald's choice of study in the mornings: Philippians, a great call to oneness in Christ and love toward one another.

In the midst of all this Donald received an invitation that he was happy to accept. One of the schools where I had been giving my weekly flannelgraph Bible lessons in released time was a black elementary school. The principal of this school asked me whether I thought Dr. Barnhouse might be willing to come and speak to her children while he was in Bradenton.

This was arranged for a morning assembly. The principal greeted us warmly. "Dr. Barnhouse, you'll never know what your radio program means to me," she said. "The mind needs spiritual food as well as the heart, you know."

One large room doubled for gymnasium and assembly hall. The children were already there when we entered. Some of them wiggled their fingers at me in greeting; some giggled. Donald was introduced to the teachers, and we were seated.

The children arose on signal, marched to the open space in front of the rows of folding wooden chairs and faced us self-consciously, awaiting the first chords of the opening song, "God Bless America." All eyes were riveted on the teacher's guiding hand; little dark faces shone above starched dresses and clean shirts; self-consciousness was gone and they sang as if they meant the words with all their heart.

"God bless America, my home sweet home!"

They filed back to their seats, and Donald, visibly

moved, stood up to give one of his wonderful stories. I had never heard him warmer, more lovingly eloquent. Who knows what fruit the seed planted that day may someday produce?

Afterward, when the principal thanked him, Donald took her hand in both of his.

"We are laborers together in God's vineyard," he told her. "When the Lord takes me to glory I'll take off my white overalls, and when He takes you to glory, you'll take off your black overalls, and He'll clothe each of us with His righteousness and we'll all praise Him together."

"Amen," she said, joyously.

Friday night the final sermon was "The Second Coming of Christ." Donald prefaced it by stating that the people whom the fundamentalists had been calling "modernists" for the past forty years—the World Council of Churches and the National Council of Churches—were meeting in August in Evanston, Illinois, to discuss, to the astonishment of the fundamentalists, "The Second Coming of Christ, the Only Hope of the World."

"For centuries," he said, "the creeds of the mainline denominations have affirmed that we believe that Jesus Christ is at present in heaven, and 'from thence He *shall* come to judge the quick and the dead,' but this fact is not often preached. I want to ground you in certain phases of a truth far more important than which of the seals, the trumps, and the vials of Revelation come first."

Seeing concern on some faces, he added. "Now I happen to be a pretribulation rapturist and a premillenarian, if that means anything to you. Yet I exchange pulpits with a friend, pastor of one of the big churches in Boston, who believes the church will go through the Tribulation. I think he's wrong, but we just stay away from these points of disagreement when preaching for each other. Of course, when the rapture takes place, I expect to pull his coattail and say, 'I told you so!' as we go up together...." The audience laughed and relaxed.

"But there are other things more important. To begin with, we must not set dates. Jesus Himself said, 'No man knoweth the day nor the hour.' He could come before the benediction, or might not come again for another thousand years."

He warned us that in 1999 the same terrible things could happen again that happened in 999 because people set dates. Believing the Lord would come back at midnight on New Year's Eve in the year 999, people crowded into the churches to wait. Many died of fright; their bodies were simply passed over the heads of the crowd and left in the street (why bother to bury what was to be resurrected at any moment?). When Christ did not come there was a great letdown. But they should never have set dates in the first place. There were many other times when men set dates and were disappointed. (He enumerated some of these. I was appalled, not knowing church history.)

"Instead of setting dates and arguing about details, we should be living so as not to be ashamed at His coming," he said.

He showed us that, like the first coming, this would not be a single incident, but a series of events. The first coming included the birth of a baby and the death, resurrection, and ascension to heaven of a man; so also the second coming would include many phases. These he enumerated: a phase in reference to the true church; one in reference to the apostate church; one each for the Jews, the nations, the Devil and his angels, "the Sahara and the Everglades" ("the desert and the waste places shall blossom like the rose"), animal life, and the sun and moon and stars.

What is the "true church"? He gave an illustration that I shall never forget: that of two tape recordings he had heard, one of the "smooth-running mechanism of the World's Most Honored Watch"—ca-lick, ca-lick, ca-lick, ca-lick, ca-lick; the other of a heartbeat—"lub-dub, lub-dub, lub-dub, lub-dub, lub-dub." Jesus Christ came into the world and founded the lub-dub, lub-dub, lub-dub—a heartbeat,

His life flowing through the believer. Then men organized this into a man-made ca-lick, ca-lick, ca-lick, that various groups made into clickety-clack and ca-lack and clackety-click, eventually fighting over them, forgetting that the important thing was the lub-dub, the heart of Christ, which after a while didn't seem to matter. "Now don't misunderstand me," he said at this point. "I believe we must have organization or the true church could not function. But it should be along biblical lines, as in the Books of Timothy and Titus. The "true church," however, is the lub-dub, that great body of believers, truly born-again, in every denomination, who are trusting Christ alone for their salvation.

"Our Lord has told us to watch, watch, watch, for in such an hour as ye think not He will appear," Donald said. "And when He comes, the day of grace will have run out. He will come with a rod of iron, and dash His enemies to pieces as a potter's vessel. The figures of speech in the Bible are terrible: He says He will put His heel on this civilization as on a bunch of grapes, and squash it. But, oh, the day of grace has not yet run out. God has everything against you, but you can still settle out of court. *Now* is the accepted time! *Now* is the day of salvation!"

Easter fell on April 18. I gave my last Bible classes just before Easter vacation, then dug into preparations for the move to Doylestown the first week in June.

With a cup of coffee and the mail, I settled myself on the porch for a brief respite from the packing. There was a letter from Donald which I saved until last. It bore no heading, no salutation:

It is Sunday night, May 9th, midnight. I have had two good services today and have come in hungry, eaten a good meal based on two lamb chops, and have come up to my room. Remembering that last night's call was six dollars and eighty-eight cents, I am resisting the temptation of telephoning Bradenton.... My type-

writer calls me to work. But I have a little argument with myself and say that if I did call Marge I would spend fifteen minutes talking to her, so I might as well take these few minutes and talk to my typewriter about Marge.

Memo from DGB to DGB about Marge:
In just thirty days you are due to marry Marge. My boy, you have hit the JACKPOT, and you are in the position of a man who has never had money and is suddenly coming into a brace of oilwells. Or of a spinster who has just inherited her sister's nine children. Or of a bull who is taking title to a china shop. In other words, you have a very valuable property with great potential that must be handled with extreme care. So stop and assess the situation.

The Bible says a husband is to love his wife. There will be no difficulty here. You love her all right, and with a love that scares you because it is so different. You loved and married before, but it was not a love that made you want to think of DGB in second place while this distinctly is. The first was selfish. You were going someplace and nothing should get in the way. Now you have been someplace and you want to travel a deux instead of alone. And it is rather wonderful and a little frightening to have a love that does all this to you at your age. . . . This, then, is something that must be watched, protected, safeguarded. Bull, watch out for that china as you walk in the aisles.

Then you read that you are to give honor unto the wife as unto the weaker vessel. So do a little appraising. Weaker in body, perhaps, so you must take the mastery in seeing that she does not overdo. She has a mind and heart that would do anything—like Mary who said to the Lord, when she thought it was the gardener, "Tell me where you have laid Him that I might carry Him hence." She was a 120-pound woman who had been drawn in her soul for three days and who had already made the trip between Jerusalem and the tomb three times. She was offering to carry the inert body of a man who weighed, perhaps, 160 pounds. She couldn't have done it, but she would have split her heart trying. Now, that's Marge, so you have to be on the watch at every second lest she try in body, mind, or spirit to pick up packages that are too heavy for her. Daily rest. Full eight hours sleep. As little mental struggle as possible. Plenty of mental exercise but no mental struggle. That means you have to watch your step lest you bruise her spirit.

She is a full-blown personality in her own right. She has been held down. You remember standing there watching as she said, "Yes, my lord" to something that was totally unreasonable and unreasoning. Yet she was submitting, because she thought this pleased the Lord. And it surely did. . . .

I stopped reading, shamed at the remembrance of that incident on our trip with DGB. Apparently he had not recognized it as a bit of swordplay. Doug had nicked me, and I was thrusting back, not in submission but in deepest sarcasm. Then, even after more than a year of being saved, Doug and I were still in competition. I had not yet heard the famous marriage tape, and was still "kicking against the goads." *(Forgive me, Lord!)* I read on:

But I think it would please the Lord more if a little . . . topsoil were taken off and the bulb allowed to flower. . . . Watch your step lest Marge become a yes-woman. Delight when she says no in a good cause. Learn to listen when her spiritual perception catches something that is even slightly off-key.

Establish a relation that will be natural. She must never strain in her eagerness to please. Teach her that if she comes with an idea and a suggestion and you seem to rebuff her that it is because you have a one-track mind and may be thinking of something else and that the idea may be very important if she can keep it there in love, nothing doubting.

Watch the growth of her feathers. She has flown for many years with wings clipped. Strengthen and encourage every little pin feather that will make her fly better, seeing to it that they balance in both wings so that she flies evenly. Encourage her to soar. You know that she has great capacities and will be hesitant because of past restraints. She probably doesn't realize the heights of her possibilities. It will be up to you to lead her gently to greater and greater heights.

Remember she is at all times her own personality, and that individuality and personality have full rights in all things. Her comfort, desires, and thoughts have equal value with your own.

See that your joint spiritual life is never neglected. Teach her your joint responsibility for this.

Now, Donald, you have been dreaming over this typewriter for almost two hours and it is well past one A.M., so get to bed. Stop and think of the hundreds of hours you have spent thinking about that Bell woman and remember that you are about to live all that you have thought. And I reckon that the separation sufferings of this present time are not worthy to be compared with the glory that shall be revealed in us.

My fatigue vanished as I read and reread that "memo." Was this the "male chauvinist" one of my friends had said he was? In Christ Jesus we were one. He gave me no feeling of inferiority, or of restriction, or of being a "second-class citizen," or a "thing," or any of the other epithets the "liberated women" were using. Perhaps it was because he really did treat me as a "full-blown personality in her own right" that submission to his headship was so right, so natural, so easy. Submission, not subjugation. Even though he had spoken of me as "property," there was no hint of domination. Instead, it was a cherishing protection. I delighted in being "his"—and was he not also "mine"?

My forgotten coffee had long grown cold. I sat as if suspended in time and space, enwrapped in his love.

TWELVE

Time seemed to rush by. During his stay in Bradenton, Donald had come out and gone over my things with me to help decide which I should take to Doylestown and which to dispose of. Because he was acquiring not only a wife but two children as well, we had decided to build a wing on his beautiful old house, with a bedroom and bath, and attic storage space overhead. I insisted on paying for this. I wanted to have one place I could know was my very own. Because the house itself was historic, Donald wouldn't consider changing even the color of one of the rooms without bringing in Mr. Petersen, the consultant for the Betsy Ross house and various other historic places in Philadelphia. I was content for his sake to assume the role of a sort of house custodian, and I accepted the fact that it would never be "my house" in the sense that my other homes were mine. It had been completely redecorated before Mother's and my visit the past fall; the new wing would be completed by the time we returned from our honeymoon in Europe, where he would be conducting his usual teaching and preaching missions.

I packed and discarded and sold furniture and equipment, and suddenly the movers were there and the day of departure had arrived. Carolyn and I were to drive to Statesville, North Carolina, for Don and Kathy's wedding on Saturday, June 5. We would then continue to New York City for my own June 8 wedding in the chapel of the Fifth Avenue Presbyterian Church. After much discussion, Donald and I had agreed that our wedding had to be either very private, with only his immediate family and mine, or else we'd have to rent out Yankee Stadium! Where would we draw the line? I invited only Mother, who unfortunately was ill and could not come, and my sister and two brothers and their spouses, plus of course Carolyn and Douglas, swearing them all to secrecy. But that rascal Donald couldn't stand not sharing his bursting joy. His children would be there, and Naomi Veit who was practically part of the family. His two sisters in California were too far away to come. So he hinted to Paul Hopkins and Russ Hitt, "It's a secret: we aren't saying where or when. But if you should happen to be walking past the Fifth Avenue Presbyterian Church in New York on June 8 at ten-thirty in the morning, and should feel an urge to go into the chapel. . . ."

Donald joined us at Statesville for Don and Kathy's wedding, where I met Kathy's delightful family and Donald's two daughters. Dorothy Barnhouse was almost six feet tall and serenely beautiful. She was deeply involved in Intervarsity Christian Fellowship and planning to attend their international convention in Europe that summer. Ruth Barnhouse Beuscher, a practicing psychiatrist in Boston, married to a psychiatrist, and the mother of two small boys, was nearer my height and had a sophisticated beauty. She joined Carolyn and me on the long drive to New York, during which she and I forged a closeness that has never been broken despite widely divergent views on many subjects.

After the Statesville festivities, Donald had flown back to Philadelphia to preach in his own church on Sunday. Monday, Douglas flew himself up from Pensacola in a small Navy plane. By Monday night the Barnhouse family and mine had convened at the St. Regis Hotel, where we all had dinner. Exhausted from the final packing and moving and all that driving, I excused myself after dessert. Donald escorted me to my room and tenderly kissed me good night, never hinting that he intended to rejoin the dinner party. An excellent orchestra was playing; the others were dancing. To the best of my knowledge, he had never danced before except in the living room of his home with his own wife. He decided this was the time to try it, all in the family!

Tuesday morning, June 8, attired in a powder blue silk suit with a small matching feather hat, and wearing a spray of blue cymbidium orchids flown in from Hawaii, the bride and her family departed for the Fifth Avenue Presbyterian Church. "The bride!" I, Margaret Nuckols Bell, about to become Mrs. Donald Grey Barnhouse!

Robert Elmore's glorious organ music was filling the shadowy chapel. I was vaguely aware that Paul and Jeanne Hopkins, Russ and Lillian Hitt, and Dwight and Ruth Small were sitting there, and Naomi Veit, along with those of our families who were not participating in the ceremony. Then Donald was beside me, and we were facing Bob Lamont, pastor of the First Presbyterian Church of Pittsburgh, the minister with a Down's syndrome baby whose poignant story opened Donald's famous sermon, "Tragedy or Triumph?" We had asked him to perform the ceremony. The Reverend Ralph Nesbitt, one of the pastors of the Fifth Avenue Presbyterian Church, was assisting.

"I, Donald, take thee, Margaret. . . ." "I, Margaret, take thee, Donald. . . ." Suddenly it was not just a ceremony. This man's whole heart was in his eyes, his whole self in his giving and taking of those vows. The Lord was there, taking over Bob Lamont's tongue as he gave a moving charge to Donald and me.

Then everyone crowded around, hugging and kissing and rejoicing.

After the wedding brunch, Donald and I returned to the St. Regis, changed to travel clothes, and had my bags put into Donald's room to be picked up later. Then we went to get my passport changed from Bell to Barnhouse for our flight to Paris. No amount of persuasion had been able to budge the authorities ahead of time: until I had that wedding certificate to show them, they would not change the name on my passport.

The place was jammed. Harried clerks were coping with all sorts of problems. Donald fumed as we waited in line, inched forward, waited again. Finally, looking at his watch for the umpteenth time, Donald said, "We dare not wait any longer, Marge, or we'll miss our flight. We'll just have to wait until we get to France to change it. Come on!"

Off we rushed. We went to his room, grabbed the bags, got a taxi, and made it to the airport in time to check in and catch our breath. Then, according to what was written on the seating plan, off to Paris flew "Dr. Barnhouse accompanied by Mrs. Bell"! It wasn't until six days later, at the consulate at Nice, that we finally straightened it out.

The days that followed were crammed with new experiences: people, places, sights, smells, sounds, adventure, blessings. I wondered if I would ever get it all sorted out. Seeing so many new facets of Donald Grey Barnhouse and finding such complete compatibility was the most exciting of all. Those who only knew him proclaiming God's Word from the pulpit would have had trouble believing what a combination he was of strong, reliable husband and naughty small boy, of sentimental dreamer and efficient organizer.

I had asked him why he hadn't brought a camera. His answer: "Marge, I have shoeboxes full of snapshots on my closet shelves, suitboxes full under the dresser. I'm so busy going to new places there never is time to sort them and put them in albums, much less ever look at them. They mean nothing to anyone else, so I've stopped taking pictures. We can always buy professional slides of places we want to remember."

This made sense, of course, but I still thought maybe

some snapshots might have helped *me* sort out the many experiences that kept crowding in, one upon another, leaving me breathless.

Among the kaleidoscope of happenings were special bright spots. Donald took me to the place in Fontainebleau Forest, where, when he was in his early twenties, he had lain beside a giant fallen tree for two nights and a day, wrestling with the Lord's will for his life. We retraced by car the walking tour of Europe he had taken right after that, during which he had finally committed his life totally to the Lord. We visited the tiny Alpine villages where he had first ministered. At the Protestant seminary at Aix-en-Provence I heard him teach in fluent French. I hadn't known that for him French was a second language! I stood beside him proudly as he was made a chevalier of the French Legion of Honor.

All of these things we did together. But when he visited the renowned theologian, Karl Barth, I sat in our hotel and wondered what was transpiring. To my yet fundamentalist mind Karl Barth and his neo-orthodox theology were to be avoided!

Donald had asked Ulrich Wever, his daughter Dorothy's fiancé, to be his interpreter. Although French was totally familiar to him, he was not so sure of his comprehension of German. "Uli" was to tutor him for a week; then they two would meet Dr. Barth at Barth's home. This would serve a dual purpose: Donald had hoped Dorothy would marry an American, not a young German doctoral student; that week would give Donald an opportunity to size up this prospective son-in-law.

Uli's account of the meeting between Barth and DGB is hilarious. Right at the entrance of Barth's home Donald asked Uli what his academic title was. Uli replied, "I have no title yet; I'm working on my doctor's thesis."

Donald couldn't understand this. "You mean to say that you've attended universities for five or six years and have no degree or title?"

Uli said that his immatriculation papers used the term *candidatus philosophiae,* meaning a candidate for a doctorate of the faculty of philosophy.

And so, when moments later Barth himself opened the door, Donald introduced himself and said, "And this is *candidatus philosophiae* Ulrich Wever, who also is interested in marrying my daughter."

Barth was amused by this and invited them in. Entering the study, he referred to Uli as the "future son-in-law," to which Donald quickly said, "Just call him "Candidatus." Barth laughed and the atmosphere seemed from that point on quite relaxed.

DGB wanted to publish Barth's views on the millennium in *Eternity.* They discussed this for some time, establishing ultimately that they were in agreement on the major aspects of the matter. Donald had brought with him several issues of *Eternity* and laid them out on the table. Barth flipped through them, and there appeared on his face a troubled expression. Barth said that he had never in his life written for such a "popular" magazine; *Eternity* seemed to appeal to "common people," and it was so American that it wouldn't even appeal to European common people. Barth asked Uli to tell DGB that he couldn't write the article. "All my life I have written only for serious theological periodicals," he said.

But there was no need for an interpreter. Donald apparently understood, and quickly replied, "Well, Dr. Barth, that's the trouble with you. All your life you've been writing for the giraffes, but Jesus said, 'Feed my lambs.' "

Barth laughed heartily. He seemed to enjoy DGB's sense of humor.

Donald pressed him once again to write for *Eternity,* and Barth suggested that his son—also a Protestant theologian —might write it instead. "My son holds basically the same views as I do," Barth said, "and he's better acquainted with America—he's lectured there extensively."

"No," Donald said. "I want *Goethe,* not Goethe's *son!"*

Barth roared with laughter, slapped Donald on his knee, and shouted, in English, "I like you!"

After a time, Uli's services as interpreter weren't really needed. The conversation was conducted in different languages—English, French, and German—and they rarely had difficulty understanding each other.

The meeting lasted an hour and a half. It ended with the agreement that Donald would report the content of the interview in an *Eternity* article.

Donald was disappointed, but understood Barth's dilemma. In the theological world it is so easy to be misjudged! Donald told me he challenged Barth on several of the doctrines that "Barthians" were teaching in American seminaries. Dr. Barth said, "Well, if that is what they are teaching, I am not a Barthian!"

What seems to have been a brief and not entirely successful meeting, given DGB's original aims, was significant in another sense. God had brought together two great Christian minds: one of the foremost Bible expositors of the era and one who is considered perhaps the greatest Protestant theologian of the twentieth century.

Donald managed to get us into the Bayreuth Wagner Festival. The festival, of course, is always sold out well in advance, and when Donald went up to the teller, he was told that the last tickets had been sold weeks before. But Donald then asked what they would do if the Chancellor of the German Republic would show up and request two seats. "In that case," the woman said, "we would naturally find two seats for him." "Well," Donald replied, "I happen to know he's not coming today, so could I please have his two seats?" They gave him tickets and we got into the festival!

And then it was over—too soon, and we were in flight over the Atlantic. This time the seating chart read, "Dr. Barnhouse accompanied by Mrs. Barnhouse."

Naomi Veit met us at the international airport on Long Island. On the way home she filled us in on what had gone on at the Farm in our absence. She had taken care of most of the mail, but there were some urgent things to be done first thing in the morning. Donald needed to see Paul Hopkins as soon as possible: first, about a proposed fall conference; and second, for briefings before the upcoming World Council of Churches meeting at Evanston, which we were to attend. Donald was to speak at the Sandy Cove Bible Conference the second week of August. Tenth Church was planning a reception for us, as was the New York Bible class, the dates not yet fixed.

Then we were nearing Barchdale, and I could sense a mounting excitement in Donald. The car crested that small rise in the road, and there lay the Farm: in the foreground the gentle, rolling meadows centered by the small lake, and beyond, the house itself, shadowed by those great maples, with fields of corn green on the rolling hills beyond. Home! And now it was to be my home, too.

We drove on up the road, past the quarter-of-a-mile of pillar roses that adorned the split rail fence along the meadow, and turned into the long, cool, shaded lane.

At the dining room entrance door, the one everyone used, the doorstep was so worn the screen door had to be specially cut, with a curve in the bottom to fit the worn place. Donald squeezed my arm with delight as we stepped across it and entered a new phase of our lives.

The next day Donald asked me to ride into the Foundation with him. After lunch Donald and I were on our way. Soon we were out of the rolling countryside and winding through the back roads and shortcuts he used on the outskirts of Philadelphia. We passed a large grey stone church.

"Let's play cathedral!" he cried.

"How do you play cathedral?"

"Just open our 'memory album' and look at cathedrals. Name one."

"Chartres!"

And as we drove to Philadelphia, our minds were back in France. In my mind's eye I could see Chartres cathedral as first I had seen it, looming up across the flat plain, enormous, silhouetted against the sky. Then a dip in the road—and it disappeared. When it reappeared it was nestled in a little village and had shrunk to proper proportion. Then we were there, and we parked and walked through the great west portal.

Gloom. Deep coolness. Quiet. Beautiful, simple sculpture. Great rose windows. Standing hand in hand, we looked, feasting on its rich beauty. Suddenly Donald said, "Marge! *Look* at that ceiling!"

I lifted my face immediately to look—and had a kiss firmly implanted on my lips. "Oh, *Donald!*" I laughed, for he was looking as pleased as a schoolboy who has just tricked a girl into her first kiss. He squeezed my hand, delighted to have found he could be silly if he wished and not be reproved. From then on it was a game: in every cathedral we visited, when we came before the altar, I would casually turn my face up, and Donald would see if he could lean down and kiss me without any of the other tourists noticing that two dignified, middle-aged people were behaving like teenagers.

He pulled my hand through his arm and we strolled on all the way around the interior, following the episodes in the life of Christ carved in marble. As we came opposite the great south doors Donald said, "Oh! You *must* see it!" He bustled off, leaving me wondering, and soon was back with the custodian, who was protesting, "But, Monsieur, it has not been opened in years! No one goes in or out that way...." Donald pulled out a hundred franc note. "But, Monsieur, we will try...."

The custodian strained at the enormous bolt fastening the center doors. It wouldn't budge. He tried again and again, working it back and forth a little as it gave slightly. Suddenly with a great screech it slid back. Donald clapped the custodian on the back and pressed the money into the hands that were laboriously pushing on the heavy doors, which slowly opened wide, protesting every inch. Beyond them a flight of steps descended to a narrow, busy street. I could see nothing special about this. But Donald had caught my hand and pulled me eagerly down the steps. He stood me in a certain spot on the edge of the sidewalk, looked back, and murmured, "No, that's not it." Then after pushing me onto the street a foot or two at a time, imperiously holding up traffic with a lifted hand and saying, 'Un moment, s'il vous plait! Un moment!" he turned me toward the cathedral. "Look!" he said.

Upon the center doorpost the beautifully carved "teaching Christ" stood serenely, and behind Him, from across the transept, the far rose window glowed like a great halo behind His head. A crowd of curious onlookers gathered, gaping. The custodian had followed us, mystified.

"Monsieur! Magnifique! I never saw it before in my life! How did you know?"

Back in the car, I echoed, "How *did* you know?"

He smiled. "When I was a young man, back in the twenties, I had to work summers to pay for my studies here in France at the University of Grenoble, so I decided to be a guide in Paris. By then my French was almost a second language. 'The war to end all wars' was over; prosperity was sweeping the United States and tourists were coming over like locusts. They would pay handsomely for a limousine, a driver, and a guide.

"I hired out as a guide, knowing the language but knowing very little about the places I was supposed to take them, so I went to the library and hunted up everything I could find.

"There were fifty castles on the 'must see' list. I would say to my patrons, 'Now in the time you have you can whiz through the countryside and *see* each of these from a distance, or you can take the time to explore five of them in depth and really have something to tell your friends about when you get home. Which will it be?'

"Of course they always chose to see the five. Then I

would say, 'I recommend castles A, B, C, D, and E.' (I had read up on them and knew I could handle it.)

"So we would start out. At the first castle I spoke to the custodian in French and made arrangements for me to be the guide instead of the regular castle guide. Then we started through. I would say, confidently, 'Down here are the dungeons,' and sure enough, there they were. 'At the top of these stairs you will find . . .' and there it was! I took the guidebooks on faith, never having seen these things before, and it was thrilling to find everything just as they said. I use this as an illustration of how it will be when we get to heaven. If we are thoroughly familiar with God's guidebook, the Bible, we will know what to expect and will feel at home there immediately.

"Well, with the next tourists I would say, 'I recommend castles F, G, H, I, and J.' I knew it wouldn't make any difference to them, so in this way *I* got to see all fifty castles on the list!

"It was through the guidebooks that I discovered the halo over the teaching Christ. But that was over thirty years ago. Meanwhile World War II has come and gone, and I guess it was just forgotten."

Recently I have seen postcards of this in full color, so apparently it is now a feature of the "tour" of Chartres, for which I am thankful. But how glad I am to have it tucked away in our "album"! What a great way to "take pictures." From then on, looking through our memories was a regular part of our lives, especially on the road.

As we climbed the steps to the front door of the Foundation at Seventeenth and Spruce Streets in Philadelphia, Donald said, "Now Marge, I want you in there with us because you'll have to understand the schedule we're working out, but you are just to listen. We don't have much time; I can do any explaining later."

We walked into the building, greeting this one and that one. Paul shook my hand warmly and led us into his office where he had a map spread out on the desk. As Donald bent over it to see what was marked, Paul seated me. Soon they were engrossed in the various details of the winter travel schedule. Finally, Donald straightened up for a moment, flexed his arms in a stretch, and suddenly realized he had a wife sitting there quietly. Putting his arm across my shoulders he drew me into their twosome.

"You know, of course, that you are to be the tail to my kite." His voice was matter-of-fact.

Immediately there leaped into my mind the picture of the wonderful kites my father had made for us as children, some as tall as a man. For these it sometimes took all five of us to carry the splendid long tail, lifting it above the entangling brush of the field where we flew it, until the kite could get up into the air, the tail swirling behind it. *Where the kite went, the tail went.* Excitement gripped me.

Donald continued to look at me steadily, as if waiting. Wasn't that what he meant? I decided not to say anything.

"You know what the function of the kite tail is, don't you?"

"Function?"

"The function of the kite tail is to stabilize the kite and enable it to fly higher."

His eyes smiled into mine. He squeezed my shoulder, then turned back to Paul and the schedule. I sat there transfixed. I, the stabilizer? Bits of Doug's words came to me: "He is a human dynamo, but he's like a truck motor with the governor broken. . . . Thank God for Paul. . . . DGB needs to have his energies channeled. . . ." Now there was Russ Hitt to reinforce Paul. Donald called them "my right bank and my left bank to keep me from inundating the landscape." Was I to be a part of this team also?

As we went back to the car Donald looked at his watch.

"We have time: let me give you a guided tour of Tenth." He led me up the driveway and through the side door.

After showing me the offices and Sunday school rooms, he led me back to the entryway and up a flight of five narrow steps that seemed to come to a dead end at a small landing. In the gloom I saw a door to the left. He put his hand on the left-hand side of the door frame and ran it up and down tenderly.

"Here is my leaning post. Every Sunday before I enter the pulpit I lean my forehead against this post and ask the Lord to take over—to keep Donald Barnhouse out of that pulpit and make it His alone, to speak through my lips, to reach out to the needs of the people." He closed his eyes briefly, then with his right forearm he leaned against the door. As it swung open the interior of Tenth Church burst into my vision.

What a sight it was from this perspective: pews, row upon row; a gallery ascending so steeply the chairs had to be in enclosed boxes, as in a theater; sunlight slanting through high, arched windows.

He ushered me onto the platform. I stepped to the pulpit with an overwhelming sense of awe, of history, of the faithful men who had crossed thus to this place and over that pulpit had fed countless people with the bread of God's Word. I glanced at the pulpit Bible, open at the fifty-fifth chapter of Isaiah. Donald told me that when he first came to Tenth that page was so worn and torn it gave mute evidence to the dependence of his predecessors on that passage upon which he, too, had wanted to build his ministry: "So shall my word be that goeth forth out of my mouth: it shall not return unto me void, but it shall accomplish that which I please, and it shall prosper in the thing whereto I sent it." The Bible had since been rebound, but the mendings on the page testified to its use.

He took my elbow and guided me down the steps to the auditorium. *(Not* "sanctuary"—I remembered how I had reacted in the Bradenton meetings in my baby Christian days when he had said that it was a place for *listening as God spoke through His Word,* and therefore an *audi*torium, that the only thing sacred in it was the indwelling Holy Spirit whom true believers had before they came and would take with them when they left.) We stood in the center aisle and Donald laid his hand upon the carved top of the end of one of the pews.

"When I first came to Tenth there were less than 200 active members. The neighborhood, once so fashionable, was deteriorating. But I *knew* God had called me to this place. One morning I was moved to kneel down and pray beside these pews—pray for those who would sit there and hear the Word. I went methodically down the aisles, kneeling at each pew, praying for a few each day. When I got to the front pews the Devil whispered, 'Don't be silly. No one ever sits in the front pews!' But I prayed there anyway. Within a few years not only were people sitting in the front pews, but there were chairs in the aisles. The Lord has blessed. . . ."

I looked back at the stately white pulpit, the soaring brown marble columns that supported the gallery and the high vaulted ceiling. He followed my glance.

"Copy of a basilica at Ravenna, Italy. . . . There used to be an enormous chandelier up there that had to be lowered in order to light it."

I looked at Donald's handsome, lifted head and could sense the love for and, yes, pride in this place the Lord had given him. How different from the great, cold cathedrals before whose altars we had stood. . . . My gaze brought his down from the lofty ceiling.

"Aren't you forgetting something?" I asked softly.

His eyes looked deep, deep into mine, and then leaning down he kissed me. But this time it was no schoolboy prank, no secret game. In the holy moment of that kiss I knew I had become for him a part of Tenth and the prayers in the pews and the leaning post and the ministry. In front of this pulpit where God's Word was lifted to feed and enrich, the words of that great hymn invoking God's Holy Spirit became real: "My heart an altar, and Thy love the flame. . . ."

III

Speaking the Truth in Love

THIRTEEN

On Saturday the Smalls, the Hitts, and the Hopkinses came out to the Farm to welcome me. It was good to be with Paul and Jeanne again and to begin to know the others better. Russ Hitt seemed to know everybody who was anybody in evangelical circles and would be an excellent public relations coordinator for Donald. Donald had known him and Lillian since before their marriage, when he had tried to persuade Lillian, a gifted writer and Bible teacher, to be his private secretary. We all—including Donald—laughed at the way she one-upped him as we were strolling around the lawns. Donald, pointing out a small flowering tree he had pruned and shaped to exquisite perfection, said, "Do you see the tree I made?" "Oh?" said Lillian demurely, "I thought only God could make a tree!" Taken aback, Donald stopped in his tracks, then recovering, laughed, "Touché!"

On Sunday, before the morning service, I went before the "Session" (the elders of the church) to answer the questions put to those who wanted to join Tenth Church. It made no difference that I was Mrs. Barnhouse; God is no respecter of persons! Having answered satisfactorily, I was received into membership during the service.

This morning, for some reason I did not close my eyes as we stood for the benediction. I had to watch as Donald lifted us up so earnestly to the Lord. He spoke with upraised arms but with head bowed and eyes closed. Then he turned and to my astonishment kept his eyes closed as he walked toward the steps leading down from the pulpit. His eyelids opened slightly as he descended and closed again as he walked confidently down the aisle toward the rear of the church. One eye opened as he passed me, and with an almost conspiratorial gesture he slipped me his sermon notes and continued, eyes closed. I stood there with the notes in my hand, feeling guilty because I had not been giving my full devotion to those last few moments of reverence before the Lord, and Donald had caught me at it. At the same time I was flooded with a feeling of oneness with him that was breathtaking. He belonged to his people; I needed to stay in the background. But this sweet gesture made me a part of it all.

The organ postlude ended. I slipped quickly out of the pew and went to the back of the church. As I reached the vestibule, I saw one of the deacons grip Donald's proffered hand, wordlessly communicating how the message had blessed. Donald placed his other hand on top, and in that silent handgrip was all the *dunamis*—the explosive power—of the Holy Spirit in deep blessing. The brief moment passed, the handclasp was loosed, and the deacon turned away to let others shake Donald's hand, but inadvertently I had witnessed one very precious secret of my husband's ministry in this church: the deep "communion of the saints."

An out-of-town visitor, a small, pretty, soft, middle-aged woman, caught Donald's hand, pressed it to her billowy bosom, and breathed, "Oh, Dr. Barnhouse, you were *wonderful!*" I could sense his inner recoil as he murmured his most formal "Thankew," extricated his hand, and hurriedly reached for the next. (*The Flesh,* I thought. *No wonder he had to build a wall around himself!*)

Later I asked him about her. "Is she a real Christian?" He groaned, "If she is, she certainly is 'carnal': 2 Timothy 3:6, 7 if ever I saw it." I opened my Bible and read: "For of this sort are they which creep into houses, and lead captive silly women laden with sins, led away with divers lusts, ever learning, and never able to come to the knowledge of the truth."

He continued. "I run into them everywhere I go. A man wouldn't even have to 'creep'—the door's wide open. They don't really listen, they just let the words wash over them, feeling smug for being in church, and looking at the minister with the same emotion a bobby-soxer feels for her movie hero. Thank God most of the people in *my* church aren't like that!" Then he shook his head as if to get rid of the whole idea.

The next few days were spent rearranging things to accomodate the furniture I had brought up from my Florida home, going through closets and drawers, and making mental inventories. I came across a notebook of speaking notes and essays his first wife, Ruth, had written. What a sense of humor! What devotion to her Lord, and to her husband and family! Being the wife of Donald Grey Barnhouse in the early years must not have been easy; nevertheless she had apparently adored him. I knew he had loved her deeply, and her death, ten years before, had been an anguish to him.

I remembered things he had told Doug and me about her on that trip. When she was forty-two she had developed cancer. Toward the end, she was in great pain, yet when each new shift of doctors and nurses came on duty, *they* would come to *her* for a joyous lift for their day. Donald had taken a Bible apart in order for her to have just a page at a time to hold in hands too weak for more than that. One day he had come into her room to find her radiant. "Just listen to this!" she had cried, *"Colossians 1:11,* 'Strengthened with all might, according to his glorious power, unto all patience and longsuffering with joyfulness.' *Joyfulness!* That's what He has given me." She had insisted that he go

ahead with his speaking engagements and conference ministry, even when it took him out of town, so he was not with
her when she died. When he and the four children were on
the way to the funeral, an enormous truck had pulled past
them, throwing its shadow across them. He had asked the
children, "Would you rather be run over by the truck, or
the shadow of the truck?" The eleven-year-old had said,
"Shadow, of course!" "Well, that's what has happened to
your mother," Donald had replied. "Only the shadow of
death has passed over her, because death itself ran over
Jesus. But He rose again, He lives—and so does she, in
heaven!" I remembered his illustration in his sermon, "Suffering," of a sovereign God deploying us, His troops in the
Invisible War: " 'Go there and take Cancer Hill!' So we go
and take Cancer Hill. 'Go there in the valley and suffer the
tears that flow inside that the world cannot see!' 'Yes, *sir,*
Lord!' " I knew he must have been there too, many times,
for his Lord, suffering the tears that flow inside.

In a box of framed pictures, put away during the recent
redecorating of the house, I found a photograph that had to
be Ruth: the resemblance to her daughters was striking.
Looking at that serene face, whose natural beauty needed
no cosmetics, I thanked the Lord that she had been part of
his life. Then I noticed something odd: instead of finger-
print marks around the edge of the glass, as would be
normal, there were smudges in the middle of it. Tears came
to my eyes as I realized those were not fingerprints: they
were the print of his lips; he had been a desperately lonely
man whose "help suitable for him" was no longer there.

My role was not "to take her place." No one could do
that: her memory had melted into his innermost self and
become a part of him. Knowing this, when I took him as
my husband, I took him in the totality of his being—and
that included all that Ruth had been to him in a happy
twenty-two years. With gratitude I realized that in the same
spirit he had married me. We could talk about Doug, or
Ruth, as easily as about any other loved ones.

That week the days began to fall into a pattern. Early in the morning I would slip out of bed, bathe, and get ready for the day. When Donald awoke, he would immediately break into song: "When morning gilds the skies,/My heart awaking cries,/'May Jesus Christ be praised!' " I would come join in the singing; then we'd have our morning devotions. He would shower and dress as I got breakfast. After breakfast he would go to our bedroom-study to work. Because this room was air-conditioned, we kept the door closed, so it was as if he really had left the house. I didn't see him again until lunchtime. Right after lunch he would go back to work, keeping at it until around five P.M. Naomi would have secretarial sessions with him, after which I could hear her typewriter clattering away. In addition to the regular household duties, I spent a great deal of time among the flowerbeds, doing the gardening I loved. In the eighteen-inch-thick fieldstone walls of the house the deep windowsills seemed to invite the arrangements of flowers or greenery I so enjoyed doing. In the evening if we had guests, or if any of the children were home, we would spend an hour or so after dinner with them, then Donald would excuse himself and go back to his typewriter and his reading and research. By the end of the week I was feeling at home and secure.

Tuesday we left for Sandy Cove.

The Sandy Cove Bible Conference grounds are on the eastern shore of Maryland, two or three hours from the Farm. As we drove, I asked: "Donald, did you realize that the first time I'd ever attended a summer Bible conference was the English Keswick this summer?"

"Oh, now, Marge. Not really."

"Really. I've only known Jesus as my Savior for slightly over three years, remember. How did you have the nerve to marry me, when I knew so little?"

He laughed. "You didn't have so much to *un*learn!"

"What will it be like at Sandy Cove? Anything like

Keswick?" I thought of that tiny English town in the Lake District where each year during the last week of July missionaries and others gather for a time of spiritual refreshing and a deepening of the spiritual life. The townsfolk double up their families and rent out rooms; the young people attending the conference camp out in tents; the speakers and other dignitaries are housed in a splendid old castle. Meetings are held in an enormous tent pitched there for the occasion. It is a time of Bible study and prayer, of deep soul-searching, of repentance, of mountain-top joy in the Lord, with messages from the best of evangelical speakers from Britain and elsewhere. W. Graham Scrogge had been the main speaker that year, a grand old gentleman with a strong message. He had not been well, so they had asked Donald to stand by and fill in, in case Dr. Scrogge could not continue. However, Dr. Scrogge's strength held and he was able to carry on. Donald was planning to use here at Sandy Cove the messages he had prepared for Keswick.

He repeated, "What's it like here? Well, it's as different from Keswick as the U.S.A. is from Britain. You'll see!"

The car swung into the conference grounds. Throngs of people were going to different activities: it looked like a summer resort.

"I see what you mean," I murmured as Donald held open the car door for me.

That night Donald's message was tremendous. I wished the Keswick people, whom I had learned to love during that brief week, could have heard it too. Afterward I was aware of curious stares. (I imagined them saying, "So *this* is the person Dr. Barnhouse married!")

The next morning Donald emerged in the wildest sport shirt imaginable. I was shocked: I had never seen him in public in anything other than a business suit and tie, looking dignified. Apparently, his sport shirts were a legend here, and people looked forward to seeing what he would appear in next!

That week, so different from Keswick, was nevertheless

in its own way a total renewal for both of us. I think Donald would have burst after preparing those Keswick messages so carefully if he had not been able to use them. Giving them refreshed him. In addition, we found rest and relaxation and exercise for the body, and food for the soul.

At the end Donald was ready to put on the boxing gloves and take on the World Council of Churches the following week.

The much-heralded 1954 Assembly of the World Council of Churches in Evanston, Illinois, was finally beginning. The processional into the auditorium was breathtaking: clerics from all over the world, in magnificent, colorful garb or simple clerical robes, coming together to discuss the second coming of Christ under the theme, "Christ, the Hope of the World."

Inasmuch as Donald was not a delegate, he had to obtain credentials as a reporter for *Eternity* magazine in order to be admitted to the behind-the-scenes meetings. He and Russ Hitt and I sat among the observers, in the main meetings, then he and Russ would leave to attend various sectional discussions.

Our Sarasota Bible class had been predominantly fundamentalist. We looked askance at the liberal National Council of Churches and assumed the World Council of Churches was more of the same, on a global scale. Donald's teaching had contributed to some of this thinking, which was why his New Year's Resolution had rocked us. *(Now I'll find out first hand,* I thought.)

As I listened to those first addresses, I found myself overwhelmed. One after another of the leaders of the European and other foreign delegations stood and magnified the Lord Jesus Christ as the only hope of a world of people who are, as Dr. Charles Malik of Lebanon put it, *"Not* only not self-sufficient, *not* only limited creatures, *not* only creatures of the living and true God, on whom we depend every minute, but fallen and sinful creatures; *not* just rebellious against this or that good and right thing, but rebellious by nature; *not* just mortal with a scientifically calculated probability of so many more years still to live, but spiritually dying every minute and physically liable to die any minute, perhaps even this very one. On this plane of sin and death which encompasses us all, and indeed the whole of mankind, we also acknowledge with tears of rapture the victory and power, the glory and forgiveness of Jesus Christ, who renews us by His grace every day."

For the most part, representatives of the delegation from the United States seemed liberal in their outlook, but many others were obviously sincere, concerned believers, convinced that the Lord Jesus Christ *was* coming a second time, in judgment, and that we would be held accountable for our proclamation of the gospel here and now.

Donald came back from the sectional discussions shaken. "Marge, it's incredible. Listen to this." He read me some notes he had taken: "Germanic voice: 'The language must be tightened up and made less vague and much more Christ-centered.' English accent: 'Terms vague. No social change is the hope of the world. Christ alone is the hope of the world.' Anglican cleric: 'Alter to stress *nature of our sin* which has brought misery upon the world, and of our duties to help.' Chairman: 'There must be a great consciousness of the possession of eternal life if we are to reach those spiritually dead.' American speaker, liberal, listened to politely, then back to conservative ideas." I was more and more astonished.

"This is something I really hadn't expected," Donald mused. "I hope some of the World Council theology rubs off on the National Council of Churches."

Outside, a group of highly vocal fundamentalist separatists were picketing the meeting, claiming that because church leaders from behind the Iron Curtain were included the World Council of Churches was under Communist influence. Inside, those leaders from behind the Iron Curtain were attesting a faith so fundamental they might someday have to die for it.

(Today, God still has His "remnant" within the NCC and the WCC—conservative Christians who work hard to steer these organizations toward the fundamentals of Christian faith and doctrine. However, the "Invisible War" is being waged in the NCC and the WCC: over the years liberals have gained control; they have become increasingly preoccupied with politics and humanitarian causes; Marxism-Leninism has become their philosophical underpinning. Is it possible, notwithstanding the valiant fight of the "remnant," that the separatists' lack of love and true concern for unsaved members of these organizations have effectively granted victory to the enemy of souls?)

Meanwhile, the dream of a television ministry, which Donald had shared with Doug when he asked him to become a board member of the Evangelical Foundation, was, through a strange set of circumstances, becoming a possibility. Members of the Broadcasting and Film Commission of the National Council of Churches—of all things!—had seen some of his films. They had come to Philadelphia to discuss the possibility of the Foundation's making some films for national television showing. In view of the controversies of the past, Donald was somewhat suspicious, but as he came to know these particular men he was convinced they were born-again men who loved the Lord. After a dozen or so meetings between them, with a cautious approach each to the other, the NCC representatives agreed that if Donald could produce sufficiently challenging films, he could have total freedom of content. However, he was not to use this as a platform to attack others. He would be one of four speakers, each of whom would produce thirteen films independent of the others. The United States would be divided into four areas. The films produced by each of the men would appear in one of these areas for thirteen weeks, then move to the next area, covering the whole of the country by the end of the year. One of the NCC men told him, "We feel that the conservative view has not been adequately represented in the NCC programs. We feel that you would face the TV cameras with a dignified presentation of the gospel, which would be welcomed by the managers and owners of TV stations and by the public." It was agreed that the Evangelical Foundation should receive and answer the mail that came in from our segment of the telecasts. It was also agreed that the Foundation would handle all gifts received as a result of the program, using them to help defray the cost of making the films, an expensive operation in itself. The Foundation agreed that we would not use the mailing lists thus built up for anything that would be detrimental to the NCC. In other words, as Donald put it, "We were both going to act as Christian gentlemen should act." Thus it was not a compromise on either side.

Because of the furor caused in fundamental circles by his New Year's Resolution and his stand on the RSV, Donald was concerned that some people might not understand this new phase of his work, and could be shaken by its connection with the National Council of Churches. He decided to prepare them, in case the program did become a reality. At each of his fall conferences, on the third or fourth night, he would tell his audiences that he had been making some films on Christian doctrine, with a strong possibility of their being shown on television. He would then tell this story: The Jewish gentleman who decided who should get free time on a certain TV chain had granted this permission for one of Donald's earlier films, because of its excellent photography, without ever seeing the entire film. Donald then would ask his audience: "Suppose a million dollars worth of free time for the gospel were offered to us by Jews without restriction. Remember, they do not believe as we do. Should we accept it?"

The audience invariably answered aloud, "Yes." Then he would say, "Suppose the time were made available to us through the National Council of Churches? Should we accept the responsibility, raise the $200,000 to make the films, and go ahead?" One pastor said aloud, "Ha! They'd never give it to you." Donald assured them of the definite possibility of this, and told of the agreement involved. But he added, "If this does go through, and you see me looking at you out of your TV screens sometime within the next year, know that I will be preaching 'Man's complete ruin in sin and God's perfect remedy in Christ.' I will not have changed my doctrines in the slightest."

On the heels of the September conferences, Donald had to be at the Foundation early one morning, so he decided to stay there the night before. After dinner in town, we went to 1716 Spruce Street, where Donald's keys let us into the dark and quiet building. He led the way through the entrance hall and up the stairs, flicking lights on and off as we progressed.

We reached the landing a few steps below the hallway leading to his office. He put down our overnight bag and started through the general office toward Paul's office, where he would leave several Romans studies to be edited.

In the general office all was ready for the next day's work: papers neatly stacked on desks; correspondence ready to be taken care of. Donald paused beside the first desk and, picking up a letter from the top of the stack, read it, put it down, then riffled through the stack. He extracted a letter or two and put them in his pocket. He did the same thing all down the line, leaving the place a shambles.

"Donald!" I objected, "you can't *do* this! You have totally disorganized everything!"

"Why can't I? It's *my* work. I have a right to do anything I please here! Every person in this place lives by my mind, my pen, my voice." He had stepped into Paul's office and laid his scripts down on the desk. He picked them up again with both hands, looked at them hard, then slowly put them down again.

"Marge, that's true! I hadn't really thought about it before. And it's not right. If anything happened to me this place would fold. We're going to have to groom some men to take over, just in case. We need writers and a stable of speakers. There are more speaking invitations right now than I can handle...." With what I called "that inward look," he started back through the general office, his mind totally occupied with this new thought. He didn't even see the mess he had made, nor have any realization of what he had done to those poor secretaries who would have to face that upheaval the next morning.

The next time we spent the night at the Foundation every desk top was bare, except for a small framed picture or two, and here and there a potted plant!

FOURTEEN

In early November, Donald prepared to go to Grand Rapids for a four-day Bible conference. Here where the Dutch Reformed churches predominated he had wanted union meetings, combining all the branches of these churches in one big teaching mission. Russ had tried to arrange this, but reported that both the Christian Reformed Church and the Reformed Church in America had turned him down. However, one of the congregations was eager to have him, so Russ had booked him there.

I was packing his bag as he was gathering up typewriter and books. "Marge, if Billy Graham can have huge meetings, why can't I? These people *need* the feeding I can give them. And the same message can feed 5,000 at once as easily as 500. I just don't understand these people in Grand Rapids." He shuffled through sermon outlines. I continued packing his bag.

"What ties do you want?"

"Any old ties will do for Grand Rapids." He put some sermon outlines into his typewriter case and closed it.

My mind went back to that trip with DGB, Doug, and me. Between two large meetings, he had been scheduled to speak in a small church in a small town. On the way to the church that evening the host pastor seemed uneasy. Finally he said, "Dr. Barnhouse, I know you are used to big audiences. We are honored that you would come to us, a small church. I'd better warn you ahead of time that there may be only 120 or so people tonight."

DGB's voice was confident, unperturbed. "I pray over all my invitations before I accept them. I know this is where the Lord wants me tonight. How do I know but what the mother of the Billy Graham of the next generation may be in this audience tonight? The Lord has a message for your people, through me. The numbers are unimportant; that's just ego-boosting. The important thing is that the *Lord* brought me here, and I *must* preach the preaching that He bids me."

What was happening to *that* Donald Grey Barnhouse? I wondered whether he had really prayed over this meeting. So many new things were occupying his mind these days, each with its own demands on his time and energy. I wanted to put my hands on his shoulders and say, "Donald, let's pray!" but just at that moment the telephone rang. When he finally hung up it was too late. Grabbing his bag and typewriter, he gave me a quick good-bye kiss and raced down the stairs to the waiting car.

(Lord, keep him! Beat back the powers of darkness! Satan would love to get Donald's ego messed up in this. Lord, don't let it happen. You have a message for these people. Use him. Don't let the channel get clogged!)

Five days later he was back, elated. The Lord had indeed used him, and the Grand Rapids trip had taken an unexpected turn.

"I preached Tuesday night to a fairly full church," he told me. "Wednesday afternoon a man called me on the house phone, said his name was Ed Kuiper, and asked for an appointment to see me. I was in the middle of an editorial, so I told him that I was sorry, that I am a radio speaker, an editor, a pastor, with a great deal of work to do, that my schedule was really full. He said, 'But, Dr. Barnhouse, I want to give some money to your work.' Immediately I asked, 'Are you a Christian? I don't accept money from anyone who isn't a Christian.' Well, he said that after hearing me the night before he wasn't sure, and that was what he wanted to talk to me about. I told him to come to the meeting that night and speak to me afterward. In the meantime, I found out who Ed Kuiper was: the wealthiest man in Grand Rapids.

"After the meeting Ed Kuiper came up to me, introduced his wife and twin sons, and invited me to their home for refreshments. I went. We talked for a while, then his wife and the boys went to bed. Right away he got into the subject of salvation, and was really open to the Lord. Before long we were kneeling beside the davenport, and he received Christ as his Savior. When we got up, he gripped my hand and said, '*Now* will you let me give you some money?' We laughed, and I told him to pray about it, and send the Foundation whatever the Lord told him to.

"He and his wife came to every meeting, bringing their friends. Marge, an influential man like that could turn Grand Rapids upside down for the Lord!"

All this while negotiations for the television series had been continuing. By November enough money had been raised to begin making the films. The one thing that remained was to secure a local endorsement either from the Philadelphia Council of Churches or from the Presbytery of Philadelphia. The Council of Churches endorsement seemed the easier approach, but it would have further alienated him from his own denomination. He would "have gone around them," as it were.

This presented an embarrassment for Donald. Because of sharp disagreement with the liberal elements in his denomination he had attended Presbytery meetings infrequently, despite the fact that many of its members were as conservative as he. How could they be expected to endorse him when he had not endorsed them by his presence at the meetings?

Paul and Russ suggested that if he really meant what he said in his New Year's Resolution and if he really wanted Presbytery to endorse his TV films, he should make the first move toward establishing a closer relationship with the Presbytery. Donald asked them to write down their thoughts on how to do this and meet with him at the Farm to work it out. It wasn't until the day before the November meeting of Presbytery that they could get together. They asked me to join them.

On the basis of his declaration in that New Year's Resolution, they had outlined their thoughts. However, to admit a wrong spirit in an article in a magazine was one thing; to do this face to face was something else again. Paul reminded Donald that the Council of Churches would endorse him for the TV program without any problem. He didn't *have* to go through Presbytery. Donald dismissed this as cowardly. After hammering at it for a while, with Donald's pride very much involved, he said to me, "Dear, I think this is something just between Paul and Russ and me, and I'd like you to leave. Do you mind?"

"Of course not." I squeezed his shoulder reassuringly and went upstairs to do some praying. This was going to take more than human effort.

At dinner Donald was preoccupied. Afterward, he worked late in the study part of the bedroom. I finally came in quietly and went to bed.

I was almost asleep when he finally rose and began to pace back and forth, saying under his breath to himself and to his Lord, "How can I do this?" He paced some more, then said, "But it should be done." He put his elbows on the chest of drawers and leaned his head on his hands. After a long time he whispered, "It must be done," and came to bed.

The next day as I sat in the visitors' section at Presbytery I continued to pray. Would he really do it?

A hush came over the gathering as he rose to his feet and went forward. He said he wanted to make a statement, but would read it so there could be no misunderstanding. He then read such a moving statement that I was in tears. When he finished, the members of the Presbytery rose to their feet, broke ranks, and rushed to embrace him as if welcoming back a long-absent brother. For a moment he stood there in disbelief, then hugged them back.

The Presbytery executive was so impressed that he asked Donald to write up that statement for *Monday Morning,* a magazine for Presbyterian ministers. It was the cover story on December 20, 1954. It read as follows:

"The November meeting of the Presbytery of Philadelphia adopted a recommendation of its public relations committee asking that the Presbytery endorse my appearance on a series of television programs, time for which would be made available through the Broadcasting and Film Commission of the National Council of Churches. . . .

"It is well known that there was great strife in our church a quarter of a century ago, and that much of this centered in Philadelphia and Princeton, and that a schism took place, largely centering around Philadelphia. I found myself somewhat alone because I disagreed sharply with the liberals on their theology and with the fundamentalists whose methods eventually separated them from the church. As the years have passed there has been a change of circumstances and of theological emphasis within our denomination which has brought to me an ever widening circle of fellowship. . . .

"Perhaps the turning point in the late years of my ministry was the publication two years ago, of an editorial, 'New Year's Resolution,' in which I confessed the need in my own life for the Lord to give me a greater experience of true humility both before Him and before men and especially a love that would surmount differences among those working for the cause of Christ.

"I have been astonished and gladdened at the way men in many camps have received this statement of purpose and desire. . . . I recognize that there is a level on which we can work together, and certain spheres where we must work together, even though we may disagree sharply in other spheres. I have found a warm, evangelical note in my dealings with certain leaders in the National and World Council of Churches, and I know that I have profited by knowing these men at closer range, finding them true brothers in Christ.

"In the course of my work I have held meetings for some pastors in the Southern Presbyterian Church who are committed to the thought of union with us and for some who are opposed to it. I recognize the serious differences that exist and the deep honesty of the men who hold opposite opinions on this subject. I once was totally opposed to the idea of union and expressed my opposition in a manner for which I am now sorry. I realize that because my ministry takes me into churches of men of varying convictions I must be willing to honor each man's position before God and to avoid taking up issues of this nature....

"Recently I had occasion to review some of the things that I said about the educational program of our denomination. I have not changed my theological position in the slightest, nor have I abdicated true Presbyterian right of dissent. I disagree with the theology of some of our denominational publications but I recognize clearly that some of the language which I used years ago in expressing my dissent was inexcusably harsh. I was speaking what I hold to be the truth, but I was not 'speaking the truth in love.' I deeply regret any wounds that I may have caused anyone by this harshness.... I now have learned that differences between true Christians can be cleared up or at least become less grievous, by face-to-face discussion. Should I have differences with men within our denomination in the future, I am determined to first of all approach the matter with love and humility in the Biblical manner. If differences cannot be thus reconciled, I am sure that after such a meeting they can at least be stated in carefully measured terms and in Christian love.

"As I travel about the country I have been frequently told by younger men that because I have been faithful to the ministry of our church it has helped them clear up their thinking about the separatist movement which is constantly wooing them. If this is true, I am delighted that the Lord has thus honored my ministry, and I believe that in some measure it has helped to strengthen the church.

"I sincerely trust that I may have the understanding of all my brethren in the ministry. As never before, I feel the need of your prayers and your love. In turn it is my hope that when our television programs shall go out over the nation it will bless many people and strengthen our hands in the tasks which the Lord has given us to perform."

The watchnight service at Tenth Church on New Year's Eve, 1954, was for me one of the highest points in a year of high points: the testimonies, the fellowship, the singing, the communion at midnight.

One of Donald's parishioners told me how, at one of those watchnight services, just as they were about to lift the cup, they could hear drunken voices passing outside, singing loudly,

Glorious, glorious,
One keg of beer for the four of us.
Glory be to God there ain't no more of us
For heaven knows I'd drink it all alone.

There was a dramatic pause. Then Donald lifted his cup and said,

Glorious, glorious,
Jesus drank the dregs for all of us.
Glory be to God there is no more for us,
For on the cross He drank it all alone.

As they all partook together of that symbol of our Lord's great sacrifice, the Holy Spirit was palpably there in great power and joy. The final hymn of praise shook the place, "I'll never forget it," this parishioner told me. "What a contrast."

New Year's Day we drove to Pittsburgh for a week of meetings at the First Presbyterian Church, where Bob Lamont was pastor. I hadn't seen him since he had officiated at our wedding. We had dinner with Bob, his wife Edna, and the children. After catching up on family affairs, Bob was full of questions about the statement to Presbytery, the TV programs, and the NCC. Donald admitted that he was having to "eat a lot of crow" these days, backing down on a lot of his former dogmatic pronouncements, and it wasn't palatable.

"But I have to be honest before the Lord: I have been guilty of dumping all members of the NCC indiscriminately into the liberal camp. Having done so publicly, I feel obliged to modify those statements publicly. And you know, I am discovering the Lord's Remnant in all sorts of unlikely places. The men I am working with on the Broadcasting and Film Commission of the NCC are true brothers in Christ, maintaining with other colleagues a witness in the midst of the liberal wing of the NCC."

Monday morning's Bible study was new to me: the first verse of chapter 1 of 1 John. Donald read it aloud: "That which was from the beginning, which we have heard, which we have seen with our eyes, which we have looked upon, and our hands have handled, of the Word of life."

He looked up, saying, "Now, to understand 1 John you must realize it is a commentary on the Upper Room. Get out of your minds Leonardo da Vinci's magnificent rendering of this subject: Jesus and His disciples were not seated at that kind of table, but were reclining on the left elbow around a low table, like the spokes of a wheel. John, probably a teenager, undoubtedly was reclining in front of Jesus; all he'd have to do would be to roll back slightly and he'd be leaning on Jesus' bosom. He could reach out his hand and put it on Jesus' hand as it lay on the table: ' . . . our hands have handled. . . .' "

Tenderly he placed his right hand on an invisible hand on the pulpit, and the whole scene sprang to life.

"Go back to John's Gospel, chapter 13, to the Upper Room. Jesus has washed the disciples' feet; He has announced that one of them would betray Him; He has told them that He is going away and that where He is going they cannot come.

"Consternation!

"He gives them a 'new' commandment: they are to love one another. 'As I have loved you, that ye also love one another.' Let's pause and consider this. What's new about it? 'Love your neighbor as yourself'; 'love one another; as I have loved you . . . love one another.' And how did He love us? Look at 1 Corinthians 13. 'Love suffereth long, and is kind; love envieth not; love vaunteth not itself, is not puffed up, doth not behave itself unseemly, seeketh not her own, is not easily provoked, thinketh no evil; rejoiceth not in iniquity, but rejoiceth in the truth; beareth all things, believeth all things, hopeth all things, endureth all things. Love never fails. . . .' John 13:1 says of Jesus, 'Having loved his own which were in the world, he loved them unto the end.' *Loved them unto the end.* Utterly faithful. *That* is how we are to accept and love one another. This isn't an option: it's a *command,* from the Lord Jesus Himself. Verse 35 says that's how people will know we're His disciples. Do we love like that?

"Now, back to this passage. Jesus had just given this new commandment; they never heard it. They were in a panic over what He had said about going away and didn't hear the rest. How do we know? Peter says, 'Where are You going? Why can't I follow You? I'll lay down my life for You!' Jesus says, 'Is that so, Peter? I tell you, before the cock crows you will deny Me three times.'

"Pandemonium! Jesus had to calm them down. John 14:1,

'Let not your heart be troubled'; and again, verse 27: 'Let not your heart be troubled, neither let it be afraid.' They hadn't heard half of what He said so the Holy Spirit had to bring it to mind, in John's first Epistle."

He continued, flipping from the Epistle to the Gospel and back again. By the end of the week in Pittsburgh a whole new segment of Scripture had opened up to me.

Home again, Donald spent a week in final preparation for the TV filming, then we started west on the 1955 winter Bible conference tour.

The first conference was in Uniontown, Pennsylvania, with C. Edwin Houk. I was informed that I was to speak at the Women's Association luncheon that week.

As I settled myself to work on my message, Donald was at his typewriter, immersed in some weighty problem, frowning over one of his reference books. I began working on my outline and was soon happily into my Bible, seeing the message take shape, reference by reference. Suddenly I hit a real snag.

"Donald?" I asked. He surfaced and smiled at my perplexity. "What does this mean?" I went to him and read him the passage.

"I don't know."

"You don't know?"

"No, I don't know."

"But... if *you* don't know, who does?"

"Dear, there are a great many things in the Bible I still do not know. That is one of the passages I intend to work on one of these days, but not right now. But the same Holy Spirit who teaches me will teach you if you really *want* to know. Now get back there and *dig.*"

"But... a woman can be deceived!"

His wonderful laugh rang out. "Get back there *and dig!* And let me know what you find." Then once more his mind was deep in his problem.

The Lord gave me what I needed, and the message went well.

Above: Barchdale, the home of Donald Grey Barnhouse, Doylestown PA.

Left: Tenth United Presbyterian Church, Philadelphia PA, the home of DGB's preaching ministry.

Donald and Margaret Barnhouse, September 1955.

Top: Marge and Donald in Europe, 1955.
Bottom: Discussion outside the tent at the English Keswick, 1955.

Donald Grey Barnhouse.   Margaret Barnhouse.

Donald, the proud granddaddy.

J. Hannay jr.   Rom 7. 32.

P. Dilhorn 4/4/13.
2 Cor. 9 : 8.

a. C. Garbutui   Rev III : 10

H B Riley
1 Cor, 13th Chap.

L. H. Kinchall
2 Tim 2:15; Numb. VI : 24-26.

Royal Doyad W.   Bolingr apica Rom

"I pray that
Thy name. O Lord.
shall be written in
my life"

THE SCOFIELD REFERENCE BIBLE

THE

HOLY BIBLE

CONTAINING THE

OLD AND NEW TESTAMENTS

AUTHORIZED VERSION

WITH A NEW SYSTEM OF CONNECTED TOPICAL REFERENCES TO ALL THE
GREATER THEMES OF SCRIPTURE, WITH ANNOTATIONS,
REVISED MARGINAL RENDERINGS, SUMMARIES,
DEFINITIONS, AND INDEX

TO WHICH ARE ADDED

HELPS AT HARD PLACES, EXPLANATIONS OF SEEMING DISCREPANCIES,
AND A NEW SYSTEM OF PARAGRAPHS.

EDITED BY

REV. C. I. SCOFIELD, D.D.

CONSULTING EDITORS:

REV. HENRY G. WESTON, D.D., LL.D.,
President Crozer Theological Seminary.

REV. PROF. W. G. MOOREHEAD, D.D.,
Prof. in Xenia (U. P.) Theological Seminary.

REV. JAMES M. GRAY, D.D.,
Dean of Moody Bible Institute.

REV. ELMORE G. HARRIS, D.D.,
President Toronto Bible Institute.

REV. WILLIAM J. ERDMAN, D.D.,
Author "The Gospel of John," etc., etc.

ARNO C. GAEBELEIN,
Author "Harmony of Prophetic Word," etc., etc.

REV. ARTHUR T. PIERSON, D.D.,
Author, Editor, Teacher.

OXFORD UNIVERSITY PRESS
AMERICAN BRANCH
NEW YORK: 35 WEST 32D STREET
HENRY FROWDE
LONDON, TORONTO AND MELBOURNE

Title page spread from DGB's study Bible.

...book must be loved to be known
...book will keep you from sin.
...sin will keep you from this book
...I don't explain it, I can't understand it, I believe

Christ is in every verse in the Bible. Your
business is to find the shortest route from each
verse to Him.   "Trust and obey"

God said it; Christ did it; I believe
       That settles it; Amen.

The Bible :—
    Man's complete ruin in Sin:
    God's perfect remedy in Christ
Bible: 1600 years, 66 books, 35 writers, one theme.
...no rest but in a nook with the book: Thomas à Kempis 1380-1471. cit.by...

The Church needs leaders today who refuse to re...
plaudits of men. or to exploit themselves. or
...to permit themselves to be exploited, o...
...names to be lauded; for it means the cruci...
...ist afresh. Nothing chokes the channels of
...E revival so effectually as idolatry of
...ders on the part of God's professing children
...for a church which tears from its heart every
...l, "and worships only Thee". G. Campbell...
...ible in its object is a whole. which presents to us God coming f...
...its essential fullness to manifest all that He is, and to bring...
...the enjoyment of this fullness with Himself. those who, havi...
...partakers of His nature, have been become capable of compre...
...ving His counsels and Himself. J.N.D. I,1.

Personal records in DGB's Bible.

Donald Grey Barnhouse

Phil 3:10 —

1700 Spruce St - Phila

17 Rue du Gouvernement Provisoire
Brussels, Belgium

1031 Walnut Street, Philadelphia, Pa

t. 14. 1919 - Brussels - Sept. 1932 Phila.

Life Texts.   Born Again July 2, 1910. San Jose, California
                   see Isa 53:6

Phil. 3:10 -   John 15:5.

Year Verses.

Year	Verse	Year	Verse
1912	Isa. 50:7.	1931	Titus 3:8
1913	Phil. 3:10.	1932	Ps. 60:4
1914	Col. 1:18.	1933	2 Tim. 2:2
1915	Heb. 2:1.	1934	2 Cor 3:18
1916	Phil. 3:13,14.	1935	Matt. 7:11
1917	Deut. 31:8.	1936	Heb. 13:13
1918	1 Cor. 7:29.	1937	Philemon 6
1919	2 Tim 2:15.	1938	1 Cor 9:27
1920	John 15:5	1939	Eph 2:6
1921	Prov. 18:10	1940	John 15:7
1922	Matt 26:41	1941	1 Th 4:3
1923	Eph. 6:16	1942	Matt 6:22
1924	Ps. 138:8	1943	
1925	1 Sam. 7:12	1944	Rom 4:20
1926	1 Cor 1:18	1945	Prov. 3:6
1927	Deut 30:14	1946	1 Jn 2:17
1928	Gal 5:16	1947	
1929	2 Chron 20:12	1948	II Pet. 3:11
1930	Isa 26:3	1949	
		1950	Prov 16:7
		1951	Heb 4:3a
		1952	

Note the listing of year verses.

MARCH 1961   MEMORIAL ISSUE   35 CENTS

ETERNITY

Donald Grey Barnhouse
MARCH 28, 1895—NOVEMBER 5, 1960

The March 1961 cover of *Eternity,* just after the death of DGB.

All that week his audiences sat there, soaking up his sermons like a sponge. Donald was warm and wonderful. We had total support from the Houks. Before the week was up we felt such a bond with Ed and Sally and their delightful family we almost hated to leave on Saturday.

Between meetings Donald had worked intensely all that week in Uniontown. I didn't want to bother him with all the questions his sermons raised for me, so I saved them for the trip to our next destination, Mt. Airy, North Carolina. Once on the highway I started to fire one eagerly at him, but he stopped me.

"Shhhhh!" he said, softly, laying a gentle hand on mine as we drove on through lightly falling snow. "These are the times of refreshing," and he began to quote a poem straight out of my schooldays: "The snow had begun in the gloaming. . . ."

"How did you know that?" I cried, enchanted.

He smiled affectionately at me. "Memorization was part of my schooling. It has stood me in good stead."

"Mine, too! Do you know . . . ?" and I was off on something from Wordsworth. By the third word he had joined me. We laughed our way through dozens of poems we both knew. I decided my questions could wait.

This tour was totally different from the summer conferences, during which I had relaxed, read, and joined the summer activities of the other guests. Shut up in the motel room with him between meetings, I was seeing the workhorse side of Donald, which I hadn't shared at home.

I was fascinated by his thought processes. Apparently he could think on several levels at once, somewhat the way a mother does when she is stirring something on the stove, talking on the telephone, answering Junior's questions, and listening for the baby, all at once—but his was much more complicated intellectually. I first became aware of this when we were driving between meetings. He was obviously thinking on a deep level, yet simultaneously at the surface level he was totally aware of driving conditions and his own responses to them.

I said, "A penny for your thoughts."

As if he had stepped into an elevator deep within a mine, I could sense him moving upward through his thinking, pausing at one level, then the next, asking himself, "Can she comprehend this?" Finally he reached a level at which he thought he could communicate with me. There was a time when this would have insulted me. Now I knew better and was grateful that he didn't say, "Oh, don't bother me," as some husbands might, but instead did share with me, each time leading me to a deeper level.

At his desk in the motel, however, I didn't interrupt. He kept to a rigorous schedule, setting himself a goal each day and pushing for it. If for some reason there was a decision that could not wait, I'd write it out and slide it wordlessly into his line of vision. He'd nod yes or no without missing a beat on his typewriter. Had I made a spoken request, he would have stopped to answer me aloud and would have lost precious minutes. Frequently we'd go all day without speaking, except at meals. I'd put little notes on his typewriter chair in the morning; he'd pencil in his answers, hand them to me, and get on with his work. These frequently had to do with his "pocket scraps," little squares of memo paper he kept in his left-hand coat pocket for jotting purposes. The jottings were put in his right-hand pocket. Every night it was my job to sort out these "pocket scraps," giving his secretary the things she was to attend to, and having him add clarifying remarks to the others to help him recall what he had in mind when he wrote it. These were then put on his desk, and he would enter them into various workbooks the next day. He had a workbook for sermons on various subjects that came up during his studies, and would jot down under its proper heading any new light as it came to him; then, when in the course of his exposition he needed something on that particular subject, the spade work was all done. Of course, being an editor as well as a preacher, he had various files and workbooks of editorial material in addition to his sermon material. He read voraciously. *Time* and *Life* magazines, the *National Geographic,* the *Saturday Evening Post, Reader's Digest,* the *New Yorker,* the *Saturday Review* and other periodicals were grist for his mill, as well as British papers such as the airmail edition of the *London Times,* the *Manchester Guardian,* the *Life of Faith,* and French and German periodicals.

He would save up the daily newspapers and read them once a week, backward from Saturday to Monday. "Saves me a lot of useless reading," Donald declared. "In Saturday's edition I read: 'Gulf coast cleaning up after hurricane.' Friday's paper tells me the hurricane has hit, with great damage. Thursday, people are battening down the hatches. I need only glance at the Wednesday and Tuesday and Monday accounts because I already know the outcome and the details. If a war should break out somewhere on Monday or Tuesday, I'll hear about it before I need to read about it."

I was discovering why Doug hadn't been able to bring me answers when he came back from Philadelphia. And to think that, on that trip together, Doug and I had wondered what on earth there was for him to do! I could also understand why, after such concentrated study and serious mental work, he needed time for play and even silliness.

He loved games. I was astonished at the seriousness with which, at first, he competed, and at how important it was for him to win—which, with me, he usually did. But I taught him a new game, "Camelot," a cross between checkers and chess, at which I could beat him until he caught on to it. My own response, which I had been taught as a child, of good sportsmanship and sincere congratulations to the winner and enjoyment of the game for the game's sake, began to change his attitude. Soon he was getting more fun out of competing, and we would have hilarious contests for a half-hour or so after returning from a meeting, to unwind him before going to bed.

The TV filming was being done in New York and was scheduled to start on a Monday morning in March. I had to make careful note of which suit Donald was wearing—what tie, what shoes, etc.—and be sure everything was the same the next day. When we got to the studio he was taken to the makeup room, where he submitted meekly to the ministration of the makeup man until the man announced proudly, just before applying the final film of powder, "This puff was last used on Marilyn Monroe" (who was then at the height of her movie career). Instead of being impressed, Donald drew back, looked at the puff, and said, "I hope it has been washed since!"

We went to the set. It suited Donald perfectly. It represented a man's study, with bookcases in the paneled wall, a fireplace, a couch with a coffee table in front of it, a man's desk and chair, and casement windows looking out on a downtown church with tall buildings in the background. On the desk was a copy of *Eternity*. On the coffee table was the Bible he had given me for a wedding gift, which he now used in the pulpit instead of the huge study Bible of the Bradenton days.

My mind flew back to the day that Bible had arrived. In one week Donald and I were to be married. In two days the movers were due to take my things from Bradenton to Doylestown. I was exhausted from the packing. I had picked up the mail at the mailbox and had gone to the porch with it, to sit for a minute and relax. I had opened the box from Donald, wondering what could be in it, and there lay that Bible. On the lower corner of its dark blue leather cover was stamped "Margaret N. Barnhouse." Barnhouse! But we weren't even married yet!

I had lifted it from its box and opened it. On the flyleaf was written in Donald's handwriting,

To my dear wife
Proverbs 18:22
realizing 1 Peter 3:7
June 8, 1954   *Donald*

I had sat there, just looking at it. "To my dear wife." As far as he was concerned it had already been accomplished in the mind of God, and of course it would be brought to pass on earth.

Now that Bible was to be part of this venture that he had dreamed of for so long. The same sovereign God could see this through too!

Donald was given a quick run-through of how the action would be. Start with elbow on the mantle. Cross to the coffee table; pick up the Bible. Talk straight into the camera. Imagine it's someone's eyes, and you're talking to them. Go to the couch. Sit down. Finish your talk. Give the closing prayer.

There was some discussion as to whether the prayer should be with eyes open or shut. They decided he would look upward, with eyes open.

Donald took his place at the mantle. The stage lights were switched on, and he blinked for a moment. Then the director said, "Take one!" and the cameras started to roll.

Donald stood for a moment, smiling into the camera. Then he started talking, easily, naturally, as to a friend.

He had decided to use for his series the stories he told as illustrations, draw a conclusion, and challenge the viewer to do something about it.

I can't remember which story was filmed first. I know one was the story of when he was in Malaysia and a small boy came alongside the train as it slowed to stop, trying to sell him a cute little caged monkey. The missionary who was with him told him how they caught these monkeys. They would take a gourd while it was still growing and bind the stem end, so that as the gourd matured the lower half swelled, but the upper half stayed small, like the neck of a bottle. They would hang the gourd in a tree in the jungle, with a small portion of rice in the bottom. A monkey would smell the rice, put its paw in and grab it, then of course would be unable to pull the paw out. When the boys returned, the monkey would chatter and tug to get away, but was trapped by its own greed. A cage would be put around it and the gourd broken. The monkey would eat its handful of rice—and be sold down the river.

Donald had been roaming around the set as he talked. At this point, he turned and, looking into the camera, said, "Are you like that little monkey? Do you have your hands so full of the things of this world—possessions, greed, lust—that you are trapped? Would you like to be free? All you have to do is open your hand, let go, and come with empty hands to let Jesus Christ take over in your life.

"If you would like to enter into the freedom and joy God wants you to have, you can. I'm going to pray a prayer, and I'll pause between the phrases, and if you really mean business with God, you pray along with me."

At this point he was sitting on the couch, his arms lay along his knees; his hands were lightly and naturally clasped as he straightened his body and looked upward.

"Oh, God . . . if there is a God . . . show me . . . how to let go . . . of all these things . . . that are keeping me from You. . . . Show me . . . how to surrender my life . . . to Your Son, Jesus Christ . . . and as best I know. . . . I shall stop trusting . . . in anything in myself . . . and put my trust in Jesus Christ . . . to be my Savior . . . and my Lord. . . . In His Name I pray, amen."

Then he turned and looked directly through that camera to the viewer, saying, "I wish I could talk to each of you personally, but since that is impossible, we've prepared a booklet called *Your Right to Heaven,* which will help you to understand what I've been saying. You can have this, free and postpaid, by writing to me, Dr. Barnhouse, at Box 8686, Philadelphia, Pennsylvania. And I'll be with you again next week, same time, same station."

He smiled into the camera; the director said, "Cut!" and beamed. Apparently it was most unusual for something like this to go right through on the first "take." Donald relaxed and stepped out from under the hot lights, mopping the perspiration from his brow. Everyone crowded around and clapped him on the back.

"Done like a pro!" said Paul Hopkins.

"It has gone much better than expected," beamed the director. "We'll see how the film looks, and take it from there tomorrow."

Tomorrow was another story. I think Donald must have put one over on Satan on Monday, because the warfare started with a vengeance on Tuesday. Something was wrong with the lights. We waited around while they were being fixed. Finally the filming began, but five minutes later the microphone went out. They chalk-marked around Donald's shoes to be sure he would be standing in the same place when they started again. By the time the mike was fixed, he was tense and nervous. When the director called, "OK, let 'er roll!" he couldn't quite recapture the original smooth flow of the story.

The sound director said, "Cut!" Everything stopped.

"What's the matter?" asked the director.

"That's not where he was," said the sound man. "Where's the script?"

"Dr. Barnhouse doesn't use a script."

"No script? We *have* to have a script. We can't work without a script!"

There was a hurried consultation. It was decided to play back the last part of the soundtrack, to where the mike went out, and have Donald do that part over. He took his position and tried to reenact the story, saying the words he had said before, but they sounded stilted, contrived.

"Cut!" said the director. "Dr. Barnhouse, you'll have to do better than that."

"I'll try," said Donald, desperately. The cameras rolled again. This time it was worse. As the disgusted director yelled "Cut!" again, suddenly it swept over me: *he can't act!* All that beautiful miming, all that portrayal of different people's voices in his stories told from the pulpit are just a natural welling up from within as he lets the Holy Spirit direct his preaching. *He can't fake it!* I leaned over to Paul Hopkins and whispered this. "I believe you're right," he said, and went over to talk to the director. After much discussion, while the cameramen and the stage crew stood around looking bored, the director said, "We'll break for lunch. Be back here at one, and we'll start from the beginning."

At lunch a chastened Donald sat looking at his plate and shaking his head. He wasn't used to failure. "I don't know why I couldn't do it," he said. "It just wouldn't come naturally."

"What we need is prayer," said Paul.

"That's it!" cried Donald. He sat up straight, recharged with energy, his nostrils flaring like those of a battlehorse. "The minute we get back we'll claim the whole place for the Lord!"—which we did.

The cameras rolled. He started from the beginning, and this time the story came with vigor and humor and spontaneity. It flowed right through to the end of the prayer and the closing announcement. The director, pleased, said, "Cut!" and the cameraman said, "My God!" "What?" cried the director, sharply. The cameraman said, "I was so interested in what he was saying I forgot to pay attention to the camera. For the last fifty feet or so we've been rolling without any film!"

The director looked exasperated. Not willing to risk having Donald tense up again, he said, "Dr. Barnhouse, under the circumstances, why don't all of you take a coffee-break while they reload the camera?"

Over coffee Donald was exuberant. "Whenever Satan tries this hard to keep me from preaching I know the Lord is going to use it mightily. Thank You, Lord, for these circumstances. We refuse to be 'under' them. By Your grace we're going to be on top of them. Lord, use this to Thy glory, and help me to magnify Thee!"

Once more they started from the beginning. Once more the entire story went with power into the eyes and the ears of the camera crew. Before the final episodes in the series were done, the cameraman who let the film run out had received Jesus as his Savior.

FIFTEEN

In 1953 a young man named Walter Martin had come into Donald's orbit. Walter was working at New York University on a doctorate in non-Christian religions that originated in the United States of America. Donald had invited him to speak on the cults at his New York Bible class. He discovered Walter could think on his feet and answer questions easily. Donald had talked with his staff. They had agreed to make Walter a contributing editor of *Eternity*, asking him to do a study of various cults. If possible, he was to go directly to the cult headquarters for first-hand information. These findings were published from time to time in *Eternity*.

In March 1955 Donald received a jolt. Preparing an article on the Seventh-Day Adventists, Walter had been welcomed with open arms at their international headquarters in Washington, D.C. Their archives had been freely available to him; he had examined their official doctrines minutely. Except for two or three of these that he could not accept, he reported to Donald that they were absolutely in line with evangelical teaching. As far as Walter was concerned, the Adventists were not a cult at all, but members of the body of Christ, and as such should be received as brethren. Donald, convinced that the whole Adventist movement was satanic, was sure this was just a ploy of the Devil, deceiving Walter. However, he decided to find out for himself. After some negotiations, he arranged a two-day conference with the Adventist leaders at the Farm in August, to explore these doctrines in the light of Scripture, and "prove whether these things be so."

The delegation of Seventh-Day Adventists arriving at the Farm on August 25 was made up of four of their top leaders: T. E. Unruh, W. E. Read, LeRoy E. Froom, and R. Allan Anderson. Donald had asked his son, Don, Walter Martin, and professor George Cannon of the Nyack Missionary College to join them.

After greeting our guests and ushering them into the living room, I went to the kitchen for a pitcher of ice water and some glasses. Returning from the kitchen, I saw that every one of them was on his knees, so I stood in the dining room doorway and waited. Donald was in the midst of asking the Holy Spirit to be present and to guide the discussion. As he finished, the others prayed in turn. Never have I heard such adoration and praise and expectancy. I could feel the presence of the Holy Spirit in awesome power.

When they rose from their knees, I took the water tray in, and was bathed with warm smiles of thanks. I thought, *Lord, these aren't at all what I had thought they'd be. Forgive me!*

In the late afternoon they broke up again, to talk out under the trees in twos and threes, stretch, and relax before dinner and the evening session. To the sixty questions Walter Martin had put to them, there were approximately one hundred pages of Adventist answers to be dissected and discussed.

That night Donald had to admit that what Walter had discovered was true: these men were his brothers in Christ. Don, Jr., had challenged him, as the two had walked together afterward under the stars; was he willing to say so publicly in *Eternity,* whose pages had so frequently vilified them?

Now again Donald paced the floor, as he had done before his statement to Presbytery. "But Donald," I objected, "what about keeping the Sabbath as a condition of salvation? I know I have read this in some of their literature."

"Marge, as they pointed out, just as we Presbyterians have men who deny the virgin birth and the deity of Christ, so they have what they call their 'lunatic fringe.' This is not the official teaching. The Sabbath-keeping is, according to them, something they do because they think it is pleasing to the Lord."

"So, what are you going to do about this?"

"We'll hammer out some more questions tomorrow. After that, we'll see."

When the Adventists left after the Tuesday sessions, cordial relations had been established. They had discovered that many of their criticisms of us, and ours of them, were a matter of semantics. It was decided that Walter should go to their Washington headquarters to pursue the study of their official teachings, and report back. Donald wanted Russ and Paul to double-check everything before making a public statement in *Eternity*.

By the following May another conference with the Seventh-Day Adventists confirmed what Donald had learned at the first one. He was convinced that they should not be considered a cult, but true Christians. He planned to publish his findings in an article in the September *Eternity*, even though he knew it would create a storm and possibly lose him some subscriptions.

The week of Dorothy Barnhouse's marriage to Ulrich Wever arrived, but caused only a slight disruption of Donald's workday. He would spend the day as usual in his study and emerge to preside over the dinner table like a benign patriarch. Then, after an hour or two with his family and the wedding guests, he would retreat to his study and attack his work once more, leaving the amenities to me.

Our first wedding guest was a new baby granddaughter,

presented to Donald the previous week by Don, Jr., and Kathy. All three were now at Barchdale. Then Donald's sister, Mabel Jean Barnhouse, arrived from California for the festivities. She was a perky, white-haired lady, fifteen years older than Donald, who had been a missionary in South America, a schoolteacher in Panama and in New York City, and now, "retired," had a full schedule of women's Bible classes. One of her pupils described her as "the twinkliest Christian I have ever known." She had never married, but had practically raised Donald and was inordinately proud of him.

Bridesmaids arrived. From various points of the compass came Donald's and my children. Wedding gifts poured in. Small tensions built up and were resolved; laughter rang all around.

In the midst of this happy confusion, Mr. Balodis, the Latvian who tended the Farm, suffered a sudden heart attack and died.

The Balodis's son, Imanz, was in the army, stationed in Korea. Donald put everything else aside, got on the phone, and tirelessly worked through all the red tape to obtain an emergency leave for Imanz. He saw to it that Mrs. Balodis had emergency cash, and he showed her his deep concern. The nearby Latvian community took the Balodises under their wing, so we had no funeral arrangements to make, but it was heartwarming to see how Donald could strike a balance between mourning with those who mourned, and rejoicing with those who rejoiced—the wedding party.

Dorothy and Uli would be living in Germany. Their honeymoon was to be a trip back to Europe by ocean liner, but a dockworkers' strike complicated everything. The guests still at the Farm after the wedding traveled to New York with Donald and me to help load the wedding gifts and Dorothy's belongings on board.

A birth, a death, a wedding, a departure had all been squeezed into two weeks." '*In* all these things we are more than conquerors!' " Donald said, as we returned home.

What more could possibly happen? We looked forward to some time of relaxation at the Farm.

It was not to be. Donald choked on a piece of meat and couldn't swallow. After some puzzling X-rays were taken, the doctors decided to operate.

Dr. C. Everett Koop, elder at Tenth, president of the board of directors of the Foundation and personal friend, came in the next morning to tell Donald what they had done. Dr. Koop had been present during the operation, although his own specialty was children's surgery. He said that after opening the chest cavity and doing a thorough exploration they found to their astonishment that Donald had been born with a web-like formation across the esophagus, much like "diphtheria throat," which should have caused death in early infancy. Apparently it had been letting food through all these years, but finally clamped on the meat so that nothing could pass around it. They had removed this web and stitched him back up; when the incision healed he would be as good as new.

"I held your heart in my hand," Dr. Koop told him.

Donald shot back, "And did you find it 'deceitful above all things and desperately wicked'?"

Later that morning I called the Hitts to tell them what had happened. On the phone Lillian sounded agitated.

"Marge! Why didn't you call me? I'd have come immediately to sit with you, pray with you during the operation. . . . What did you do?"

"As a matter of fact, I took a nap."

"You *what?*"

"I took a nap."

"How *could* you?"

Indeed, how could I? I, the compulsive worrier; I, who had thought that if you didn't worry you didn't really care; I, who, if I had nothing to worry about, looked for something to worry about? My mind raced back over the events of that evening.

They had readied Donald for the operating room. As

they wheeled him out into the hall he said, "May I speak to my wife privately?" Immediately I was at his side, and the orderlies withdrew.

"Marge, you know of course that they have no idea what the trouble is. You know that the Lord could take me home to heaven. . . . It's all right with me . . . is it all right with you?"

Shock waves rushed through my mind; then came peace. "It's all right with me," I said. I kissed him, and they trundled him away.

Back in his room, assessing the situation, I thought, *Lord, it's in Your hands. If You do take him home to heaven I'll need all my strength; if you don't, I'll need more than all my strength. I'd better get some rest.* Whereupon I stretched out on the bed and was immediately asleep, without one worry.

Thinking about it, delight swept through me: I was free! Donald's teachings on Isaiah 26:3 had really taken hold. His words reechoed in my mind:

" 'Thou wilt keep him in perfect peace, whose mind is stayed on thee: because he trusteth in thee.' Now this is a mathematical equation. 'Thou wilt keep him in 50 percent peace whose mind is 50 percent stayed on thee, because he 50 percent trusteth in Thee.' 'Thou wilt keep him in 75 percent peace whose mind is 75 percent stayed on Thee, because he 75 percent trusteth in Thee.' 'Thou wilt keep him in 99.44 percent peace whose mind is 99.44 percent stayed on Thee, because he 99.44 percent trusteth in Thee.'

"But, if your mind is 100 percent stayed on Him (and that word 'stayed' derives from the picture of a tent peg firm in the ground, holding fast) because you trust Him completely, you will have 100 percent peace."

I felt like a child whose loose tooth had just fallen out in her hand, who, fearful of pulling it, hadn't realized that all that had been holding it was a tiny bit of flesh, and that the edge of the new tooth was already pushing its way through the gum. Worry was gone, trust was pushing through, and I hadn't had to do a thing about it. *Thank You, Lord!*

Two weeks later Donald was home, shaky, but on his feet. As he stood in front of the mirror combing his hair he said, "Marge, I've just got to get a haircut."

I decided to mention something we never discussed. For years he had been coloring his hair. I think this started when they dyed his hair for the first of his movies. I felt there was nothing wrong with a man's coloring his hair, but it should not be obvious. When we were first married I had asked him why he didn't have it done professionally and was astonished that he seemed hurt. He said the colorless liquid he used on his hair was "vitamins." I let it go at that. Now, after two weeks in the hospital the roots needed more "vitamins."

I came up behind him, put my arms around him, and said, "Darling—why don't you let it go gray?"

He pulled away from me, went into the study, and shut the door.

For a while there was silence, then I heard him dial the telephone, and I caught the murmur of his voice. I heard him typing. Then the telephone rang; he answered. Then he typed some more. I sighed and went down to the kitchen.

As I was getting lunch I heard him come out of the study and lie down on the bed. I let him rest for half an hour, then took his tray up. He was awake and cheerful.

"Marge, I called the doctor and he says it's all right for me to go get a haircut. Will you drive me in after lunch?" Of course I agreed, glad his hurt mood had passed.

For Donald, with a thirty-six-inch scar back to front around the rib cage, riding in the car was still very painful. I cushioned him with pillows and with extra care drove him to the barber's. On the way he told me that a concerned friend had offered us both a week or two at the shore so he could recuperate. This sounded to me like a good idea.

I waited in the car, writing letters, while he was in the barber shop. Home again, he came into the house but didn't take off his coat and hat. He roamed around from window to window, looking out and making remarks about the things he wanted done outside while we were at the shore. Finally he went to the coat closet, took his coat off and hung it up, but left his hat on. Puzzled, I watched him. Then he turned, looking like a prisoner about to be executed, and, eyes pleading with me, took off his hat.

His hair, cut very short, was snow white.

He looked older, yes, but so distinguished. I rushed over, threw my arms around him and cried, "Donald! Darling, you look so *handsome!*"

Relieved, he hugged and kissed me, then went to look at himself in the mirror. "It'll take a while to get used to it," he said. But I could tell he was already beginning to like it.

These were the times of the great healing campaigns. The healer would set up a huge tent; people would come by the thousands to listen, then queue up in the "healing lines," hoping to be cured. Everywhere Donald preached these days there would be inquiries about this in the question and answer sessions.

He considered these healers to be "quacks and crooks," preying on a gullible public. "If this person really can heal," he would say, "why isn't he at the Home for Incurables, healing the unfortunates there?" He conceded that people with psychosomatic illness and those with "suggestible" minds could be helped, but he warned his listeners not to put their eyes on a man (the healer) but on Christ, the Great Physician.

"Don't forget," he would say, "it is perfectly possible for the Devil to make you sick, and then remove the sickness, hoping to deceive you into thinking a special place, or statue, or person is responsible for your healing so you will give the glory there instead of to the Lord."

So vitriolic was he against these healers, many people missed the fact that he did believe God could, and often did, heal in answer to prayer. "But," he said, "the death rate is still one per person."

Concerning the healing gifts in the Book of the Acts, he

would remind us that this was a time when the Old Covenant was shifting gears into the New Covenant. The Apostles could not point, as we can, to the New Testament as their authentication: it hadn't been written. They had to have the miracle gifts to attest to the fact that they were God's men. But as the New Testament draws to completion, we find Paul with a "thorn in the flesh" (probably near-blindness) which God chose not to heal despite Paul's prayers; Epaphroditus was "sick nigh unto death"; and Paul gave Timothy a prescription for chronic stomach trouble. Apparently, later New Testament Christians were not immune to sickness and disease. What had happened? The New Testament Scriptures were then the authentication of God's power, not the signs and miracles.

DGB did believe in "intercessory prayer," that is, believers uniting their petitions on behalf of the afflicted person, or against satanic attack, but this was quite different from "going to a healer." "We do not need any intermediary between us and our Lord," he would say, "except in the case of the person whose sin is so grievous he cannot pray for himself. James 5:14 directs such a person to 'call for the elders of the church; and let them pray over him.' Note, it does not say, 'Go to a healer.' "

What should a believer do when he is sick? "Pray earnestly for recovery," he would say. "Ask the Lord to show you if this illness is the result of unrepented sin or wrong attitudes toward your Christian brothers. The Bible warns that these things can make you sick or even bring on an untimely death. Sometimes the Lord has to put you on your back to make you look up. Ask Him to forgive and cleanse and heal. If healing does not take place in spite of repentance, thank Him for the ministry of suffering. His strength is made perfect in our weakness. His grace *is* sufficient.

"But if any man takes credit for the healing, the glory is given to him, and not to the Lord, and this is *sin*. There is no special 'place of healing'—not a tent, not a grotto, not a shrine. *Any* place can be a healing place for one who is yielded to the Lord. The important thing is our yieldedness to Him in whatever circumstances He has placed us. We are betrothed to Him, 'in sickness and in health, in plenty and in want, in joy and in sorrow'—and He is faithful."

The day after Christmas we set out for the winter conference tour of 1956. There had been no time to open our Christmas cards, so I stuffed them into a paper sack and brought them with us. As we drove along I opened and read them. Donald would describe the people I didn't know, so I made their acquaintance before I actually met them. Reading each one, we prayed for them and their immediate needs, leisurely enjoying these yearly communications in a way we never had before. In a sense, our friends rode with us on that journey.

By New Year's Eve we had reached Amarillo, Texas, where on New Year's Day the first of the conferences would begin. As Donald and I sat quietly in our motel room in Amarillo that night, the very end of the year, Donald lifted up before the Lord in prayer all who were associated with the ministry, thanking Him that through the ministrations of these men and their wives he was free to concentrate on study and missionary travel.

The First Baptist Church of Amarillo had at that time a membership of more than six thousand, and it was jammed Sunday morning. An expectant, receptive, overflow crowd like that is bound to draw from a man great preaching. Donald preached his sermon on "The Scales of God," with warmth and wit and love. The congregation lapped it up; Dr. Carl Bates, the pastor, hung on every word. At the end Donald sat down, and Dr. Bates stood and gave an invitation. Many people came forward. Immediately, information about them was taken by co-workers, including name and occupation. Dr. Bates went down from the platform, welcoming each one individually. With the first person, Dr. Bates looked at the information card, then said,

"Oh, so you're a lawyer." Then he looked out over his audience and called, "Andy, you're a lawyer—you and your wife come down here and sponsor these folk," whereupon an attractive young couple came and stood beside the lawyer and his wife. This he did for each one, matching him or her with someone who shared a similar occupation or interest. We learned later that the sponsors served for a month; then the newcomers were considered to be seasoned enough to be sponsors themselves. I could see that Donald, watching from his seat on the platform, was impressed. Here was a man with a large congregation who knew his people so well he could call them by name and occupation!

During our stay in Texas one of the things Donald hoped to accomplish was to interest some of the oil millionaires in helping put Christian-oriented literature in the hands of the thousands in emerging countries who were learning to read. In an editorial in a 1951 *Eternity* he had expressed his concern about this: "The greatest foreign missionary is the printing press, and we must use it more," he wrote.

His concern had crystallized some months before. I walked into his study to see him poring over what had just arrived in the mail. Spread out on his desk were a number of Russian magazines, of the *Life* magazine format: excellent quality paper and beautiful photographs. He looked up.

"Marge, look at this!"

"They're gorgeous! But where in the world did you get them?"

"Because of 'scholar's privileges' I got permission to import them. One of our missionaries told me about them. It seems that the Christian missionaries are reducing spoken language to writing, then teaching the backward nations and tribes to read. Naturally their minds are reaching out for *any* reading matter, and there's nothing to read but the Bible. And just portions of that. Into this vacuum the Communists are pouring their own literature, and through it shaping the thinking of the people. *We have got to count-*

eract this. We have got to get literature to them that will relate the Bible to all of life, instead of having them think of it merely as an exercise in reading."

He leaned back in his chair. "Now if we could just get translators to do a condensed version of *Eternity....*"

I could sense his mind going a mile a minute as he picked up the phone and called Paul at the Foundation to discuss this. Soon "The Christian Literature Project" was under way.

All was not that simple, however. Donald was confronted with the difficulties of transcultural communication. For instance, there is a tribe in Africa that does not "feel" with the "heart." For them, the seat of the emotions is the liver. So, for them, "Let not your heart be troubled" had to be translated, "Do not shiver in your liver"! Donald had encountered this problem in foreign countries when preaching through an interpreter but had not thought of the implications in written communication. It took a while for him to relinquish the direct-translation idea and accept literally what he had always preached: that Christianity must be indigenous to each culture; that Jesus was not "the white man's God," nor was it necessary to worship Him in the American manner, in a church building with pews and pulpit, and the other accoutrements that we Christians in the United States associate with Sunday worship.

Before the winter conference tour, Donald had approached a wealthy Christian gentleman in Philadelphia about his literature idea. The man had seemed very much interested. He had given Donald a letter of introduction to a friend in Texas who could put him in touch with various Texans who might also be interested.

With great enthusiasm Donald returned from his meeting with the Texas contact person. "Marge, it was terrific! When I was ushered into his office he shook my hand and seated me opposite him across a desk that must have covered an entire acre. Everything in Texas sure is *big!*

"He said to me, 'Well, Dr. Barnhouse, what is this project that our friend thinks is worth looking into?'

"I answered, 'I do have a project that I know will help stem the rise of Communism in the emerging nations, and we do need financial help. But before I talk to any man about money I talk to him about his soul. Are you born again? If the roof caved in and killed us both right this minute, do you *know* you'd be in heaven?'

"He leaned toward me and said, 'Dr. Barnhouse, I don't know. I've often thought about it, and I know all the "right" answers, but I just don't *know!*'

"And right there I led him to an assurance of his salvation, and he's coming to my meetings and is thinking of a bunch of others who ought to hear me."

"Donald! How wonderful!... Did he give you any money for the project?"

"Oh. Well, we never got around to *that.*"

The next day the gentleman called Donald and made a luncheon appointment. There Donald explained what he had in mind. The man gave him a sizable list of names and a generous check for the work.

Donald was jubilant. One by one he contacted these oil magnates, using the same approach: "I never talk to a man about his money until I have talked to him about his soul." The reactions were varied. He watched one man feel surreptitiously for the call button under the edge of his desk as Donald asked the question. Immediately a secretary knocked, entered, and said, "Excuse me, sir: Mr. Johnson is waiting to see you," and left. The man stood up and told Donald he was sorry, but he had forgotten this appointment; he'd call and make another date with him. Donald shook his hand, silently asking the Lord to forgive this obvious lie, and left, knowing he wouldn't hear from him again. Another man also called his secretary, but it was to tell her to cancel all his appointments for the rest of the morning; he had important business with Dr. Barnhouse. He too was led to the Lord, then asked about the project with great interest. Many of the men contacted said their charitable giving was all apportioned for the next year or two, but they'd figure how much they could give after that and let him know in a couple of days. With most of them he felt confident this was not just a brush-off.

Donald waited for their calls, working sporadically at other things, but with one ear listening for the telephone. After several days of this, he began pacing our motel room.

" 'My God *shall* supply all your need,' " he said quoting Philippians 4:19. "Why hasn't the need been met? They all but two or three agreed it was a good idea. They seemed interested. But only three have committed themselves to give to it. Lord, why?" He paced some more, then sat down, put his head in his hands, and prayed silently, in great concentration. I sat across the room and prayed too. This was one of those times when he obviously had to struggle privately in prayer.

After a long time his head snapped up; he slapped the arm of the chair, and cried, "I've got it! Of course, of course! When the Philippians were promised their need would be met, it was because they had stripped themselves to supply Paul's need. Before these fellows can be expected to give, *I* must give. But I don't have anything. . . . Yes, I do. I have that land up on Pebble Hill Road, where the apple orchard is. Where I planted all those Christmas tree seedlings. I could give that!" Looking relieved, he sat down at his typewriter to report to Paul Hopkins what had been happening.

SIXTEEN

In early May one of my friends who had been closest to me when we were growing up spent the night at the Farm. After lunch the next day Donald had gone back to his study to work. She and I strolled out into the spring sunshine.

"Well, what do you think of him?" I asked.

She looked at me with a "Shall I tell her?" look, then said frankly, "I don't like him. I don't like the way he treats you."

I was astonished. He treated me as if I were the angel on the top of the Christmas tree. I was his ewe lamb, his precious treasure, his "good and perfect gift from the Lord"—to the point of embarrassment.

"The way he whistles for you, and you have to come running like a little dog...."

"Oh no!" I laughed, "You don't understand!"

I told her that my mother and my father had had a private little signal that had been as much a part of my life as the house I grew up in. When they wanted to locate one another, one would whistle a lilting little questioning tune; the other would reply with a four-note answering whistle. In telling Donald about my childhood, I had taught him the signal. Being a romantic, he loved the idea.

On our honeymoon, as we milled around in the crowded Orly airport outside Paris, I couldn't keep up with his long stride, and we became hopelessly separated. I stood still, looking for a shock of reddish curly hair towering above the lesser mortals. Then I remembered he was wearing a hat. How in the world would we ever find one another? Then above the other conflicting and confusing sounds my ear caught the lilting "Where are you?" whistle. I answered back. Again his whistle, closer. I answered back. Within moments we were together again, and from then on the whistle was ours. Sometimes it meant, as then, "I'm lost! Where are you?"; sometimes, "I'm finished with my work and ready to be with you again—where are you?"; sometimes, "Come share something beautiful with me!"; sometimes, "Come quickly—I need you!"; sometimes, "I just wondered where you were. I love you." It became so much a part of our oneness that whichever of us heard it immediately dropped whatever he was doing and went to the other. I hadn't even thought how this might look to our friends.

The Christian Literature project became DGB's top priority. Translators to do the work were next on the agenda. When Bob Pierce of World Vision asked him to be the speaker for his summer series of pastors' conferences in Korea in 1956, everything fell into place. Donald would take this opportunity to strengthen the national pastors spiritually, and at the same time would put out feelers for gifted national translators in the various countries he would visit en route. He would fly to the Orient July 7—and the kite tail would accompany the kite! ("Don't let him commit himself, Marge," warned Paul. "You know how impulsive he is at times. Far better to move slowly and solidly than to get himself out on a limb.")

It was nearly time to leave for "those far-away places with strange sounding names." We had had our inoculations; our passports and visas were in order. In three days this newest adventure would start. Then the telephone rang: long distance for Donald.

Donald hung up the telephone, looking grave. "Maddy has died, and Naomi wants me to preach his funeral. Can you be ready to leave for the Orient three days early?" He turned from my dismayed face, picked up the telephone again, and began putting into action an acceleration of his own plans.

"Maddy" was General Louis Wilson Maddox, husband of Donald's sister, Naomi, whom I had not yet met. He had been a member of General MacArthur's staff in the Pacific. For some time he had suffered from a rare tropical disease which had resulted in his retirement. For the past eleven years they had lived in Palo Alto, California. Undoubtedly a great many high-ranking military personnel would be there.

In casual California what did one wear to the funeral of a retired army general? How could I possibly get ready? I had counted on those three days to wind up my own affairs, balance my checking account, and try once more to find a dress in that new miracle fabric that washed and dried looking freshly pressed. *(Lord, You have promised to supply all my needs. Help!)*

On Monday, Donald left on schedule to teach the New York Bible class. He would go from there to the airport, with time to spare. Friends would drive me over to join him at take-off, giving me a bit of needed extra time. I was still madly packing when the friends arrived. It took me almost an hour before I could zip closed our suitcases, hoping I had everything. I stuffed my accounts into a paper sack and got into the back seat of the car to do the final balancing of my checkbook on the way over.

We made good time over the now-familiar back roads, the stretch of U.S. 1, the New Jersey Turnpike, the tunnel, the city—but as we emerged on the other side and headed for the airport, traffic began piling up. By then I had found the error that had thrown my books off, had happily balanced them, and had put everything neatly into the sack for my friends to take back home again, but my happiness evaporated as I saw the jammed highway, and we slowed to a crawl. I knew we could not possibly make it to the plane in time. How could I have let Donald down so? Why hadn't I just spread over into another suitcase instead of taking the extra time to pack properly? My one consolation was that we had agreed if I was late he would go on without me. I was hoping he would do just that, leaving my ticket at the counter, and I'd take a later plane. *(Lord, please don't let him be angry or upset. . . . Lord, at least get* him *on that plane.)*

It was almost half an hour after take-off when we finally arrived at the airport. Towering over the others at the luggage weigh-in stood Donald, face enigmatic but slightly pale. I searched his eyes but found no clue to his inner feelings.

"Oh, Donald, I'm so sorry. Traffic jam. I thought surely you'd go on ahead. . . ." He turned to the business of weighing in the bags and changing tickets to a later plane. Then he picked up his typewriter, overcoat, raincoat, and tote bag, whereupon I also gathered up my carry-on paraphernalia. He took my elbow and propelled me forward, still not speaking to me. He was calm and impersonal. My heart hurt. What a way to start off on our long-anticipated Oriental trip!

He guided me into the restaurant, chose a table, held my chair. I stowed my gear on the adjacent chair. Without consulting me, he ordered dinner. The flight we had missed was a dinner flight: obviously the one we would take would be much later.

"Donald, have you notified Naomi of our changed time of arrival?" I asked.

"No."

"Wouldn't it be a good idea? I mean, she has enough on her mind without this extra worry and suspense. . . ."

"I'll handle it."

Mentally I kicked myself for not simply waiting and calling her myself after dinner. Having asked him, I now could do nothing. I didn't know that we were on stand-by and he had no definite flight information to give her.

He opened the *Saturday Review* and started working the anacrostic puzzle, shutting me out as if he had closed a door between us, whereas usually he shared the anacrostic conversationally. Then suddenly it dawned: everybody else always managed the impossible for him, but I had failed. His "good and perfect gift" from the Lord was not perfect after all, and he didn't know how to cope with this. Perhaps if I were obviously very, very miserable he would relent.

I have always despised women who use tears for a weapon. Until that moment it had not occurred to me that they could be used for communication. I looked at him, no longer fighting back the tears, and let one trickle down my cheek. I added just a tiny sniffle. I was truly sorry and overwhelmed with remorse, as much for the dreadful uncertainty I had put Naomi Maddox in as for the inconvenience I had created for him. He glanced up and back down quickly, and I knew that tear had gotten to him. He sighed and called for the check, rolling up the *Saturday Review* and putting it in his coat pocket. We were on our feet, gathering our belongings, when over the P.A. system we heard our names called, asking us come to the airline desk. "Dr. and Mrs. Barnhouse." Hurriedly he paid the bill, took my arm with urgency, and off we rushed. By some wonderful alchemy, in the calling out of our name, we were one again, imperfections and all.

Like all the Barnhouses Naomi Maddox was remarkable. Everything was militarily precise: "No eulogy, just the regular funeral service, which begins at ten A.M. at the funeral parlor, and must be over by ten-thirty in order to start the cortege toward the Presidio as soon as possible for the military service there at twelve noon. It takes more than an hour at the slow funeral pace to get from here to the

Presidio Cemetery.... Do be careful: there will be all faiths and some no-faiths at the funeral." She was so controlled, so in command of the situation, we did not sense that she was at the breaking point after an exhaustingly long period of coping with the illness and a nerve-wracking night of not knowing when we would arrive.

In her guest room we changed clothes, freshened up a bit, and rested briefly. Then the limousine arrived to take us and the rest of the family to the funeral parlor, and we entered precisely at ten A.M. After the usual opening formalities, Donald announced that at the request of the widow there would be no eulogy, that all knew General Maddox as an honorable gentleman and good friend. Instead, he said, his message was to the living, to those here in this room. Then for forty-five minutes he fired with both barrels. He spoke about the conditions God has laid down for men; how far short all of us have come; how despite this, God, acting in love, intervened for us at the cross; the necessity for us to believe Him in order to receive Him. Then he gave the illustration that had so blessed me when I first heard it, in Coatesville after Doug's death, Psalm 23: "Yea, though I walk through the valley of the shadow of death... *thou* art with me...."

Naomi fidgeted, looked at her watch, and cleared her throat. But Donald kept preaching. The importance of timing had been completely lost on him: he had seen this simply as an opportunity to show honorable, upright men and women that "your character can take you to hell but not to heaven," a chance to challenge them to stop depending on themselves and take hold of Jesus' outstretched hand. For him there were only two kinds of people in that room: those who had believed and were saved, and those who had not believed and so remained lost. Denominations, "faiths," had nothing to do with it. And he desperately wanted them to believe.

In a turmoil I sat there thinking, *Ah, Donald, you who could be so unbelievably kind and perceptive to others, your own flesh and blood are so close you find it difficult to see them as persons, and not extensions of yourself!*

The three days lopped off of the Philadelphia end of our preparations for the trip to the Orient were spent as guests of Donald's sister, Mabel Jean Barnhouse, at the Mount Hermon Bible conference grounds. Here, under towering redwoods, Donald had spent the summers of his boyhood; here he had sat under the teaching that had established him in the sure Word of God. Fascinated, I watched him gulp in the morning fog as if it were a life-giving elixir. (Indeed, in this place the fog was strangely exhilarating, not damp and depressing as it usually is.) I struggled to keep up with his confident stride down the steep path from our cabin to the dining hall. Everything he did was with vigor, joy, "heartily, as unto the Lord." He once said, "The Lord would not have given me the work of a horse without also giving me the constitution of a horse."

What a combination he was of sophistication that knew its way around the world and child-like (not childish!) wonder at everything in that world. His curiosity was insatiable. When he was a small boy he had decided there ought to be a book that would tell all about everything there was to know about anything, so he set about collecting facts for such a book. Imagine his amazement when, at age 10 or thereabouts, he discovered the Encyclopaedia Britannica! Although a bit disappointed that someone had beaten him to writing those volumes, he had plunged gratefully into them and soaked up into his memory facts that would later return as illustrations for his sermons.

The incident of missing our plane to California apparently was forgotten, as if it had never happened. I tried to put myself into his shoes as he had waited for me at the airport, and remembered a time when one of my children had been "missing." Annoyance had turned to worry, and worry to panic as I had imagined all sorts of horrible things that could have happened to him. Then my son had wandered in, astonished that he had caused any furor. Immediately my mood had changed to outrage that he could have been so irresponsible.

Poor Donald must have gone through much the same thing when I was "missing." He was such an old hand at world travel he couldn't conceive of the problems that had faced me in preparing for such a trip into the unknown and had been compounded by the updating of our departure.

All that was now a thing of the past. Once more Donald was tender and loving, sweeping me into the orbit of all his doings. It was overwhelming to realize that he *needed* me to enter joyfully into every phase and emotion of his life; this included his disappointment at how, since his childhood, "the enormous family home" in Watsonville had "shrunk" to normal size, as well as his feeling of reverential awe as we walked among the giant redwoods that were like a cathedral, reaching up and up toward God.

How could one record all the happenings of our trip to the Orient? It was a blur of impressions: Spiritually hungry listeners wherever Donald preached; new sights and sounds and textures and scents for our "memory album"; a whole new culture opening up before me; Hawaii, Wake, Guam, the Philippines, Taiwan, Hong Kong, Japan, Korea, then back to Japan before leaving for Alaska and home; Donald's white hair commanding instant respect in these lands where the elders were revered; five to six thousand Korean pastors at once crowding to hear him through an interpreter; a trip by jeep to the thirty-eighth parallel that divided North and South Korea, with, as our guide, Harold Voelkel, the missionary who was directly responsible for the conversion of thousands of North Koreans in the prisoner-of-war camps during and after the Korean conflict; Donald, as always, alert to every new learning experience, every source of an illustration; the depth of Christian commitment in these lands where to be a Christian really cost something.

In his search for translators Donald ran into difficulty.

Too many wanted to be "translators" when they discovered they would be paid for it; very few were really qualified. We had the same discouraging results in each of the countries we visited.

Then, in Sapporo, on the island of Hokkaido, Japan, where Tenth Church had helped build and maintain a Christian girls' school, we met Toshii Shimoda. Toshii, a young teacher at the school, had been recommended to us as a possible translator. We interviewed her.

Donald asked the first, most important question: "What is your heart relationship to Christ?" Not expecting such a question, she hesitated a moment, then answered simply, "I live for Christ, and . . . I . . . would die for Christ."

Donald and I looked at one another, and I knew his heart was answering mine. He then told her about the Literature Project. "We need an educated person who can translate English into Japanese without its even *smelling* of English," he said. "Would you like to try it?"

She said modestly that she really didn't think she would do well at translating: she had a friend who perhaps would do better. Donald asked her what she would like to do if she could do whatever she wished. Her eyes fastened on a faraway dream.

"I would like to go to America, to obtain the education that would qualify me to teach at the university level, where the students are so in need of Christ," she said. "But the only scholarships open are designated for girls who are members of another denomination."

Again Donald's eyes locked with mine, in wordless communication. He said, "Toshii, we are leaving for America in ten days. Would you like to come with us and get that education?"

Her eyes widened in astonishment. "But Dr. Barnhouse, Mrs. Barnhouse, that would be impossible!"

"If the Lord makes it possible, will you come?"

"If *He* makes it possible, I will come."

We conferred with the missionaries heading the school.

Passport formalities were begun. Every impossibility became possible in miraculous ways, even to having a seat cancellation on the plane taking us back to the States, which allowed Toshii to fly with us. We even found it wasn't too late for her to enter Princeton Seminary for the term starting that fall, to work on her Master of Religious Education degree. When the Lord opens a door, no one can shut it.

The missionaries and all the girls from the school came to the airport to see us off. Toshii would not be returning for three years. She had said good-bye to her mother; now her father approached her for his good-bye. He bowed a polite Japanese bow. Toshii bowed to him, only lower, as befits a daughter. They did not touch, yet between them one could feel deep affection flowing. Then it was time to go. We picked up our flight bags and other luggage and went aboard, Toshii turning for one last look before stepping into the plane. She lay back in her seat in a happy daze.

"To think," she breathed, "I am going to a *Christian* country!"

I looked at Donald. "You'd better tell her," I said.

"Toshii, America is known in other countries as a Christian country, but it is very pagan."

Toshii's eyes widened. "How can this be?" she asked. After a while she brightened. "Well, at least I will be in a Christian seminary."

"Dear Toshii," he said, "people go to seminary for all sorts of reasons, and many of them do not know Christ as you and I know Him. You will find believers there, yes, but don't be surprised if you find you are a foreign missionary to Princeton Seminary! But you *will* get a good education, and you will find a loving home with us."

As the plane droned on toward home and Toshii slept in her seat, Donald and I began reviewing the status of the Literature Project. He had been deeply disturbed by one confrontation. Two nationals had approached him, interested in becoming involved. They had given him a pamphlet in English listing all the books that had been published by the literature committee of the Council of Churches there. Reading it, he had been appalled. We had gone to see the head of the publishing house, and Donald had shaken the list in his face.

"Sir," he had cried, towering over the smaller man. "Do you realize you have nothing on this list but liberal, modernist trash? I tell you, a man who acts as a procurer for a house of prostitution would not mislead young Christians more than one who publishes literature stating that the Bible is full of myths and legends, and that the deity and resurrection of our Lord are not to be taken too seriously. Our Lord had terrible words to say to men like you, who mislead the Lord's little ones: 'Whoso shall offend one of these little ones which believe in me, it were better for him that a millstone were hanged about his neck, and that he were drowned in the depth of the sea. Woe unto the world because of offences! for it must needs be that offences come; but woe to that man by whom the offence cometh!' "

The gentleman stood there, impassive, palms pressed together in front of him. When Donald finally stopped his tirade, the gentleman bowed slightly, in Oriental deference. When he spoke, his voice was reasonable.

"Dr. Barnhouse, I am honored by your visit. I have heard your words. But obviously you have not informed yourself of the nature of the work done here. The committee meets; the decisions are made; all I do is execute the decisions. The conservatives are eligible to come, *but they do not come to the meetings*. Thus it is that the liberals make all the decisions." Once more he bowed slightly.

The wind was taken right out of Donald's sails, all but enough for him to bluster, "Do you mean to tell me that you would print and distribute conservative literature if the conservatives were at the committee meetings and voted it in?"

"Certainly, sir. I would be obligated to do so."

"Well. Well, that puts a different light on the matter.

But, sir, it does not excuse you nor discharge your obligation to exalt the Lord Jesus Christ not only as the Son of God, but as God the Son. Good day," he said, and he stalked out.

Sitting there in the plane, Donald brought up the problem of non-participation by the conservatives. He could understand their lack of desire, but they did have an obligation to get the truth to the people. Perhaps by attending the meetings they might find a neglected mission field: the liberals themselves.

Donald put his typewriter on his lap and tapped out a long editorial, ending with: "We must hold fast to the gospel of our Lord Jesus Christ in all its divine fulness and scriptural purity. And if our stand is certain and unshaken, we will never be misunderstood. I believe that the conservatives who take such an attitude will find that many they have thought liberal are more interested in conservatism—with love—than in liberalism. It is conservatism without love that has caused too many divisions."

At the beginning of the year Donald had begun a new financial arrangement: at his conferences, once the expenses were met, all offerings of any sort would go directly to the Evangelical Foundation, and he would be paid a direct salary. That way everything would be open to the scrutiny of anyone who might question the financial set-up. His obligations to Tenth Church and to the Foundation, and theirs to him, were spelled out, easing a tension that had been growing because the work was getting so big. Tenth was to pay a third of his salary, and the Foundation the rest, out of the offerings taken on the conference tours.

For a while the offerings fell off: people who had been blessed by his ministry wanted to give to *him,* not to some far-off "Foundation." A person would press a large check into his hand, saying, "Dr. Barnhouse, I want *you* to have this." He had to explain that he *would* "have" anything given to the Foundation because it existed to implement his work, and without that back-up he could not possibly do all he did. Of course under the new arrangement any such personal checks would be signed over to the Foundation. This simplified his life considerably: he knew exactly what his income would be and could plan accordingly.

Between an income I had from Doug's estate and what Donald could spare we financed Toshii until a scholarship could be established for her, through the pages of *Eternity*, where she was introduced as *"Eternity's* Daughter." It was explained that anyone who gave to the scholarship would be training a national missionary to go back to her land better equipped to witness.

Toshii was overwhelmed by the abundance of everything in the United States. Donald kept reminding her: "Enjoy it here, but don't let America corrupt you. Don't get so used to it that it will be a hardship when you go back."

Toshii particularly relished her large glass of orange juice at breakfast, and all the coffee she could drink. One morning as she passed her coffee cup to me for a refill Donald said, with mock severity that dissolved into a big smile, "Don't . . . let . . . America . . ." Toshii, who had drawn back her cup, passed it to me again, saying, "I think I will let myself be corrupted this one time!"

Tenth Church had an important outreach to the large group of foreign students in the various universities within a radius of thirty or forty blocks of the church. These were the pick of the university level young people in their own countries, the leaders of tomorrow. If they could go back home as committed Christians they would have far more impact for Christ than any American missionary could. Indigenous "missionaries," indigenous magazines: these could spread the true gospel and glorify our Lord Jesus Christ.

The same concern he had for Toshii filled Donald for these foreign students who flocked to this country. He wrote in *Eternity:* "This land has a terrible power to corrupt the foreign student. It is difficult to live in a dormitory in college, seminary, or Bible school, and then return to a hut in Africa, a mud house in Korea, or a bamboo house in Japan. But this return is necessary if the plan for the student is to be fulfilled.

" 'You must not let America corrupt you,' I tell foreign students. 'You must go back and be the Word made flesh among your own people.' It is true that these returned students, living as pastors on less than forty dollars a month in Asia or Africa, will be tempted to remember the fleshpots of America; but they must learn that they are living for Christ and must remain, in the economic scale, what they were before they went to America."

It was at this time that Dwight Small was called to another church and Edwin Houk of Uniontown, where Donald had held such good meetings the year before, became the co-pastor at Tenth Presbyterian Church. Ed and Sally were just right for Tenth, giving the people warm pastoral care.

Donald found he could roll the cares of the church onto Ed's capable shoulders and be free for the exacting study that backed up his ministry. Someone once asked him how long it had taken him to prepare a certain sermon. His answer was "Thirty years and thirty minutes!" He had immersed himself in the Bible from the time he was fifteen years old, when he memorized the Book of Philippians a verse a day until he knew the entire book by heart, then went on to other passages. He felt it was not enough to learn *by rote*—it had to be *by heart,* because you loved and believed it. He never did commit the entire Bible to memory, but he was thoroughly familiar with all of it. Everything he read—the newspaper, a magazine, a book— he read in the light of what the Bible teaches, gearing his thinking to eternity and God's over-all plan, rather than to time. His great gift of illustration was based on the belief that we existed in the mind of God before the foundation of the world, and that therefore everything God created was to illustrate for us some spiritual truth. All one had to do was to recognize the particular truth a given thing or circumstance was illustrating. His encyclopedic memory and agile imagination made the application in an unforgettable way.

For his own congregation at Tenth Church he used mostly verse-by-verse expository preaching of various books of the Bible. As he came across some new truth in God's Word, he would first track down every other reference to it in the Bible, then find what various commentaries had to say on the passage, then see what he could find on the subject in other sources: encyclopedias, books of proverbs of other lands, hymnals, literary references (many in French and German as well as in English). Of course he'd check the original Hebrew or Greek of the passage itself. Once on the trail he would work through to completion if possible, often keeping at it until two or three in the morning. If he had a particularly knotty theological problem, he would think it through in French, then translate his conclusions into English. This provided a clarity that made it understandable to the simplest minds. He typed, whenever possible, at such a speed it sounded like rain on the roof. If interrupted, he would always leave his manuscript in the middle of a sentence in order to pick up the thread of his thought more readily.

His radio sermons were typed out, and he read them before the microphone, but the prayers that followed were always extemporaneous. In the pulpit he used only an outline, which could be expanded or contracted according to the time given him. He said that once he had the "feel" of his audience, he preached to their need as he was led by the Holy Spirit, not according to a preconceived idea (except for the outline, which gave structure and continuity).

By the time we had arrived home from the Orient, the September *Eternity* had dropped Donald's blockbuster, "Are the Seventh-Day Adventists Christians?" with his conclusion that they are. Reaction was immediate: outraged canceling of subscriptions or grateful commendation because DGB had had the courage to tell the truth and admit he had been wrong in the past about the Adventists.

At his New York Bible class questions abounded. He had Walter Martin on the platform to give the answers to the Adventist questions but handled the others in his usual manner. He let Walter go first.

"On what basis do you claim that the Seventh-Day Adventists are true Christians and not a cult?"

"Adventists hold all the basic doctrines of Christianity," Walter replied, "although they have secondary teachings that I question. But that would not keep me from fellowship with them, because they believe in the Trinity, the miraculous conception and virgin birth of Christ, the perfect, sinless human nature of Christ during the incarnation, His eternal deity, His vicarious atonement on the cross for all sin, His bodily resurrection from the grave, His literal ascension, His present priestly intercession for us before the Father, and His visible second coming to judge the world. On these doctrines, Seventh-Day Adventists are solidly in the tradition of historic orthodox Christianity. Also, they accept the Bible as the inspired revelation of God to man, the only infallible rule of faith and practice."

The second question focused more on what Adventists believed concerning salvation.

"They believe in the necessity of the new birth," Walter said, "justification by faith, progressive sanctification by the indwelling Holy Spirit, and salvation by grace *alone* through the blood of Christ, *apart* from the works of the law. It's true that many of the teachings of the early members were off-base in some of these doctrines, but they have been repudiated by the present General Conference of the Seventh-Day Adventists."

"Don't the Seventh-Day Adventists say you have to keep Saturday instead of Sunday to be saved?"

"Some of their early writers and some of their extremists have said this. But the present position is that, whereas they believe the biblical Sabbath should be kept on Saturday, Christians who keep Sunday in good faith are as much members of the body of Christ as they are."

"Please explain the Seventh-Day Adventist doctrine of soul sleep. Do you believe in this?"

Walter thought carefully before answering. "This is the belief that at the death of the body the spirit, or principle of life in man, returns to God who gave it, and man as a 'living soul' lapses into a state of unconsciousness, oblivious of passing time, until the resurrection of the physical body. They base this doctrine on the various texts in the Bible where the word 'sleep' is used as a synonym for death, as 'Lazarus is not dead, but sleepeth,' or 'they which have fallen asleep,' and so on.

"I do not hold this doctrine. Second Corinthians 5:8 says that to be absent from the body is to be present with the Lord. Paul writes to the Philippians that he desires 'to depart and be with Christ, which is far better.' But my disagreement with this doctrine doesn't bar my fellowship with them. For me, the basis of fellowship is mutual belief in Jesus Christ crucified, risen, and coming again, and *not* the nature of man or the intermediate state of the soul pending resurrection. But in all fairness I must admit that Martin Luther held this doctrine. So did several of the great translators of the Bible: William Tyndale, John Wycliffe, and others. But this doesn't make the doctrine true. You have to balance it with everything else the Bible has to say about the afterlife."

(By this time some in the audience were looking like the little girl whose book had told her "more about penguins than she cared to know!")

Then Donald took the first from his own stack of questions.

"This person asks, 'How can you tell a cult from the real thing?' The same way a bank teller can spot a counterfeit bill. A bank teller once told me that to do this they don't study counterfeit money. Instead they are given the real thing to handle and count, handle and count, handle and count, until it is so familiar that if a counterfeit is slipped into the stack they can feel it right away. Just so, you should get into the Bible, read and reread, read and reread, asking God to show you Himself. Be so familiar with His Word and His ways that when the false tries to sneak in you can spot it right away. Don't depend on what *people* tell you is false: go to the Word of God and let *Him* tell you. And don't just use little spot checks: check it with *all* the Word."

He answered other questions, then paused for a moment and studied the last one. He said, "This question seems to imply that I do not like to be challenged. It has three parts." He read the first: " 'Does not 1 Thessalonians 5:21 say we are to prove all things, hold fast to that which is good?' " He looked up and said, "Yes, sure," then looked back at the question. " 'Should we not apply that to all teachings?' " (I thought, *Someone is really gunning for him!*) Again he looked up. "Of course. Including mine. You have heard me say many times, 'Don't you ever dare to say you believe something because Barnhouse said it.' That's the biggest insult you can ever give to a teacher. You are to be like the Bereans in Acts 17:11 who 'received the word with all readiness of mind, and searched the scriptures daily, whether those things were so.' Now the last part of the question: 'Must we not have to debate to get at the truth?' Yes, and I welcome this. But it is unfruitful to argue the mere opinions of men. If you think I am wrong in any way, phrase the question, 'You say thus-and-such, but does not *the Bible* teach thus-and-thus?' and give the Bible reference. Then I will discuss it.

"And incidentally, this can be very valuable to me. For instance, the reason my book *Meditations in Genesis* has not yet been published is because a person in this class questioned something I had published in *Eternity* and I have not yet found the answer. I cannot accept their answer, but it did destroy one answer that I gave concerning the twelve tribes of Israel and I simply haven't had time to go into it.

But I consider very carefully anything that is put before me."

The 1956 *Eternity* Conference at Princeton had been postponed from the usual Friday and Saturday after Thanksgiving to two days between Christmas and New Year's. During the conference Wallace Erickson, a close friend of Donald's and one of the directors of the Evangelical Foundation, stayed with us at the Farm. He and DGB and David Barnhouse, who with his family was home for the holidays, got involved one night after dinner in a spirited scientific conversation. Normally Donald knew more than anyone else on a given subject and tended to dominate a conversation. But he was no match for a doctor and a scientist who were talking on a technical level. He tried interjecting some of his illustrations and anecdotes, but as these were not really germane to what was being discussed he found himself little by little shut out of the conversation. For almost an hour Donald sat, very quiet, listening intently. Then he said, "Well, carry on. If you'll excuse me, I have to get back to work." He smiled and left the table.

(I made a mental note to be sure to check on whatever editorials or other writing he would do that night, to "get his word in edgewise" in spite of them!)

Our winter conference tour took us to the West Coast. Donald's preaching was so enthusiastically received that I didn't know until years later there had been serious doubts in some places about inviting him because of his controversial stand on so many issues.

It was at conferences in San Diego that for the first time I heard Donald's sermon series "The Five Points of Calvinism," under the acrostic TULIP: Total depravity; Unconditional election; Limited atonement; Irresistible grace; Perseverance of the saints—a combination of much that I had heard him preach before, put together in a new way. Such eminently theological, incomprehensible-sounding doctrines were made so clear no one could misunderstand.

During this week Russ Hitt, in Los Angeles on Foundation business, drove with Donald to Glendale where Donald preached to the staff of the Seventh-Day Adventist "Voice of Prophecy." The next day he spoke at Fuller Seminary, where questions about the Adventists came thick and fast. One had the feeling that people loved the preaching of Donald Grey Barnhouse, but were not quite sure how to take the man. Donald sailed through all of this unperturbed. The Lord had called him to love the brethren, and shall the eye say to the ear, or the hand to the foot, I have no need of thee? "It's like that orphanage in Taiwan, Marge. Remember? Where they paired a deaf child with a blind child, so the deaf could be eyes to the blind, and the blind could be ears to the deaf. In Christ's body the eye and the ear need one another."

He and Russ had appointments with a publisher and with Dick Ross, the Christian movie producer who had made Donald's initial films. We had lunch with Ethel Barrett, a talented young woman and long-time friend who was "The Story Lady" on a television station and did marvelous monologues of biblical characters. We spent a delicious hour wandering in a nursery that had trees and shrubs of every description; here, Donald ordered some redwood seedlings for the Farm. I have never known anyone who could shift gears so easily and completely from work to recreation and back again. After each of these excursions, refreshed, he would return to the pulpit and preach with power.

Starting east again, with six days before he was due to preach in Tucson, Arizona, we decided we should visit every one of the national parks on our route, even if it meant zig-zagging around to reach them. From Tucson we drove to Texas, collecting a lengthening list of "National Parks visited" as we went. Because he had preached before in many of these cities, people knew what to expect and the churches were packed. Between preaching and studying and writing he made contact with more wealthy Texans about the Literature Project, but again received encouragement without much financial backing.

One of these gentlemen invited us to dinner. He had heard Donald preach, had really been touched, and wanted his wife to meet him. Dinner was a banquet in lavish Texas style for our hostess and Donald and me, but our host had to be content with an elegantly served poached egg and a glass of milk because of stomach ulcers. What price wealth!

Our hostess told us of several religious movements that interested her. She asked Donald what he thought of them.

"Well, they're cults," he said.

"Oh." She reflected a moment, then said, "But which of these 'cults' would you say was the best?"

He spread his hands and shrugged his shoulders. "Which is the best of five counterfeit twenty-dollar bills? They all look pretty, but they are false religions." He then explained what each taught, and why that was false teaching. She still looked unconvinced.

"Religions are like a see-saw, with God on one end and man on the other," he told her. "When God is up, man is down; when man is up, God is down. Any religion that brings God down to man's scrutiny, for man to decide whether or not God is just or right, has not taken into consideration what sin really is."

"Well—what do you mean? How would you define 'sin'?"

"The basis of all sin is insisting on your own will instead of God's will. Every one of these cults, subtly or blatantly, exalts man and man's will."

From Texas we worked our way north week by week until we finally reached Holland, Michigan. Here at last Donald was to have the city-wide meetings in the Civic Auditorium that he had tried to arrange in Grand Rapids in 1954.

In his afternoon meetings at Western Seminary, Donald gave the exciting series of messages—"First John as a Commentary on the Upper Room of John 13 and 14." The evening messages, appropriately for a town settled by the Dutch, were on the TULIP. By this he could show them that his theology was Reformed, and at the same time bring life to what too easily can become "dead orthodoxy." Throughout the week the meetings built up, until by Friday there were nearly five thousand people in the Civic Auditorium. I was puzzled when he reacted to this with uneasiness instead of elation. "The intimacy is gone," he said. "It's just a sea of faces. I know the Word is blessing, but there just isn't the same feeling there is when I can get the audience interaction. A gigantic crusade is all right for an evangelist like Billy Graham, but for the kind of teaching I do it just doesn't work as well."

The last meeting of the conference was the Thursday night before Good Friday. I was to start ahead with the car Thursday morning, spending the night en route. Friday morning Donald would fly to Pittsburgh and rendezvous with me at the Pittsburgh airport. Then together we would drive the rest of the way home along the beautiful Pennsylvania Turnpike, burgeoning with spring.

A grateful conference committee had given him a thousand daffodil bulbs to naturalize in the front meadow at the Farm; these were stowed in the rear seat of the car. My bags, the books, the dictating machine, the tape recorder— all our paraphernalia except his typewriter—were packed in the trunk. We had said good-bye at the door, and Donald had returned to some urgent work at his typewriter. I should have left, but I kept finding things I should do for him before taking off.

With some irritation, Donald cried, "Marge, go! Go!" and looked up at me. My face evidently betrayed my feelings, because immediately he gave me his full attention. He stood, put his hand under my chin, and searched my face with concerned eyes.

"I know what the trouble is. You don't want to leave me." As he spoke he put his arm around me and started walking me toward the car.

"Marge, listen carefully. You know I will fly over you tomorrow morning and be in Pittsburgh before you even get there. Don't think of this as leaving me, but as coming to me." He opened the car door and I got in.

"Now just remember," he said, "you aren't leaving me, you are coming to me!" He kissed me through the open window and waved as I put the car in gear and started off.

Sure enough, he was at the Pittsburgh airport before I got there, holding up an enormous pair of Dutch wooden shoes, carved to order, that had been presented to him as he was leaving. On the side of one shoe was "Dr. Barnhouse"; on the other, "Holland Classis Reformed Church, April 14-18, 1957."

"My feet are shod with the preparation of the gospel of peace!" he cried, as he climbed into the car. "They fit perfectly." For days he clopped happily around the house in them. Then he put them in the deep windowsill of his study to remind him to pray for those in that "sea of faces" who had heard the Word and been quickened by it.

IV

The
Invisible
War

SEVENTEEN

For several years the theology concerning the church had been an issue among evangelicals. At the staff meetings at the Farm, Paul, Russ, Ralph, Ed, and Donald had wrestled with it: What, actually, is "the church"? What is *Eternity's* position on this?

Throughout 1956 and early 1957 Donald had been led to preach frequently in his Bible conferences from 1 John and from John's Gospel concerning this theology. In the preparation and the giving of these sermons the Holy Spirit seemed to pinpoint the lack of love among the brethren, and Donald was made even more aware of Jesus' new commandment to His disciples, which called them to love as Jesus loved—unconditionally. Jesus Himself had said that this was how the world would recognize His true disciples. From time to time, as I sorted Donald's "pocket scraps," there would be a notation on this. And the shock of seeing, during our visit to the Orient, what harm the divisiveness at home in America was bringing to new believers in foreign lands, was still with him.

Of course this for him was not a new thing: the seeds of it appeared years before. Back in 1932, one of his radio sermons, subsequently made into a booklet, "Separated Christians," stated that the important thing for a believer was not *what* he was separated *from,* but *whom* he was separated *to:* the Lord Jesus Christ.

Now, *whom* the believer was separated *from* was troubling him.

In one of his early books, *Guaranteed Deposits,* Donald had listed what he considered "the irreducible minimum of Christian truth which must be accepted if one is to call himself a Christian and yet remain honest." These doctrines were: "First, Jesus Christ is none other than the Second Person of the Godhead, and before His human birth He existed eternally as God. He took upon Himself a human body of His own creation in order that He might grow up to die on the Cross. He shed His blood as an offering which could satisfy all the demands of His perfect justice and holiness. At the same time His love was given the freedom to reach down to mankind and save those individuals who would accept the fact of their own unworthiness and consequent condemnation, and the fact that all of His righteous demands were satisfied by the death penalty which He paid. All this is sealed to us as factual by the resurrection of that body which was crucified, which resurrection is a certain guarantee to us that we are accepted and that we shall live eternally with Him, reigning with Him forever and ever."

He had pointed out that other distinctive doctrines *having nothing to do with salvation* separated believers into denominations, but should not separate them from fellowship with others who believe the "minimum." In his New Year's Resolution of 1953 all of this had crystallized.

In the early days of our 1957 winter tour he had hammered out his beliefs about the doctrine concerning the church in an article titled "We Are One Body in Christ," which appeared in the March *Eternity.* In it he had said that, sweeping through the New Testament, he had not been able to find one verse that taught separation from another true believer because of doctrine. Separation because of *immorality,* yes, but because of *doctrine,* no!

"When in 2 Corinthians 6:17 the Bible says, 'Come out from among them and be ye separate,' for the Corinthians it meant, 'Come out from the temples of Venus and Jupiter; be separate from the evil of Devil worship.' . . . Don't draw any smaller circle than Christ did. After all it is not our duty to draw the circle of fellowship; our duty is to live in it. We are not to pull out the tares; Christ has assigned that job to the angels at the end of the age—*'Lest in gathering the tares you root up the wheat along with them.'* To us this means, 'Don't go calling another man "liberal" or "modernist" and thus relegate him to hell. He may well be one of My sheep who has had too little teaching and too much criticism. Deal with him in love and leave the judgment to God.' "

Under the heading "Communion of the Saints" he had written, "Where does this lead us practically? It means that if the Episcopalian and the Pentecostal Christian are true believers, walking in the light of God's Word, then each needs the other. Each, confessing that the other is a member of the body of Christ, must acknowledge that every other true believer is a member and that they need each other whether they be Baptist, Presbyterian, Methodist, Lutheran, or any other denomination. And so we all need each other. The church in America needs the ministry of the churches abroad, and believers in the free world need those who dwell behind the Iron Curtain, and vice versa."

The response to this article, and requests for reprints were so numerous that it was made into a booklet. Donald was gratified to see that positive letters to the editor far outweighed negative ones.

Practically on the heels of this great call to oneness in Christ came, in the May *Eternity,* another article by Donald, entitled "Billy in Manhattan." At one time he would have printed a scathing denouncement of those ultra fundamentalists who criticized Billy Graham for allowing to sit on his platform, in addition to Bible-believing Christians, clergy who were so liberal in their theology one could doubt their being born again. With the approach of the 1957

Billy Graham Manhattan Crusade had come attacks against Billy more vitriolic than usual. But Donald's article, instead of burning with wrath against the attackers, had a new note: concern for the attackers. It said:

"With mingled joy and grief I look forward to Billy Graham's New York Crusade which opens May fifteenth in Madison Square Garden. I rejoice because the gospel will be preached in New York. I know and love Billy Graham and am confident that he will not pull any punches when he declares the Word of God to the most critical audience of his career.

"I grieve because true Christian brethren, some of whom I know and all of whom I love, are criticizing Billy and are even writing and circulating scandalous untruths about him. There seems to be in these brethren another spirit than that which moved Paul to write to the Philippians, 'Christ is proclaimed; and in that I rejoice. Yes, and I shall rejoice' (Phil. 1:18).

"Billy's detractors use insidious means. They use half-truths and insinuations to draw false conclusions. They instill doubts in the minds of believers and stir up enmity among brethren. They cry out with loud voices that they are the true defenders of the faith; but the net result of their campaign proves that they are just the opposite. . . .

"I say, as deeply and sincerely as I know how, that the half dozen men who have banded together to attack Billy Graham give no evidence of being impelled by the love of Jesus Christ or led by the Holy Spirit. . . .

"Are Billy's detractors praying for him each day? Do they ask God to bless him and his work and the New York campaign? . . .

"Let every Christian pray for Billy in these days, and for all members of the team. Let us pray for every minister and layman who works for the crusade. I say, 'Lord, bless those ministers and strengthen their faith as they see souls saved; bless these critics with their dwarfed love, and fill them with Thy love.' After all, there is nothing wrong with these men that cannot be cured by the love of Christ. . . ."

In April and May, Donald preached a series of sermons at Tenth on the subject of Christ in the Old Testament Scriptures. He began with Luke 24, where Jesus encountered the two disciples on the road to Emmaus.

"Don't let anyone tell you the Old Testament is 'myth, folklore, and legend.' Jesus Himself authenticates it. Listen to verse 27: 'Beginning at Moses' (that's Genesis, Exodus, Leviticus, Numbers and Deuteronomy) ' . . . he expounded unto them in all the scriptures the things concerning himself.'

"What were these things? Turn with me to Genesis 1." We flipped back to the first book of the Bible. " ' . . . and God said . . . and God said . . . and God said . . .' over and over. Now look at John's Gospel, chapter 1, verse 1: 'In the beginning was the Word, and the Word was with God, and the Word was God.' Verse 3: 'All things were made by him. . . .' Therefore, when God spoke in Genesis 1, it was the preincarnate Christ in action."

He took us to Genesis 3:15, where the Seed of the woman (Christ) is named as the One who would eventually destroy Satan; then to verse 21, where the "coats of skins" speak of "the Lamb of God" who would die in our stead in order to clothe us with His righteousness. His sermon that night focused on Adam and Eve and the fig leaves of their own works with which they had tried to cover their disobedience to the known will of God. It was funny but poignant, and the truths hit home.

Next in the series was Genesis 4. Abel brings a sacrificial lamb, believing and obeying the instructions God had obviously given Adam. This symbolized what Ezekiel 18:20 verbalizes: 'The soul that sinneth, it shall die,' and God's solution, 'the Lamb of God which taketh away the sin of the world' (John 1:29). Cain brings the fruit of his own works, is reminded by God that the sacrificial lamb must come first before his works can be accepted, refuses to believe God about this, and so is sent away from the presence of God."

Week after week DGB showed us what Jesus must have brought to the Emmaus disciples' remembrance. No wonder their hearts "burned within them"! Abraham believed and obeyed when he was willing to sacrifice Isaac, confident God would raise his son from the dead. For this prefigured the crucifixion, when God the Father slew His beloved only Son in order for us to have eternal life.

He spoke at length about Jacob, whom God had renamed "Israel." At the end DGB took us to Genesis 47:31, in which Jacob, knowing he was dying, made Joseph swear to take his body back to Canaan for burial. "Then follows an inspired picture of an old, old man—for Jacob was now 147 years old. You see him leaning on his bed, in weakness, in this verse. In Genesis 48:2, on being told his son Joseph was coming, he 'strengthened himself, and sat upon the bed.' Hebrews 11:21 adds that he was 'leaning upon the top of his staff.' He recognizes Joseph and the children, Ephraim and Manasseh. He claims these boys, not as grandchildren, but as sons, to share with his other sons in the inheritance of the land. As he talks, his mind wanders; he reminisces about Rachel and her death; he rambles. He looks at the children he had recognized earlier and asks, 'Whose are these?' Then his mind clears, and with full authority he knowingly blesses Joseph's younger son, Ephraim, instead of Manasseh, the firstborn. He calls all of his sons, prophesies concerning them, blesses them, and charges them to bury him with Abraham and Isaac in the cave at Mamre. In his prophecy concerning Judah, he predicts: 'The sceptre shall not depart from Judah, nor a lawgiver from between his feet, until Shiloh come; and unto him shall the gathering of the people be.' Christ in the Old Testament Scriptures! This is a prophecy of the coming Messiah.

"Then, the Bible says, 'When Jacob had made an end of commanding his sons, he gathered up his feet into the bed, and yielded up the ghost, and was gathered to his people.'

"Now let me read it to you." As he reached verse 7

DGB's voice trailed off, wandered, cracked a bit; his body bowed and seemed to shrink, and yet it held itself with dignity. Suddenly, as he read on in the narrative, he *was* Jacob, pulling himself back from forgetfulness, exercising authority to the very end, ruling his household, totally in charge even in weakness. I could see DGB at ninety or a hundred commanding his own four children, then tucking his feet up into the bed and dying triumphantly, in full control. How that man Barnhouse could make the Scriptures live!

Russ had been talking to Donald about the Pentecostals. For years DGB had sniped at their doctrines, lumping them together with the Holiness groups, yet mentally accepting them as brothers in Christ. Russ had decided the time had come for him to meet with the Pentecostal leaders and make that mental acceptance a heart acceptance. ("And for goodness sake, Donald, don't keep calling them 'Pentecostalists.' They are *Pentecostals.*") With some reservations Donald agreed to such a meeting.

After three days of discussion in Springfield, Missouri, at the headquarters of the Assemblies of God (one of the major Pentecostal denominations) he was astonished to find the agreement in doctrinal matters far outweighed the disagreement. As usual, when entering into discussion with other denominations, Donald used the formula he had found worked best: on the first day they discussed only their areas of agreement, saving the disagreement for the following day, and using the third day to wrap up. He came home humbled. Convinced he had wronged them in the past, he wrote an article that appeared in the April 1958 *Eternity* that ended: "So strong was our agreement on essential truths... that before this article appears I shall have held a week of meetings in the Central Church of the denomination in Springfield, Missouri. It is good for the whole body of Christ to notice that a Presbyterian minister who adheres to the Westminster Confession is an acceptable guest in a Pentecostal Assembly....

"What is the value of this exchange of ideas and experience of fellowship between the editors of *Eternity* and the leaders of the Assemblies of God? Each group has acquired confidence in the other as men of honesty and integrity. Each feels that the other will not make light of our differences which separate us but will both seek to emphasize the wonderful truths which we hold in common. And even though we disagree, we accept the fact that God can work wonderfully with believers who hold opposite opinions. . . ."

Previously in the article Donald had stated his "views about the Person and work of the Holy Spirit." Shortly after the article had appeared in *Eternity* a letter arrived from one of the Pentecostal leaders, thanking him and stating, "You have represented us very fairly and well. . . . You have stated our position correctly. . . . You will allow me one further comment concerning the statement of your own belief concerning the Holy Spirit. Let me quote: 'I believe the Scriptures teach that upon the entrance of new life every true believer is born of the Spirit into the family of God, baptized by the Spirit into the body of Christ, indwelt by the Spirit and sealed with the Spirit, and all this happens at one and the same moment.' I thought that we had made it clear that we believe identically with you in this regard. We believe that 1 Corinthians 12:13 is indeed baptism by the Holy Spirit into the body of Christ, but we also believe that there is a baptism into the Holy Spirit by the Person of Christ as stated in Acts 2:33 and Matthew 3:11 and Acts 1:5. I do not wish to open any further discussion, but thought I would merely reiterate the above for the record's sake. We agree with you that 'No man is born again without simultaneously being baptized by the Holy Spirit into the body of Christ.' "

To this, after a paragraph of personal greeting and appreciation, Donald answered:

"I take note of what you say concerning the 'baptism of the Holy Spirit' and as I see that this is a point of difference, I propose in the near future to write an article in which I take up this matter and present what we believe to be the biblical position. I think this interchange is very profitable because we are all members of the body of Christ and anything that can be done to minimize the differences and magnify the points of oneness in Christ is all for the good of the whole body. . . ."

Another letter, also expressing appreciation, arrived within a few days of the first, from the dean of men at a theological school of the Assemblies of God. He had sat under DGB's ministry when he was doing undergraduate work in Philadelphia.

He said: "Incidentally, the 'baptism of the Holy Spirit' is a work done *by* Christ (Matt. 3:11, Luke 3:16, John 1:33) when He brings us into a new relationship with the Holy Spirit. The verse, 1 Corinthians 12:13, which you referred to, is the baptism *by* the Holy Spirit when He brings us into a new relationship with Christ by putting us *into* the body of Christ. . . ."

This letter, which did not say, as did the first, that no further discussion was invited, received this answer from DGB: . . . "I note what you say about the difference between the supposed baptism done 'by' Christ and another done 'by' the Holy Spirit. I believe that you are in error here because the Greek will not allow the translation that is in the *King James Version.* If you look in the *American Standard Version* and the English *Revised Version,* you discover that the correct translation of the Greek word *en* is *in* and that the passage must read, 'For in one Spirit we were all baptized into one body.' . . .

"I believe that there would be a much greater basis for unity in the body of Christ if the people who believe in the general position held by the Assemblies of God would accept one correction in their vocabulary, namely *never* to use the word baptism of the Holy Spirit for any experience other than that which puts a man in Christ. In this way it is understood that nobody is in the body of Christ without having been baptized in the Holy Spirit and that everyone who is in the body of Christ has been baptized in the Spirit. For any further experiences of the work of the Holy Spirit use the word 'filling.' This is the scriptural vocabulary and this is what should be used. . . ."

In the first letter the writer had not quoted all of that paragraph from the article. Donald had said, " . . . No man is born again without simultaneously being baptized by the Holy Spirit into the body of Christ. Any later experience is the 'filling' or 'fulness' of the Holy Spirit. Such filling may take place many times."

Semantics again! To me the crux of the problem is, "What do you mean by 'baptize'?" DGB's explanation in his studies in Romans 6:3 and following makes sense, to me. He points out that the word "baptize" was taken over into the English directly from the Greek, transliterated instead of being translated. The original word has both a literal meaning: to plunge, to dip, to immerse, and a metaphorical meaning: to change the identity, or, to identify. In explaining it to Doug and me, DGB likened it to dying a garment. You have a vat of purple dye into which you plunge a faded pink dress and a faded blue dress. Both come forth from the dye bath royal purple, changed from their old "identity" and now identified with the color of the dye bath. Just so, when we are "baptized into Christ," God considers that we are "in" Him. Our identity is changed, and we are "identified" with Him. This is what happened to the thief on the cross. He identified himself with Jesus, calling Him "Lord" (and 'no man calleth Jesus Lord but by the Holy Spirit') and showing faith in His resurrection and His coming again in power. Thus, although water was not applied at all, he was "baptized," identified as a believer, and owned by Christ Himself.

DGB explained to us 1 Corinthians 10:1, 2, "On one side of the Red Sea the Children of Israel were complaining against Moses; on the other side they said, 'Moses, you are our leader.' As they passed through the Red Sea on dry ground they were 'baptized unto Moses,' identified with him. The only people who were *immersed* were Pharaoh's army!"

First Corinthians 12:13 says, "For by one Spirit were we all baptized [identified] into one body." DGB's studies in Romans show that our 'identification' is not only into Jesus' death, burial, and resurrection, but also into every phase of His life on earth and in heaven.

When we first heard DGB teach on the filling of the Spirit, he pointed out that the disciples "were all filled with the Holy Spirit" on the day of Pentecost, but a few chapters later they were "filled" again. What happened to the first "filling"? "In the meantime," he said, "they leaked!"

Years later he was to retract this: "I used to think of the infilling of the Spirit as a sort of liquid, flowing into me. Now I realize He is a Person, coming into my personality, filling all my vision, all my desire, pushing farther and farther and farther into the innermost reaches of my being. The reason I need frequent refillings is not that 'I leak,' as D. L. Moody put it, but that I, Donald Barnhouse, intrude self into what I had surrendered to the Holy Spirit, and must get self out of the way to make room for Him. 'He must increase and I must decrease.' "

In May we had acquired a new secretary to replace Naomi Veit Fink. She was a wonderful woman, a highly qualified secretary, totally committed to the Lord. She had been attending Tenth Church for some time, and felt it would be an honor to work for, as she put it, "such a man of God." While Donald was in Cleveland for meetings, she settled in, forming close, warm friendships with Toshii and with Al Wever, and fitting beautifully into the household.

Then Donald came home, and her work went into high gear. Donald, used to Naomi's long familiarity with his work methods, was at first unreasonably demanding. Then, because he had set aside May and June to research *The Invisible War,* he began to dig deep into that. He didn't call for her, and suddenly she had nothing to do. Mail began to pile up; she didn't know she should insist he give it his attention. Finally, although I didn't like to interfere in his business relationships, I spoke to him about it. He looked up from his reading with desperation in his eyes.

"Marge, I can't work with her—she's in awe of me! I cannot have a secretary who is in awe of me. I need someone to organize me and keep me on the track."

"But it's not fair to her. She's a good secretary. Give her time. She'll work into it, I know. And there's mail that *must* be taken care of."

"Well, why don't I tell *you* what to tell her, the way we do on the road?"

"You are putting me in an impossible position, Donald. All I did on the road was forward your dictation to Naomi, but when we were home you worked directly with her."

"No, Marge, *she* worked directly with *me*. She organized my day; she told me what to do. This girl cannot do that. Marge, she's in awe of me!"

At his insistence we began taking the letters with us on the drive to New York Monday nights. I'd read them to him and he'd dictate. I'd turn the dictation over to the secretary, who would then do the typing. Hurt and puzzled, she had no way of knowing why he ignored her. I tried to tell her tactfully how to cope. Paul, who had hired her, tried to explain. But when Dr. Barnhouse ignored someone, *she was ignored*. I could have kicked him. Yet I understood his dilemma. He had tremendous work pressures and deadlines, and needed a different sort of secretarial help than she was able to give. She *was* in awe of him. Finally the situation became unbearable. We parted by mutual agreement.

For a while we struggled along, sending the dictation to the Foundation for processing. We prayed. Donald tried to get Naomi to come back, but having made the break she wisely refused.

Then along came Wanda Ann Mercer! A well-organized, flexible, happy person, with a brilliant mind and a wonder-

ful sense of humor, she was not in the least intimidated by
DGB. Shortly after her arrival, the relationship was established on the right track. He had been planting some of our
daffodil bulbs that afternoon, using a tool somewhat like a
spade curled into a cylinder, which he would press into the
ground with his foot. By the time to leave for his New
York class his foot was so sore he couldn't drive. I had gone
off on a speaking engagement. Wanda, instead of riding
along doing the mail, had to drive. He was obnoxiously
"backseat driving" all the way, but really poured it on as
they swung down the ramp to the Lincoln Tunnel in the
midst of the usual rush-hour traffic. At that point Wanda
stopped the car, opened her door, put one foot out, and said
calmly, "Dr. Barnhouse, would you care to drive?" Cars
piled up behind them, horns honked, a policeman started
toward the car, blowing his whistle and wildly gesturing
them onward. Donald realized she really meant business.
"No, no, *you* drive," he said hastily. Calmly she got back
in and started into the tunnel. He was meek as a lamb the
rest of the way, and never again did he treat her conde-
scendingly.

Wanda knew how to draw from Donald a tremendous
amount of work production. She and I worked together as
a team, to keep him running smoothly. It made me think of
the relationship, in the musical *The King and I,* between the
Number One Wife and Anna, the British governess for the
children. The wife sings of the difficult king, who suddenly
will do "something wonderful" that makes everything all
right. DGB demanded so much of himself it never occurred
to him that often he was asking the impossible from those
who worked for him. Yet incredibly they accomplished
the impossible!

One day Wanda's father died of a cerebral hemorrhage.
"DGB was unbelievably kind to me," Wanda said later. "I
flew home to Louisiana immediately after Mother called,
and DGB made all the arrangements without my saying a
word. He called the travel agent, had Paul send me $100,

had Al drive me to the airport, and then called Louisiana to see how things were. It's one of those 'something wonderful' things he did."

She recalled a time when, scheduled to fly to Michigan, DGB decided he would go to Newark, New Jersey, and from there take the shuttle helicopter to Idlewild Airport, where his plane was scheduled to depart for Detroit—all because he had never ridden in a helicopter! I had cooked breakfast for the three of us at four A.M., then crawled back into bed while Wanda drove DGB to the airport. "In that predawn trip DGB decided to give me a lesson in French pronunciation," Wanda said. "Un soldat, un officier; deux soldats, deux officiers; trois soldats, trois officiers, etc., demonstrating the sliding sound when the noun begins with a vowel. He didn't get to ride in the helicopter because of heavy fog, and had to be taken by limousine to Idlewild. But it was one of many memorable trips." Another time, DGB insisted on playing Twenty Questions because he thought Wanda needed practice in logic, feeling she shouldn't rely on intuition so much!

How often Donald was the compulsive teacher! Wanda wasn't the only pupil. He had a tendency to impose himself and his views on others and was amazingly unaware that he was doing it, sometimes insensitive to the real problems that other people had.

Whenever we were at the Farm we often had overnight guests. Sometimes these were pastors or young men seeking career guidance or counseling. One Saturday morning Donald included me in one of these sessions. Our guest was a young man who was deeply involved in a mission work that frequently took him out of the country. He complained that his wife, alone at home, was "not being supportive," and he was at a loss as to how to deal with the situation. After discussing the problem, Donald assured the young man that he would go personally to talk to the wife when he was in their city the following week.

Years later the wife told me her side of this encounter.

She was in bed with a cold; head stuffed up, Vick's Vapo-rub smeared on her chest, she felt miserable. The telephone rang.

"This is Dr. Barnhouse. I am in the city for a Bible conference and I must see you. May I come over?"

Dr. Barnhouse! She had never met him, but knew a great deal about him; her husband knew him well and had spent some time with him in Philadelphia recently. She was dismayed.

"Oh, Dr. Barnhouse, I'm in bed with a dreadful cold, and it would be most inconvenient. Another time, perhaps?" (Her *m*'s were all *b*'s; her *n*'s, *d*'s. Surely he would understand.)

"I'll be over in fifteen minutes!" he said and hung up.

Slow rage began to engulf her. She got up, wiped off the Vick's, threw on some clothes, ran a comb through her hair, and had just managed a touch of lipstick when the doorbell rang. She went to the door and somewhat icily greeted the huge man who stood there.

"Come in, Dr. Barnhouse."

And the bull entered the china shop.

She ushered him into the living room. He sat on one end of the couch, she perched at the other, looking him over distastefully.

He plunged immediately into the purpose of his visit: his time was "limited," he had told her husband he'd see her when he was there, inasmuch as, being a "pastor's pastor" he had had poured out to him by the young husband a great many things that were "wrong" with their marriage; she would ruin her husband's ministry if she did not change; this, this, and this were wrong; she was not being a biblical wife; she should be doing such and such.

The nerve of him! she thought, becoming angrier and angrier, knowing the anger was showing but at this point not caring.

She let him go on. Then she said, shaking her finger in his face, "Now you let *me* tell *you* a thing or two!" and she poured out her side of the story. He looked at her in aston-ishment, then suddenly really listened. When she was finished he threw back his head, laughed uproariously, slapped his knee, leaned forward and said, "I like you!" and like sunshine after rain the air between them miraculously cleared. Her anger evaporated, for intuitively at that moment she knew that he had acted out of real love and concern for her husband, *caring* that this marriage be smoothed out. He was genuinely sorry he had not taken the time to learn both sides of the story. From then on he was her firm friend, able to give a more balanced appraisal of any difficulties she and her husband might have.

"*Time* was your husband's problem," she told me later. "I guess he really never had enough time. There were so many demands on his life and ministry. If people could have understood this they might have been less critical."

One day I was in our bedroom putting away laundry. Donald, returning from a recording session at the Founda-tion and a meeting with Paul, came up the stairs three at a time, grabbed me, and swung me around.

"The reports are in on audience response to the TV series, and guess what?" His voice was so jubilant it was easy to guess. "More letters came in for my segment than for all the others combined, which shows that people are hungry for the true gospel. . . . But Ralph Sockman was voted 'Most Philosophical Content.' "

I hugged him. "But philosophical content doesn't feed the sheep!"

"Oh, Marge, I am bursting with ideas for a regular, full-time Christian TV station. The possibilities are endless. What do you think of these?" He ripped some pages out of his pocket memo book and handed them to me. Then he started getting into his gardening clothes.

His notes had been written in ink from several different pens; two entries were in pencil. Obviously he had been collecting these ideas for a day or two, in different places:

Invalid of the Week (sponsored by greeting card company)
Hymn
Hymn story
Personalities
    Billy Graham
    Van Cliburn
    Policeman
    Rose Bampton
Art Development
    Picture of the Week
    (LIFE magazine tie-in)
Bible Passage
Prayer
Story-ette
News paragraphs and illustration
Missionary Story
Foreign Student
Oversupply of Food (suggest buying)
Etymology of Words
Travel Story
Book of the Week
Education & help for children
Stories to make you THINK
What happened on this date?
Museum re Bible
Stamps and Coins
Art Objects from Morgan and other libraries
Fed. Reserve Head

"You left out gardening!" I cried, as he put on his old shoes. "After all, the history of man began in a garden!"

Another kind of history was being enacted in a garden: Madison Square Garden in New York City. The Billy Graham Manhattan Crusade had begun.

EIGHTEEN

Despite the bitter attacks dividing believers on whether or not they should support the Manhattan Crusade, Madison Square Garden was packed to the rafters by the third day. "Babes in Christ," newly born again or brought to a new commitment after years of indifference, began pouring into the New York Bible class.

From the pulpit Donald greeted them by saying, "Billy Graham is the obstetrician; I am the pediatrician. Billy assists at the new birth; I fix the formula, help the babes in Christ grow up, and see that they get enough vitamins. I am delighted to welcome you here."

The questions that were asked made me think of my own baby Christian days in Bradenton. Many were prefaced by, "This may sound foolish, but . . . ," to which he would say, "The only foolish question is the un-asked question. Questions are like splinters. The ones you get out never bother you, but the ones that are left in are apt to fester." You could almost see the light dawn, as they listened to his answers:

"Please explain the virgin birth. What difference does it make whether or not Mary was a virgin?"

"The sin principle in the human race is carried from one

generation to the next in the genes of the father. Romans 5:12 states that 'by one *man* sin entered into the world, and death by sin,' and 1 Corinthians 15:22 says, 'In *Adam* all die.' If Jesus had had a human father, He would have inherited through that father the sin of Adam, 'original sin.' He therefore would have had sin of His own to be paid for, and so could not have qualified as the sin-bearer, the Lamb without spot or blemish. It was necessary to God's plan of redemption that Christ should be born of a virgin, without a human father. It was necessary that the infinite God should be the Father of Jesus the Christ, in order that His sacrifice would be infinite."

"Aren't all religions good? You seem to be very narrow."

"One of the lies of the Devil is that all religions are good. Let's face it: Jesus said, *'No man cometh to the Father but by me.'* So that means any other way, no matter how good it looks, is the Devil's path to lead you away from Christ and the necessity of His atoning blood.

"Another lie of the Devil is that God is the Father of all men, and that all men are brothers. There are two distinct families and two fatherhoods. Here in a group, for example, you may have an Ethiopian, an Englishman, a Russian, a Chinese, and any other assortment you wish, and in a duplicate group the exact same assortment. All in the first group are believers in Christ and they are brothers to each other. All in the other group are unbelievers and they are brothers to each other. *But those in the first group are not brothers to those in the second group.* They are our *neighbors,* and we who have the life of God in us through the new birth will love them, and feed them, and clothe them, but the unbeliever is not a brother, a true child of God, until he has become a partaker of the divine nature through faith in Christ Jesus."

"I went forward at the Billy Graham Crusade and received Christ. I know I am born again, but I find myself still being pulled back into the same old sins. Why?"

"If you want to know what a real, born-again, Bible-believing Christian is capable of doing—read what the Bible tells him *not* to do. These warnings would not be there if Christians—*Christians!*—weren't doing them: 'Let him that stole steal no more'; 'Flee fornication'; 'Be not drunk with wine but be filled with the Holy Spirit'; and on and on.

"The old nature is still there, just waiting for a chance to take over, and the only way to 'keep your body under' is to keep your new nature on top. Just take your eyes off the Lord for a moment, and up pops your old nature. You have to slap it down immediately or it will take over. Whatever was your weakness before you were saved will continue to tempt you after you are saved. There must be a continual yieldedness to the Lord's will as revealed in this Book, a *willing* bringing of every thought and imagination under the scrutiny of His holy gaze, to be approved for action or disapproved and discarded."

"Second Peter 3:9 says that God is not willing that *any* should perish. Doesn't that mean that everyone will be saved?"

"Read the first part of that verse: 'The Lord is not slack concerning his promise, but is longsuffering toward *us.*' Who are the 'us'? Well, to whom is the epistle addressed? Look at the first verse: 'To them that have obtained like precious faith with us.' This is speaking to the elect of God. He is not willing that any *of us* should perish. Verses 3 and 4 of 2 Peter 3 tell us that they were being scoffed at by unbelievers: 'Humph! If your Jesus is going to return, why hasn't He? Everything is just the same as before. You are fools!' Verse 9 reassures them: He isn't coming *until all of His elect are in the fold.* Verse 8 tells them that his return could be today, or not for a thousand years, but *He will come.* And verse 14 warns, 'Be ready!' If He should suddenly appear, right here in this room, right now (and He could!) would He find you 'in peace, without spot, and blameless'? The elect *will* be saved, but many of us will stand before Him ashamed. But as you can see, this does not teach universal salvation."

"Is it sinful to be wealthy? Are we supposed to sell all our goods to feed the poor, as Jesus told the rich young ruler to do?"

"Having wealth is not sinful: it is a gift from God, as is the ability to make money, as we see in Deuteronomy 8:18. Having it your god *is* sinful. First Timothy 6:10 tells us that the *love* of money, not the money itself, is 'the root of all evil.' But if God has given you wealth, verses 17 and 18 are for you: use it wisely; be willing to share; and don't *trust* in 'uncertain riches' but in the living God, who gives us richly all things to enjoy."

Soon the class was bursting at the seams and had to be moved from the Lutheran church on 46th Street to Calvary Baptist Church, which had a larger capacity. Enthusiastic members brought their friends, who in turn brought theirs.

One evening a famous voice teacher and his wife were persuaded to come. Nominally Roman Catholic, they said their "faith" had meant little to them other than fear and restriction and was "an insult to our intelligence." Years later the maestro told me their story.

"We were (please pardon the expression) 'hooked' on Dr. Barnhouse. We could hardly wait for Monday to come. Our souls craved his teaching the way a drug addict craves drugs. He made good sense. It was the first time I really *knew* Jesus. I now knew He was the only One, the only intercessor. It was like breathing fresh air for the first time. It filled my body, my soul, my mind. When I went out of there afterwards, it was as if I were floating, my feet hardly touching the ground."

He slipped into a third person account: "Before long people began kidding the maestro: he no longer made sly, off-color jokes. Then it became apparent that his life had *really* changed: watching him they began to realize they were missing something vital in life, and longed to have this for themselves."

That Bible class produced many surprising results. Once, after the meeting, someone stepped up to Donald and said, "As you know, I am with one of the leading pharmaceutical firms. I found out the other day that they are going to dump $25,000 in pharmaceuticals, still usable, but for some reason no longer marketable. Isn't there a missionary outlet for something like this?"

Donald, still gripping the hand he had shaken, clapped this man on the shoulder and boomed, "Of course! Of course! And I know just the man you can send them to: Ray Knighton, executive director of the Christian Medical Society. He knows more missionary doctors than any man I know. Here's his address."

The man wrote down the information and went away elated. Donald turned to the next person, unaware that he had just set off for Ray Knighton a delayed-action bomb.

The man telephoned Ray, told him the story of what happened, and informed him the shipment was already on its way and could be expected in a few days. Had he asked first, Ray would have said they couldn't possibly accept: they had no machinery set up for such a distribution. Nevertheless, the shipment was on its way.

It arrived, *eleven tons* of it, and was unloaded into their office, a room maybe thirty or forty feet square. They had to shove desks back to the wall; the stuff towered to the ceiling and overflowed the room. At that time the Christian Medical Society was just the home office of a loosely organized fellowship of believing medical men, without any sort of warehouse or any place to put this fabulous white elephant. They began franticly telephoning every missionary they knew, told them what had happened, and asked them to help out. They came eagerly, and as they did an idea began to percolate: here was an untapped source of God's bounty, an answer to the medical missionary's chronic crying need for pharmaceuticals. Perhaps this group could be an avenue of service, not just a fellowship. Perhaps. . . .

And out of this was born MAP, the Medical Assistance Program, a voluntary international agency that sends tons of life-saving medicine to missionary physicians who are attempting to meet the health needs, both spiritual and physical, of people in eighty-one developing countries.

Once, DGB asked Ray Knighton to work for him at the Evangelical Foundation. DGB's dreams were always ahead of his rapidly expanding work. He was somewhat miffed when Ray, instead of jumping at the chance, thanked him but told him he'd have to talk it over with his wife, Beth, and pray about it.

Even after much prayer, he and Beth could not seem to discover the mind of the Lord for them in this. They discussed it with some friends, a young doctor and his wife who were among Donald's ardent followers. The wife cried, "Why Ray! If Dr. Barnhouse has the mind of the Lord as he says, you don't even need to pray—just go with him!"

Ray shook his head. "That's not the way I am. The Lord has to show *me* His clear will for me. I cannot take another man's word. Not Dr. Barnhouse's, not anybody's." Which is of course precisely why DGB wanted him.

A few weeks later, at the Billy Graham Manhattan Crusade, we had bumped into the Knightons. DGB, with a warm handclasp for Ray and an affectionate shoulder squeeze for Beth, said to her, "You and Ray are coming to work for me." It was a positive, quiet statement. He was sure what the Lord would do. But Ray said, just as quietly, just as positively, "When the *Lord* tells me, OK."

To our disappointment, the Lord did not give his OK. Instead, because Ray Knighton insisted on waiting, MAP became a reality. Today more than a thousand missionary physicians and dentists, working in eighty-one countries under 136 boards, benefit from MAP's services.

These days the Literature Project and ways to promote it seemed to be a continual undercurrent of Donald's thinking.

He was convinced that the best missionary in a turbulent Third World could be the written page. He had been deeply concerned about a monthly Christian magazine called *The New Nation,* being published in Ghana. The periodical was having problems: money was short; the local committee could not get government recognition as a non-profit corporation; newspapers were saying that Prime Minister Kwame Nkrumah was behaving like a despot.

All of this was on Donald's mind as we returned to our hotel room in Boston the first Sunday in November. Donald had preached at Park Street Church that morning and would preach there again that evening.

"This Kwame Nkrumah is an enigma to me, Marge," he said. "At Presbytery the other day I was talking to Dr. George Ellison (pastor of a black Presbyterian church in Philadelphia). He told me Nkrumah had spent ten years in the Philadelphia area in his student days, and had attended his church. Nkrumah had worked his way through college, getting a B.A. and an M.A. degree. I think he may also have studied at the Presbyterian Theological Seminary of Lincoln University. He has preached in Dr. Ellison's church. According to Dr. Ellison, he is a real Christian. Yet he calls himself a Marxian socialist, and won't support a Christian magazine. I don't understand it."

He sighed, stretched himself out on the bed for the nap he always disciplined himself to take between two preachings in one day, and was soon fast asleep.

Suddenly he sat bolt upright, eyes wide open, as if lightning had just struck him.

"Marge!" he cried. "I'm going to Ghana to see Kwame Nkrumah!" Seeing my look of incredulity, he added, "Don't ask me how—I just *know*. I must take Dr. Ellison with me."

He swung his feet off the bed, went to the desk, and began planning excitedly. He called a gentleman whom he knew to be greatly concerned about the Communist influence in Ghana. Before we left Boston the next day for the

New York Bible class, he had the promise of finances for the trip, and Dr. Ellison had said he would go. Within a few days an exchange of cablegrams with the Prime Minister assured them of a welcome and visas. It was all so smooth we knew the Lord's hand must be in it.

In an article he wrote for *Eternity* after the trip, Donald stated that Nkrumah's remark about being a Marxian socialist had been misunderstood, destroying the objective view of many Americans, including journalists. He wrote, "They ignore the fact that [Nkrumah] has never recognized Russia and would not invite Russian delegates to the independence ceremonies. . . . He used the word 'Marxian' in a purely philosophical sense; it had no overtones of Leninism, Stalinism, or any similar destructive force. Individual capitalistic enterprise, state socialism in large ventures, and full cooperation with the Western nations—especially with the United States—are the future course of Ghana. Private industry in the United States, finding atomic development too costly, has yielded it to government control. This is the only type of Marxism that Nkrumah had adopted for Africa. . . . The average journalist could not draw from this man what he revealed to his former pastor and to me, a Christian friend. Nkrumah is a committed Christian. On his breakfast table he has a Bible from which he reads each morning. As long as I live, I can never forget an expression that was torn from him late one evening in the castle at Accra. After the three of us had prayed together, he spoke with tears about his loneliness. He said, 'Do you understand there are times when the pressure is so great that all you can do is to cry, "O God, O God!" and there are times when you can't even bring yourself to the point of crying His name, but can only groan?'

"Nkrumah is greater than Ghana. This is the fact that the West must realize. What he has done in turning the Gold Coast into a republic will be followed in East Africa, Uganda, French Africa, and Belgian Africa, perhaps in that order. Most sure is the fact that there will be no retrogression toward colonialism.

"There is a great need of continuous prayer for Ghana, for Prime Minister Kwame Nkrumah, and for all the missionary forces of Africa."

Donald returned from Ghana with the assurance that the Christian publication could continue if financial support were forthcoming. Nkrumah said he was confident that he would not be betrayed, and that what would be printed would be for the advancement of his people and the proclaiming of Christ to them.

(I have been asked if DGB was wrong in his evaluation of Nkrumah. I don't think so. Nkrumah did what he thought was best for his country. As have so many of the leaders of Third World countries, Nkrumah became disenchanted with the West and turned toward socialism. He lost his leadership in a military coup and died in exile.)

Donald had barely caught his breath after the trip to Ghana when the winter conferences were upon us. Our first stop on this tour was a four-day conference at the University of Illinois campus at Urbana, ending on New Year's Eve. He was to be one of the speakers at the Intervarsity Christian Fellowship Fifth International Student Missionary Convention, sharing the platform with Dr. Harold Ockenga, Dr. Billy Graham, Dr. Kenneth Strachan, Reverend Israel Garcia, and Dr. Masumi Toyotome. The theme was "One Lord—One Church—One World." While preparing his messages, Donald had become even more deeply convicted of the need for Christian unity-in-diversity.

Those were four strenuous days, every moment action-packed. Between addresses by the various speakers, Donald was in his element, standing in the midst of a thousand students, answering questions as fast as they were fired at him. In his messages he hit hard, pressing the point of unity, confessing his former lack of love toward believers who differed with him doctrinally.

He told how his life had been dramatically changed by his resolution to get together with everybody who truly believed that Jesus Christ is the Lord God Almighty, not only the Son of God, but God the Son, and that He died on the cross for their sins. But then, although adding that he loved them nevertheless, in the same breath he would point out, as sardonically as in the old days, what he thought was wrong with their doctrine. Apparently old habits are as hard for a preacher to break as for us ordinary mortals!

Reversing the order of the theme, Donald preached first on "One World," then "One Church," then "One Lord." His sermons soared, and my own heart soared with them. This was Donald Grey Barnhouse at his best, glorifying the Lord Jesus Christ, lifting us to worship and adore.

On New Year's Eve, the last night of the conference, Dr. Billy Graham took a few moments before his final message to explain why he couldn't stay for the communion service that would follow. With a twinkle in his eye he said, "Usually at a conference I am the only speaker, so it isn't often that I have the opportunity to sit and listen. Well, this morning I sat on one of *those benches.*" Laughter rippled through the audience. "I assure you that my message will be much briefer tonight than it was last night!"

The students roared with laughter, then applauded.

"If you keep applauding I may pronounce the benediction *now!*" Again they laughed. "But I sat on one of those benches, and the first five or ten minutes I squirmed a bit. But after I got used to it and the calluses began to form, . . ." (the students looked delighted: was this the great Dr. Billy Graham?) "I found myself wishing it could go on longer, because my own soul was being fed.

"To have the privilege of sharing the platform with Dr. Barnhouse is a frightening experience," he bantered, "because when he gets through, you feel that nothing else can be said. He has been a wonderful friend and counselor and advisor of mine for many years, and tonight I am going to have the hazardous experience of driving with him to Indianapolis or Cincinnati or points south, and we need your special prayers—not because of his driving but because of the road conditions! I wouldn't drive on those icy roads, but Dr. Barnhouse is a Calvinist and if he thinks it's safe and decides to go, I'll ride with him!"

Refreshed by a glimpse of Billy Graham, the man, the audience then turned their undivided attention to Billy Graham, God's messenger. When he flung forth his challenge at the end of the sermon, some fifteen hundred students rose to their feet as evidence that they were willing to go wherever the Lord might send them, in this country or abroad, to serve Him. Billy warned, "Don't get carried away by emotion. This is not a pledge or a vow to man, but to God. Don't make it unless you really mean it." One student, obviously struggling with himself, sat down and put his face in his hands. To the others Billy gave a solemn charge, then slipped away to join us for the trip to Indianapolis.

There had been an ice storm that day. It was still sleeting as Donald, Billy, and I got into the car. Despite the generous width of the front seat, it was a squeeze. Our heavy overcoats didn't help matters either, except later to cushion me a bit when the car would start to skid, then would right itself under Donald's careful driving. On another trip Donald had told Doug and me, "The closer you get to Jesus Christ, the more on-target you become." I had an uneasy feeling that, for the Enemy of Souls, we were all very much "on target." We started out into the night after Donald briefly committed to the Lord the car, the tires, the brakes, the roadway, the trip, and each one of us.

To be wedged between Donald's massive bulk and Billy Graham's lean, broad shoulders was a little like sitting between a wrestler and a prizefighter. Each of these mighty champions of the Word had scored heavily for the Lord Jesus Christ during the past four days. Satan certainly wouldn't be happy over that. If he could get rid of both of them at once what a victory he would win! Was it Satan's hand that was flinging that sleet so viciously against the windshield? Twice we had to stop to scrape off the ice, before the defroster warmed the glass enough to keep it clear.

Donald had started out very cautiously. Every time he put on the brake, so did Billy and I!

Suddenly the car went into a bad skid toward an enormous tree. Instinctively I braced myself for impact. *(Lord, don't let it happen.)* Satan wasn't fooling around: this could be "it." But in the nick of time the tires crunched into gravel on the shoulder of the road, and we stopped inches from a terrible crash.

"Praise God!" said Donald, edging the car back onto the road.

We didn't talk much until we got out onto the main highway, where the road had been sanded and heavy traffic had worn it almost clear of ice. As we swung eastward Donald breathed a relieved prayer: "Thank You, Lord, for bringing us safely thus far. I know we are not supposed to talk directly to our guardian angels, because they work for You, not for us—but will You please thank ours for keeping us safe?" Billy said a hearty "Amen!"

For a while they talked about the conference at Urbana, and what the other speakers had said. I listened, fascinated, as they discussed the theology of a book Billy was writing. Then Donald turned up the radio, which had been on at a very low volume. It was eleven o'clock where we were, but on Times Square in New York, 1958 was being ushered in.

We listened to the countdown, the "Happy New Year!" the horns and whistles and general drunken hullabaloo. Donald shook his head, and said, "Well, Billy, you were in Manhattan just a few months ago. They can never say they weren't told the gospel." Billy's arm was stretched across the back of the seat to make more room. His hand reached out and pressed Donald's shoulder in reply. I sensed that these two men were as close as two brothers, each aware of the other's weaknesses, each perhaps a little envious of the other's accomplishments, but appreciating and loving one another nonetheless.

Just before midnight our time, we pulled off the road.

The sleet storm had ceased. In the midnight silence we prayed for the students back at Urbana as they lifted in communion that symbol of the life-blood of the Lord Jesus Christ shed for them. We knew that many of those who had dedicated their lives there might have to pour out their lives, for Him.

In Indianapolis we dropped Billy at his hotel; then, continuing toward our next Bible conference, Donald and I drove on through the night, running ahead of a new storm.

As daylight came I was at the wheel, with Donald dozing beside me. He looked so peaceful no one would have guessed that he had just gone through a skirmish with Satan. But a mighty Savior had been present with us all the way through the sleet storm and through the night, giving that "peace that passeth understanding."

When I had read that first chapter of *The Invisible War,* I had been interested intellectually in how to use "the whole armor of God." I never dreamed that someday I would be drawn into the thick of the fray, nor that it really was possible to have "in the midst of wrestle, rest."

Ever since my introduction to *Eternity* magazine I had looked forward to Donald's "Survey of the Year" and his "Man of the Year," patterned on that of *Time* magazine and featured in the January issue. *Eternity's* survey always began at Jerusalem and went from there in widening circles to the "uttermost part of the earth." How Donald pulled everything together always amazed me.

The Survey of 1957 began: "The second most important year of the Twentieth Century is drawing to a close. 1945 was the year of the first atomic bomb. 1957 is the year of new companions in the sky. The word *companion* in Russian is *Sputnik.* Two *Sputniks* were now circling the globe, and man was beginning to conquer outer space. Some bold minds even envisioned *man* in a capsule in outer space some day."

In the question and answer period before Donald's evening sermons during the winter conference tour, anxiety over current events was reflected in the questions. One of the most frequently asked concerned man's exploration of the universe: "Aren't we tampering with things beyond us when we go into outer space? Won't God judge us for this?"

Donald's answer: "Turn with me if you will to Psalm 8:3. 'When I consider thy heavens, the work of thy fingers, the moon and the stars, which thou hast ordained. . . .' What is the work of God's fingers? The moon and the stars. All right, now look at verse 6. This is speaking of man, and it says, 'Thou madest him to have dominion over the works of thy hands.' So man is *meant* to have dominion over the moon and the stars, and conquering space is quite proper."

These were times of tremendous racial upheaval in the United States. The Supreme Court decision banning segregation was having violent repercussions. *Eternity* had run several articles on the racial question, by authors on both sides. Now our 1958 winter conference tour was taking us into the deep South and the midst of that upheaval.

In January Donald was scheduled to be in Atlanta, where he had a loyal and enthusiastic following. However, because of the *Eternity* articles and something he had said on the radio that had been misunderstood, the friend who had arranged his meetings there wrote him, deeply disturbed. In response to this letter Donald explained his position:

"Now with reference to the racial issue, what I said on the radio is in print and you can see that it is in no wise what your friend said it was. I did not 'chew anybody out.' With great searching of heart I presented such matters as pacifism, as submission to authority, etc., and said that each individual must follow his own conscience and that it was perfectly possible for people to be sincerely led by the Lord and come to opposite positions. I gave a lengthy story of two young men, one of whom is an officer in the navy ready to drop an atomic bomb and the other a pacifist who would consent to be lined up and shot before he would bear arms. I gave the story of two men at the time of the Revolutionary War, one of whom sincerely believed in following the authority of the king and the other who went with the Continental Congress. Each was answerable to the Lord. I specifically stated that what I was saying about conditions in America today (the North as well as the South) was a question of submission to law. I did not go into the racial issues as deeply perhaps as my conscience would have liked to have pushed me. I am still quite convinced that the matter of racial differences, like that of war and prostitution, etc., is going to be settled only by the second coming of Christ. Each individual must be absolutely sure in himself as to the nature of his conduct in each individual instance."

The dictates of his conscience made him believe that segregation was unbiblical. I remember his telling how he had tried to integrate his own church. He kept praying about it.

One Sunday one of the deacons saw a young black man standing on the sidewalk, looking longingly at Tenth Church. (Later we learned that he had been listening to DGB on the radio, and found he made so much sense he'd like to talk to him.) The deacon invited him in, and to the young man's surprise instead of being shooed up into the balcony he was taken unconcernedly into the church and seated beside two white ladies. Because he was a stranger, they helped him find the place in the hymnal and treated him as if he were one of them. From that moment it was his church. In the course of time he became a deacon and eventually went into the ministry.

From then on Tenth always had a small number of blacks, although never very many. Some of these took leadership positions in the church. Donald always felt that the ones who did come were sent by the Lord for a special purpose.

As we left the snow behind, embarking on our trip south for the winter conference tour, I asked Donald what he was going to say about the race issue in these meetings.

"Marge, you know I've never preached against behavior.

I'll do what I've always done: magnify the Lord Jesus Christ, get His Word into their hearts, and let *Him* do the work. You know how this worked with Doug, who had been so prejudiced against the blacks and the Jews. I didn't have to say a word against his attitudes. The Holy Spirit within him gave him a love and concern for all men, especially for those toward whom he had been most prejudiced. I'm counting on the Holy Spirit to do that same work in all who hear me. But I don't expect it to happen tomorrow!"

And so it happened, in Salisbury, North Carolina; in Atlanta, Georgia; in Chattanooga, Tennessee; in Birmingham, Alabama. I was amazed at the tact the Holy Spirit gave him, when the bull could have so easily wrecked the china shop.

In Birmingham we were invited to stay with Doug's sister, Eleanor Bell Page, and her husband George ("Buzzy"). Donald decided a motel would be more conducive to plowing through the workload he had that week, but we did accept their invitatioin to dinner in a restaurant not far from the church where Donald was preaching.

While we were waiting for dinner to be served, Eleanor lit a cigarette. Donald looked at her through the curl of smoke and asked, "Do you want to stop smoking?"

My mind flew back to that trip Doug and I had made with DGB. Doug had been under deep conviction that his smoking was offensive to the Holy Spirit indwelling him, a *Holy* Spirit. At dinner one night DGB had said, as he watched the smoke drift up from that cigarette resting on the edge of the ashtray, "You *can* overcome your problem, Doug. All you have to do is say no to your sin and yes to the Lord."

To that Doug had shaken his head. "I want to stop smoking, but I just can't." He started to reach for the cigarette.

DGB had said, "Let me see you open your hand." Doug's right hand stopped in mid-air and opened to a wide stretch as he looked quizzically at DGB. Then Doug picked up the cigarette and inhaled deeply.

"All right," said DGB, "every time you find a cigarette in your hand, just go like *that,*" and he opened his hand as Doug had done.

Puzzled, Doug started to transfer the cigarette to his left hand, preparatory to opening his right hand. DGB stopped him.

"Oh, no, not that way!" he cried. "Just open your hand!" DGB meant for Doug to open his *cigarette* hand, so that the cigarette would fall out. Doug, seeing the point, ground out the cigarette and said, "It just isn't that easy!"

Now DGB was confronting Doug's sister with the same question: "Do you want to stop smoking?"

Eleanor answered, "Yes! Ever since I began!" She put out her cigarette, then immediately lit another.

Donald continued to look at her steadily. "Are you a Christian?"

"Yes!" Her voice was defiant.

"Is your body the temple of the Holy Spirit?"

"Yes!"

"Knowing that cigarette smoke can cause cancer, are you deliberately defiling the temple of the Holy Spirit?"

Her answer was to grind out that cigarette, then compulsively light another. Donald pressed his point: "Better read the rest of that verse. First Corinthians 3:17 says, 'If any man defile the temple of God, him shall God destroy; for the temple of God is holy, which temple ye are.' If you really want to stop, just *stop.*"

Through the haze of smoke surrounding her, she said, "Dr. Barnhouse, have you ever smoked?"

"No," he replied, "I haven't."

Dead silence.

Eleanor lit another cigarette. You could almost see the smoke coming out her ears—and it wasn't cigarette smoke. She was obviously in a rage. I heard her mutter under her breath, "Meddling old man!"

Buzzy, who had been watching this interchange with amusement, looked at his watch and said, "Dr. Barnhouse, the deacons want you to join them in prayer before the service. I think we had better get going." He rose, squeezed Eleanor's shoulder affectionately, gave her some money, and asked her to take care of the bill, then steered Donald toward the coat room. Eleanor's baleful glance followed them.

That was the last week of January. We didn't hear from them until the end of April, when a note came from Eleanor, ecstatic over some of Donald's books we had sent them. In the course of the letter, Eleanor wrote, "Donald, I was furious with you for exposing my bad habit, but I prayed that if you were right the Holy Spirit would *make* me stop smoking. You must have been right, for I haven't smoked since."

Visiting her some time later, I got the full story as she told it to a group of us. Starting with what had happened in the restaurant, she continued: "So I stuffed what was left of my pack of cigarettes into my handbag, and Marge and I stood in line to pay the bill. By the time we reached the church the message had already begun. I slipped into a seat just in time to hear repeated verbatim our dinner table conversation! I could feel myself going stone white. That was the first time I had ever been preached at from the pulpit. I don't remember what the message was. How *dare* he accept our hospitality and then turn on me like that!

"At home, on my knees, I told the Lord, 'I can't stand that man. I don't want to do anything he says. But if he was speaking for You, Lord, and if he's right, then You will have to do the whole taking away, because I can't. I give it to You. Do whatever You want.'

"That was the first time I ever surrendered anything to anyone. There had never before been a problem I couldn't solve myself. Well, He didn't take away the *desire,* but He diverted my normal habits that involved cigarette smoking, step-by-step, moment by moment. I'd reach for a cigarette and the telephone would ring, or the doorbell; or one of the children would need me, and I'd hurry off without the cigarette. He just kept diverting me until I was no longer in the habit! What a Savior!"

The New Year's Resolution was now being challenged by what Donald called the "ultra-fundamentalists" and the "hyper-dispensationalists": "Are you going to extend the hand of fellowship to us too?" In the past he had sharply criticized them for being separatists, dividing the body of Christ along doctrinal lines. He admitted that he himself used to do this, but as he had progressed in his studies in the Book of Romans for the radio broadcasts the Holy Spirit had been convicting him that he had no right thus to judge his brother: "To his own Master he standeth or falleth."

In the September 1957 *Eternity*, Donald had published an article entitled "Thanksgiving and Warning," in which he outlined his present stand: Premillenarian? Yes. Dispensationalist? No. Asked why he was unwilling to identify himself as a dispensationalist when he obviously was one, he said, "The dispensationa*lists* insist on separation from those who don't agree with them. I can accept them as Christian brothers, but I am not one with them on the basis of separation. Dispensationa*l*? Well, it's a matter of semantics. If by 'dispensations' you mean the different ages in which God has tested men by various means, let's just call them 'tests' and agree that there has never been but one way of salvation: by grace through faith plus nothing. In that case, yes, I believe this. But if you say that the means of salvation varied from test to test, I do not believe this and never have. In the Old Testament, faith in the shed blood of Christ was represented by the slaying of a lamb. In the New Testament it is faith in the same shed blood, that poured-out life of Christ as our substitute, that brings salvation."

At Tenth he began a series of sermons on these "tests." When he got to the final test, "The Millennium," he summed up the others that had gone before:

"Remember, the purpose of these tests was to demonstrate to man that he could not be good without God. Jesus did not say, 'Without Me you can't do very much.' He said flatly, 'Without Me ye can do nothing.' When God put the man and the woman in the Garden of Eden, they were perfect. Their wills were in tune with God's will. The test: 'Believe Me. Obey My word. Don't eat of this one tree, for if you do, you will surely die.' They disobeyed. The judgment was immediate *spiritual* death (i.e., separation from God) and eventual *physical* death. But note this: As they were being put out of the Garden, God showed the way back to fellowship with Him: He killed an animal (and I believe it was a lamb), shed its blood, and clothed them with its skin, symbolizing the future coming of the 'seed of the woman,' Jesus, who would shed His blood to pay for our disobedience, then clothe us in His righteousness.

"So now willful disobedience (sin) had entered the world and had become a part of the human make-up. They now knew the difference between right and wrong, good and evil. The next test: Conscience. 'You know what is right. Do it.' But Cain, knowing it was wrong, killed Abel, and by the time of Noah, Genesis 6:5 tells us 'every imagination of the thoughts of [man's] heart was only evil continually.' They failed the test, all but Noah, who preached the way of salvation *for 120 years,* and still they would not turn to God. The judgment: the flood. The first thing Noah did when he stepped out of the Ark was to build an altar and offer the sacrifices that showed he believed God's Word.

" 'But, God,' someone could have said, 'You wouldn't let us judge sin. You put a mark on Cain and wouldn't let us punish him.'

" 'Very well,' said God, 'you may now govern yourselves. Whoso sheddeth man's blood, by *man* shall his blood be shed.' So the next test was Human Government. Result: Man said, 'I can do it all by myself. I don't need God,' and he tried to establish a civilization without God at Babel. The judgment: the confusion of languages, resulting in many separate nations. Don't forget that nationality is a curse from God, and no attempt to unite the nations can succeed apart from God.

"After that God let mankind go its own self-centered way and chose to work through one man, Abraham. He said, 'Abram, go out to a land I will show you, and I'll make of you a great nation.' Everywhere he went, Abraham built an altar to God and made the appropriate sacrifice. As long as he obeyed, all went well. But he left the place of blessing and landed in Egypt. Years later the judgment was slavery in Egypt for his descendants.

"When these 'Children of Israel' asked, 'But God, how were we to know Your will?' God answered, 'Here is My will' and gave them the Ten Commandments. 'But,' said God, 'I know you cannot keep them.' So at the same time that He gave Moses He gave Aaron the priest; at the same time that he gave the Law He gave the lamb whose shed blood would cover their sin until the Lamb with a capital *L* would come and wash that sin away. They promised, 'Oh, yes, we'll keep the Commandments,' but immediately broke them. Over and over God warned them through His prophets. When they listened and obeyed and brought the sacrifices that foreshadowed Christ there was blessing. When they went their own way they were in trouble. Finally God sent His own sinless Son. They rejected Him and killed Him (and our civilization today would do the same thing). Their judgment was the destruction of Jerusalem and the scattering of the Jews throughout the nations.

" 'But God, You knew we couldn't keep Your Law,' they might have complained. 'I know—that's why I gave you the sacrificial lamb, so you could show you believed My word that sin means death. Now I'm through with the Temple, the shewbread, the candlesticks, the incense, the altar, the animal sacrifice. I have torn the veil of the Temple in two *from top to bottom*. My sinless Son has become the supreme sacrifice. I count His poured-out life a full and sufficient sacrifice: your sins are paid for. Next test: Believe this, and receive Him into your life, and I will make you

My sons and daughters. If you will not believe this, then you will be cast away from Me forever.' 'You mean—I don't have to *do* anything? Just believe?' 'That's right.' 'But then I won't get any credit.' 'That's right. I will not give My glory to another. If you try to add one iota of your filthy works as a part payment on your salvation, I'll subtract Christ. Just believe My word, and prove that you believe it by receiving Him into your life as your Savior.'

"Well, it has been almost two thousand years since God said that. We are now in what is called 'the day of grace.' But that day is running out. When it does, God will remove all believers from this earth. Then, as Jesus Himself tells us in Matthew 24, there shall be poured out on this earth 'a great tribulation such as was not since the beginning of the world to this time, no, nor ever shall be.' This ends with the battle of Armageddon, at the height of which Jesus will return, not as the lowly Savior, but as the conquering King to rule with a rod of iron and bring the last and final test, which we will consider tonight: the millennium.

"You see, man might say, 'But God, I couldn't help disobeying You: the Devil made me do it.' Well, the Devil never made anyone do it: he can only tempt you to do it. 'All right,' says God, 'I'll remove the Devil and shut him up for a thousand years. I'll have peace on the earth.' The lion will lie down with the lamb; there will be a perfect environment, with the desert blooming like the rose, two chickens in every pot and two cars in every garage. If anyone tries to sin, an angel will be right there to keep him from it. Death will be so rare that the sacrifices will be reinstituted in the rebuilt Temple at Jerusalem, as a memorial, so people will know what My Son has done for them. Jesus will be right there for all to see and know in His divine majesty. But will people be happy? They'll still want their own way instead of God's way, and they won't be able to blame it on the Devil. The drunk will reach for the bottle: an angel will grab his wrist and say, 'Sorry, Buddy.' A couple will want to commit adultery: an angel will stand between them, preventing it, reminding them of God's righteousness. A man will hate to the point of murder: an angel will flip the gun out of his hand. Far from being the utopia it has been pictured, for these people who still insist on their own way, the millennium will be the most horrible time in the history of mankind. It will be like the time a man came running full speed to the dock, jumped on board a boat just as it was pulling away, finally caught his breath, and said to a man standing by who had given him a hand, 'Well, I made it! I'll be there in time for the third race!' only to find that he had jumped on board a harbor cruise ship taking a Sunday school group on an all-day outing.

" 'Oh, *no!* Well, where's the bar?' 'The bar is closed.' 'Oh, this is awful!' He finds the captain and tries to bribe him to turn back and let him off. 'Mister,' says the captain, 'We're fifteen minutes out. It would take fifteen minutes to take you back, then another fifteen to return to where we are now, which would take half an hour of these kids' day. I won't do it.' So there he is, trapped, with Sunday school songs ringing around him, and innocent games, and wholesome food and drink. Does he say, 'Oh, how sweet. This is for me.' No, he does not. When the ship docks that evening he can hardly wait to jump off and head for the nearest bar.

"That's the millennium. Man will be tested to see if he will do God's will, with no excuse for not doing it, and he will still want his own way. At the end of the thousand years the Devil is loosed for a little season and people will flock to him by the thousands, saying, 'Thank God for the Devil!' joining him in a final battle against the forces of righteousness. Then comes the Last Judgment, after which God will create a new heaven and a new earth wherein dwelleth righteousness.

"But those of us who have believed His Word that without Him we can do nothing, who have received Jesus as our Savior, have found that 'we can do all things through Christ who strengthens' us. We will be heirs of God, joint-heirs with Christ, reigning with Him during the millennium and throughout the ages to come. Our old sinful nature will be gone forever and our delight will be to do His will.

"Oh, come now to this Savior, and receive all He wants to pour out on you in blessing!"

NINETEEN

When planning his schedule for 1958, Donald had included a time of concentrated study at the Spanish Language School in Costa Rica. However, there arose the possibility of visiting Red China for a first-hand look at the situation behind the Bamboo Curtain. His reporter's nose twitching, Donald was pursuing this possibility eagerly. Because the People's Republic of China was not recognized by our State Department at the time, the whole thing would have to be very low-key, and there was much red tape involved. This uncertainty upset his schedule to a point at which he finally wrote to Dr. Kenneth Strachan at the language school, postponing his studies there.

When the plans for China did not materialize, we went to Germany to see Dorothy and Uli's twins, who had arrived in April. This was a time of much-needed unwinding for Donald, with only one preaching engagement scheduled the entire time. In addition to our week with Dorothy and Uli in Marburg, we spent a whole week, leisurely, in each place we visited: Paris, Vienna, Brussels, and Amsterdam. We browsed through the great museums, went to concerts and symphonies, picnicked in the woods and beside picturesque rivers, took boat tours on the canals. We came home refreshed, he with important insights on the international scene and many new sermon illustrations, and I not only with new pictures for our "memory album," but with actual snapshots of a very proud granddaddy holding a twin on each shoulder.

That fall Donald spoke at the Rotary Club in Grand Rapids. He decided to record his talk, experimenting with a new recorder called "Midgetape," which ran on batteries and was much smaller and more portable than the bulky reel-to-reel machines we had been using. It's a good thing he did record it: the furor that speech caused had repercussions for weeks afterward, so it was helpful to have on tape exactly what he did say.

When he returned to our hotel afterward, we listened to the recording together. Donald had opened with some good-natured ribbing of the Rotarian who had introduced the guests, who himself had done some ribbing, then launched into "The Scales of God." Donald told me that as his talk had progressed the room had become quieter and quieter. Cigars died out unnoticed. Many looked as if a sledgehammer had hit them. When it was over, Ed Kuiper (who now was on the Foundation's board of directors and was making quite an impact on the Grand Rapids community) had said to him, "You've probably made some mortal enemies, but they can never stand before God and say they never heard."

The newspaper account was surprisingly accurate, summing up neatly what Donald had said. It pulled no punches:

NO EASY WAY UP
PREACHER TALKS TO ROTARY CLUB
ON TOPIC OF HIS LORD OF LIFE CRUSADE

"I am a definite believer in heaven and hell and that there are men in this room who will go to hell."

Dr. Donald Grey Barnhouse, speaking Thursday before the Grand Rapids Rotary Club in the Pantlind Hotel, soon made it clear that this gloomy prediction was not limited to his audience of the moment.

The pastor of Philadelphia's Tenth Presbyterian Church who is conducting the Lord of Life Crusade here this week compared the attainment of grace and salvation with the individual's being weighed against God's perfection. "If God demanded only 90 percent perfection, then heaven would be 10 percent dirty," he said.

WARNS AGAINST CONJECTURE

Conjecture on how salvation may be insured is a hazardous pastime, according to Dr. Barnhouse. "The fellow who says 'If God were just, He would do such and such,' is reeling God down from heaven and subjecting Him to the two-by-four supreme court of his mind and I say God will send him to hell.

"Resort to solutions suggested by history, tradition, and personal experience is equally futile," he continued. The ultimate test is being weighed against God's perfection, and earthly character as we understand it is weightless; "your character can take you to hell, but not to heaven," he said.

The report continued, summarizing several of Donald's illustrations and concluding with his quoting of two lines of a hymn: "My hope is built on nothing less than Jesus' blood and righteousness."

After reading it I said, "But Donald, on the tape you said that there were men there who would be in hell, *and you were going to show them how to get out of this.* Unless they realize that was what you were doing they'll miss the whole point. The reporter should have given the whole quote, right there at the beginning."

The following week, *Spokes O' the Wheel,* the Rotary weekly news bulletin, showed that the message had hit home but the point had indeed been missed by many.

Two weeks later someone sent Donald a clipping from that week's *Spokes O' the Wheel,* which said, "In introducing the guests John Collins called attention to his new suit. He said it was made of asbestos and after what Dr.

Barnhouse had said about Rotarians going to hell he thought he should be prepared. President Sam asked him where he got the suit because he felt he, too, needed one."

That same week, in Muskegon, during the preliminaries of the Kiwanis Club meeting where Donald was to be the speaker, a rousing song was sung about "The King of the Cannibal Islands" who "dined on clergymen cold and raw"—and died as a result!

It was early on a Sunday evening, the end of October. Donald was hard at work in his office at the Foundation. After his nap, thoroughly refreshed, he had plunged into research on an idea for his evening sermon. He tracked down word meanings and compared the translation of a Bible passage in different languages, his typewriter chattering happily as he found what he needed. I fixed some supper and fed him at his work, and he didn't even know he had eaten.

At about seven-thirty he pulled his sermon notes triumphantly from the typewriter. "There!" he said. "And it's a good one!" He glanced over them, folded the paper, and slid it into his inside breast pocket. As he stood and stretched, I perched his hat on his head and stood ready with his overcoat. As he began to put his arms into the coat sleeves he stepped through his office doorway to the hall. He looked so pleased with himself I couldn't resist taking him down a peg: "Preach in love and *humility!*"

He wheeled around toward me, and I could tell I was about to get one of his I'll-show-you-who's-boss-around-here kisses, but in a flash his feet went out from under him on the newly waxed floor. His arms, half into the coat sleeves, were useless to break the fall, and in a moment he was face down on the floor, a widening pool of blood pouring from his nose.

I yanked off the coat, tossed it aside, grabbing his pocket handkerchief to staunch the flow of blood as I helped him to his knees. Groggy, he got to his feet and went to the bathroom basin: the blood continued to flow. I fished the ice out of his water glass, wrapped it in a piece of paper towel, shoved it under his upper lip and made him come sit in his swivel chair with his head back, as I called the church office.

Within minutes the study was crowded with elders and doctors from his congregation. He directed proceedings like a wounded general of the army: "Fred, you lead the singing—go! Get them started!" Fred left. He named another: "You preside, tell them I've been delayed, I'll get over as soon as I can."

"Ralph, you—" He sat bolt upright, with a look of bewilderment. "Where am I? What are you fellows doing here?" One of the doctors took him by the shoulders and gently pressed him back into his semi-reclining position. "You've had a fall and a bad nosebleed. Just relax. Everything's under control." Expert fingers probed gently across his face, his nose, his forehead.

"Marge, take him to University Hospital for X-rays as soon as the service is over—I'll make an appointment. He may have a broken nose. But everything seems to be all right otherwise. Let's have a round of prayer." Fervent voices thanked their Lord in brief prayer; all but two or three then left; by a little after eight Donald was in the pulpit. And it *was* a "good one."

Ralph Lingle, a Philadelphia policeman, was waiting to drive us to the hospital. I had never before whizzed through the streets in a police car, sirens screaming. Despite the pain of a nose that was indeed broken, Donald was loving it, enjoying "special privilege" as if he had not just preached against the pride of life!

During this whole year the pressure of getting out the gospel, through foreign magazines, through his spoken and written word, through the radio, "that he might by all means save some," weighed heavily on Donald. He determined that the time had definitely come for him to retire from Tenth Church and go into full-time writing and conference work. The church had functioned well with him there only twenty-six Sundays out of the year, first under Dwight Small, and now under Ed Houk. It would do even better with a full-time pastor. He informed the church leadership of his intentions (emphasizing that it was *definite* this time), and asked them to appoint a pastor-seeking committee as soon as possible. This was done half-heartedly; they didn't believe he really meant it. He had been at Tenth for thirty-three years; of course he wouldn't leave them.

As 1958 had progressed, Donald had become more and more convinced Americans needed to realize that on the clock of time it was past the eleventh hour and approaching twelve. He began preaching a series of sermons on current events in the light of the Bible, teaching what the Bible said about the rise of Russia and the Powers of the North. He wrote an article that appeared later in the May 1959 *Eternity,* in which he said:

"Sit down with your family today and talk calmly about what to do if a missile strikes *near* you. If you are under a direct hit, you will be in heaven. But if you are at a point where you have time to get away, arrange with your family where you will leave news of your whereabouts. Families will be separated. It may be weeks—or months—before any mail can be delivered, but do the best you can. Keep a pair of low-heeled shoes in the car. Gas will run out if you are driving; and there will not be another drop; main roads will be closed for defense purposes. . . .

"We do not know what is in the future. But always remember *Who* is in the future. There shall be wars and rumors of war; see that ye be not troubled."

Donald began preparing a four-part series of articles for *Eternity* on the second coming of Christ. It was during this period that I began to be aware of a change in our prayer life. When he ended our morning prayer, he would say musingly, "Maybe He'll come today." At night, it was "Maybe He'll be here before morning." Little by little this changed to part of the prayer itself: "Lord, maybe You'll come today!" and "Lord, You didn't come today, but maybe it will be before morning!" I felt a rising excitement.

Long ago when his preaching had first exploded into our lives there in Florida, he had said, "Plan as if the Lord were not coming again for a thousand years—but *live* as if He were coming tonight! If you *knew* He were coming at a given moment today, would it change your way of living? What would you be doing differently? Would you be ashamed to have Him find you doing what you are doing?" I think this gave new perspective to many of us and changed many of our priorities, but now suddenly the imminence of His actual return became real. He really could come at any moment. Though He might not come for a thousand years —*He could come at any moment!*

This feeling of urgency seemed to spur Donald on to an even more prodigious amount of work, to even more drive and power and capacity. Joyful anticipation of each day, being a conscious part of the implementation of God's great plan, was both exhilarating and sobering. For me this added a new dimension to living: a tip-toe expectancy, an urgency for the task of each day. There might not be a tomorrow, and would I really be glad to see Him, at any moment? *(Lord, may I not be ashamed at Thy coming. Lord, establish Thou my priorities.)*

A four-day Bible conference at a small church in Radnor had been tucked into the schedule for the first week in December. The last night tragedy struck: the youngest of the pastor's thirteen children, a toddler, was accidentally drowned in the bathtub. Someone's callous remark, "Oh, well—they have twelve others," brought tears to Donald's eyes. He gathered the family together and told them about the arithmetic of Job: in the opening chapter we are told that Job had *seven* sons and *three* daughters, plus *seven thousand* sheep, *three thousand* camels, *five hundred* yoke of oxen, and *five hundred* she-asses, all of which were swept away. In the last chapter, in verse ten, after much tribulation, "the Lord gave Job *twice as much* as he had before." The text enumerates: *fourteen thousand* sheep, *six thousand* camels, *a thousand* yoke of oxen, and *a thousand* she-asses, doubling the number given in the first chapter. Then verse thirteen says, "He had also *seven* sons and *three* daughters." Why not *fourteen* sons and *six* daughters? Because he had never *lost* the first ones: they were alive in heaven! "And that's where your little sister is. Whenever anyone asks how many children are in the family, say, 'Thirteen: twelve here and one in heaven.' "

At Tenth the Sunday School Curriculum Committee had, with DGB's blessing, been doing an exhaustive study of available Sunday school materials. They were seeking literature which was faithful to the Reformed tradition and trying to correlate what would be used in order to give continuity from grade to grade instead of letting each teacher choose what suited him or her. Narrowing down the field, they had finally concluded that at the elementary and junior high levels, the material of the Presbyterian Church in the U.S.A. was superior to all the rest—and that included the various denominational, nondenominational, and evangelical sources. But for years DGB had blasted this "Faith and Life" curriculum, in the magazine and from the pulpit; he had warned his hearers away from it and had said, "I wouldn't have it in my church." How was this committee to get him to reconsider it?

Finally, one member of the committee challenged him to read some of the material, then sit down with the men who were responsible for it and discuss it with them. Would he, in all fairness, do this? Reluctantly, Donald agreed.

So it was arranged. Donald dug into the box of "Faith and Life" material the committee had supplied and skimmed it, making copious marginal notes. At the meeting, following Donald's formula, they first discussed the points of agreement. Then for a good half-hour Donald held forth on what was wrong with the material. The men representing "Faith and Life" listened patiently, then refuted Donald's arguments, showing how the main problem was not one of scriptural fidelity, but of Reformed versus Dispensational theology. From then on it became a dialogue instead of a monologue, and both sides profited from it. At the end Donald agreed to have Tenth Church try the "Faith and Life" curriculum up to the high school level, where higher criticism began to be evident. Back home, he made a second examination of the material, this time looking for its virtues.

That was December 30. On New Year's Eve, after the watchnight service at Tenth, we started west on the 1959 conference tour.

This year's circuit took us, in reverse order, to almost the same cities the 1958 tour had covered. We started in Oklahoma, beginning with Tulsa, then Bartlesville, Muskogee, and El Reno.

In each of his 1959 conferences that winter, Donald's theme was "Faith for a Day of Missiles and Bombs," undergirding the fearful with the Everlasting Arms, but showing the obligation of those in whom Christ was dwelling to show forth "the Word made flesh" to those around them, no matter what the circumstances.

To watch these sermons evolve was, to me, intriguing. They were first preached at Tenth Church, where, except for Thanksgiving, Christmas, and Easter, he rarely did topical preaching, but based his sermons on verse-by-verse Bible exposition.

The advantage of this was that no one had hurt feelings when he came to a passage that castigated: they realized it was all in the course of God's message to them and learned from it. Out of this verse-by-verse exposition would come some very outstanding sermons. These he would preach on Monday nights in his New York Bible class. By this time they were tightened up and streamlined, and the best of these he would use in his Bible conference tours.

In his conferences the question and answer session before the sermon each night was a unique feature. Every once in a while I'd hand in a question myself, for otherwise it might never get answered! His choice of Communist China's leader, Mao Tse Tung, as *Eternity's* 1958 Man of the Year had to be explained over and over: DGB's Man of the Year wasn't necessarily the *best* man of the year, but the person who had most influenced history, whether for good or for bad.

After the final meeting in Atlanta, the pastor was thanking Donald for his ministry and commented with a laugh, "My preaching will seem awfully quiet next Sunday." Donald answered, "Wait a minute. Remember that after the thunder and the lightning came the still, small voice, and the Lord spoke through that still, small voice!"

In March, while we were still on tour, the Bible Study Hour celebrated its tenth year on the air. An interesting little booklet commemorating the event gave its history, its purpose, and an informal snapshot with a brief vignette of each of the staff and their work, accompanied by an appropriate Bible verse. A copy of this was forwarded to us from the office. Donald perused it and said, "Who would have thought that a man could spend ten years in one book of the Bible, and still have treasures to dig from it!"

Of course what he really was doing was an exposition of the whole Bible, based on the Book of Romans. His system, as explained in the preface of volume one of the messages in book form, was "to take the whole Bible and place the point of it, like an inverted pyramid, on that passage, so that the weight of the entire Word rests upon a single verse, or indeed, a single word."

What eventually turned out to be a ten-volume set was later reissued in four fat volumes. Into the preparation of each of these messages went many hours of concentrated study. I remember one in particular, on that winter tour, when he had been at it since immediately after lunch, utterly absorbed. It was far past time for his usual afternoon break and rest—dared I interrupt?

He raised his head slowly, closed his eyes, put back his

head and took several slow, deep breaths. Then he shook his head, as one awaking from a dream, sighed, and turned back to the typewriter.

"What is it, Donald?" I was alarmed.

He turned to me, as one still partially in that dream.

"Oh, Marge . . . this Book! I was doing some routine checking for the Romans passage I'm working on, and I ran into something in Isaiah. . . ." He took another deep breath. "I feel as though I have been methodically exploring the central passageway of a complex cave. Then that Isaiah passage caught my eye. It was like a crevasse beside my passageway, into which I peered, out of curiosity. Then I let myself down into it—and suddenly I was in a chamber glinting with crystal, dazzling, going up and up and out and out. I so longed to explore it—but that was not the passageway I was assigned to follow. So I withdrew to where I had been; I had to keep on with my assigned task. But, oh! someday I shall return and really get to the far reaches of that chamber."

Again he shook his head. Then under his disciplined fingers the typewriter keys began to respond, slowly at first, then faster and faster as his mind returned to the assigned passageway.

For months we had been looking forward to a trip to South America. Donald had bought Spanish phonograph records with accompanying grammar books over which he pored in his spare moments. The phonograph records were turned on first thing in the morning after our devotions, and sounded in our ears as we dressed and prepared for the day. Although unable to translate the Spanish into English, I found myself beginning to *understand* the recorded conversations. I suppose this is how a baby learns any language. We set apart a certain time each day for me to drill Donald in grammar, so I learned a little from that too. Speaking through an interpreter is frustrating at best; Donald wanted to communicate directly if possible. In Brazil, where Portuguese is spoken, he would of course have to use an interpreter.

Our itinerary was now settled. Donald would attend the World Alliance of Reformed Churches, in Saõ Paulo, Brazil, as an accredited visitor, the last week in July and the first week in August. The rest of the trip was planned around that. We were to visit sophisticated cities and fly over vast jungles and great rivers into remote tribes with one of our missionaries in a little Cessna 220. We would visit all ten of the South American republics, making important contacts for the Literature Project and holding meetings in many places.

One day in mid–May we were in Donald's study, tracing our route on a map of South America. It was sounding more and more exciting. The element of danger made it even more challenging.

I heard the timer in the kitchen ring, and rose to put a casserole on the table. He stood and stretched. I paused and then spoke aloud something that had been bothering me.

"Donald, if that little missionary plane we'll be in should go down in the jungle, they'd never find us. That would be the end, wouldn't it?"

He nodded but smiled as if it couldn't happen.

"Darling," I said, "you *must* make a proper will! That scrap of paper in your dresser drawer would never be valid. It really isn't fair to your children or mine to leave them with the legal mess of dying intestate. My will gives you the use of any or all of my worldly goods until you no longer need them, then all reverts to my children. You should do the same for your children."

"But the Farm is already theirs, in irrevocable trust. I don't have anything else."

"What about the furniture, and your china and crystal and silver from your first marriage that should be willed to your children? If you should die intestate, that would come to me or be sold so the state would have its intestate share. That's not right, Donald."

Seeing my seriousness, he, too, became serious.

"I suppose it could happen. All right, I'll take care of it this week."

Hearing him say the words, "It could happen," made the possibility suddenly imminent. For a moment I panicked.

"Oh, Donald! What would I ever do without you!"

He grasped my shoulders. "Listen, Marge! You lean on the Lord, and I'll lean on the Lord, and then no matter what happens we'll each still have our Leaning Post!"

Then swiftly he drew me to him, one arm shielding my shoulders, his other hand protecting my head as if from an invisible blow. An agonized prayer wrenched from him: "But, oh, Lord, don't put us to the test! Don't put us to the test!"

TWENTY

It was Sunday morning, May 31, a sizzling hot day. Donald would preach at Tenth Church, then we would go to the airport, board one of the new airplanes called "jets" —only the second of such flights ever made!—and be in Rio de Janeiro the next morning. Imagine traveling in one night a distance that years ago took months by sailing ship!

Donald stood to preach. "In thinking of the dangers of the coming trip, I began wondering what I would wish to have said if this were my last sermon in Tenth."

The congregation stirred uneasily. Dangers? Last sermon?

"We'll be flying in a little missionary plane over great jungles. I just might not come back. Or the Lord could return before I see you again." He stepped forward in the pulpit as he spoke. Suddenly sparks and smoke arose around him. Some in the congregation rose to their feet, fear, apprehension, and joy chasing across faces at the thought that the Lord could be coming right now!

Ed Houk, seated behind him on the platform, could see what was happening: Donald had stepped on the worn old wires to the ancient electric fans under the pulpit; they were shorting out. Ed rushed to unplug the fans as Donald stepped back out of the way. The sparks stopped; the smoke drifted away. Donald reassured his congregation: "For a minute there I thought I might not even start on this trip! Apparently I stepped on some wires. Everything's all right now." He then resumed his sermon.

(What would he wish to have preached, if this were indeed his last sermon? The sovereignty of God.)

South America! How astounding it was for me to be living the adventures I had read about in books and dreamed about all my life, but never thought I'd realize!

Donald was asked to be one of the speakers for a convocation of leaders of more than eighty Protestant missionary societies, gathered to celebrate the one-hundredth anniversary of Protestant missions in Brazil. What a master of adaptability he was! At the convocation he gave a doctrinal study in depth; a few weeks later, when we were visiting an Indian tribe in the heart of the jungle, he gave one of the simple stories he had used on TV, one that could translate easily and reach any age group and any culture. He told me afterward that it was a strange feeling to preach in English, then have our missionary host translate what he said, sentence by sentence, into Portuguese (the official language of Brazil) after which a bilingual Indian interpreter put it, sentence by sentence, into the tribal tongue. It made him wonder what his audience actually heard! But the response was positive and joyful.

Outside of Portuguese Brazil, wherever we went Donald would ask our hosts to converse with him in Spanish, so he could practice the language. After a while it began to come easily. In Buenos Aires, he finally attempted a sermon directly in Spanish. He explained to his audience beforehand that this was his first try, and asked their indulgence. Our host helped him when occasionally he was stuck, but it went fairly well, in an atmosphere of eager acceptance. Donald was elated.

"But I must, must, *must* get to language school," he told

me. "It's all right to converse in Spanish, and make a few mistakes, but it's risky to *preach* in another language unless you really know the theological terms. Did I ever tell you what happened to me the first time I tried to preach in French?

"I began to learn the language when I was in Brussels with the Belgian Gospel Mission. Out walking with my professor one day, I was arguing, 'Why should *things* have gender, in French? Why is "table" feminine, and "chair" masculine? Why. . . .'

"My professor stopped stock still, and looked up into my face, shaking his finger at me for emphasis.

" 'Monsieur,' he said, 'une langue, c'est *un fait!'* (A language is a fact.)

"After that I didn't question, but learned French just as it is, even though it seemed illogical.

"But how that business of neuter things having gender did get me into trouble! When I was in France I was asked to speak at a boys' school. *'I'll do it directly in French,'* I thought; *'I'm pretty good at it now.'*

"So I got up and began to give my testimony. But I hadn't realized that the word for 'faith' and the word for 'liver' sound exactly alike, although one is feminine and the other is masculine. Possessive pronouns and articles (a, an, the) must agree in gender with the noun.

"I told them how when I was in my early teens I had had strong faith. Only, I actually said, in French, 'liver.' I proceeded to tell how for a while I lost my liver, then later the Lord brought me back and my liver was stronger than ever . . . well, you can imagine how funny this was to the boys, and how humiliating for cocky young me when I found out what they were laughing at! Never again, unless I *know* what I'm saying!"

The staff of the Evangelical Foundation had been rapidly expanding. In January, William J. Petersen had come to us as managing editor of *Eternity,* of which Russ Hitt was now editor, with DGB editor-in-chief. Antha Card was DGB's editorial secretary, editing his *Romans* series and other writings. In October, Herbert Henry Ehrenstein, who for two years had written the Sunday school commentary for *Eternity* and frequently reviewed books, became a contributing editor and full member of the staff. In the expanding Bible conference ministry he was to join DGB, Ralph Keiper, and Walter Martin in conference work. Herb, like Ralph, knew Greek and Hebrew well, and, like Ralph, did research for DGB. He tells me that he and DGB had a tacit understanding, never actually discussed: Herb would hear DGB coming down the hall with a visitor he obviously wanted to impress. DGB's voice would boom, "Now in the next office is our Greek expert." He would open the door, and there would be Herb, surrounded by Greek reference books, regardless of what he had been doing moments before. If DGB said, "Our Hebrew expert," Herb would hastily pull down his Hebrew reference books!

Meanwhile, Donald's four-part series in *Eternity,* "What Is the World Coming To?" beginning in the August issue, was again sounding the warning, "It is later than you think." Over and over in his church he was telling women to keep a supply of dehydrated food on hand and a pair of low-heeled shoes in the trunk of the car, because the international situation was truly serious. The bombs could fall.

Tenth Church's young adults couldn't take it seriously. A song about "Dried Beans and Walking Shoes" evolved at one of their meetings and was sung with gusto behind DGB's back.

In fact, DGB didn't want people to be frightened or pessimistic, just prepared. *Watch* and wait. The last paragraph of his 1959 Survey of the Year read: "It would seem that the one who had had the most influence on world movements as a whole is Khrushchev. From a secular point of view he is probably the man of the year. I have called President Eisenhower the man of the decade.

"Over it all, thank God, thank God, is the man of all Eternity, the Lord Jesus Christ. Though all is wrong with the world, God is in His heaven. From there He rules and from there the Lord Jesus Christ continues to make Himself known in the hearts of all those who trust in Him. Event of the year in the spiritual realm is that there has been peace that passes all understanding in the lives of numberless believers who were going through all the trials the race is capable of knowing, and finding in Christ the fullness of joy and peace. To Him be the glory!"

It seemed that 1960 was rushing toward us. Donald finally squeezed his annual physical check-up with Dr. Thomas Durant into his schedule just before Christmas.

The weather reports were ominous, so immediately after the service on the Sunday night following Christmas we drove back to the Farm, packed the car, and were on the Pennsylvania Turnpike going west by eleven P.M. for another winter conference tour. We pushed on until after two A.M., fighting heavy snow before stopping for the night. We arrived in El Paso, Texas, on New Year's Day, 1960, for the first week of meetings.

A wire from Tom Durant awaited us, telling Donald to have extensive blood tests as soon as possible: his blood sugar was dangerously high; he might have diabetes. Donald pooh-poohed it, but finally did have tests done the following week.

When the results of the tests had arrived, Tom called us. Donald did indeed have a diabetic condition that at this stage could probably be controlled by diet. Tom had sent a diet sheet to our next stop, San Diego, and Donald had to adhere to it strictly. Donald groaned. Everywhere we went, people invited us to lavish dinners. This would be difficult.

Saturday we packed up and drove on toward San Diego. We had been carrying with us the pot containing one of the giant amaryllis bulbs which friends in Michigan had sent him. It had sprouted in early December. Donald had watched its progress with fatherly solicitude; he couldn't bear to leave it behind. It had gone with us into the various motels; it had been shielded from the bitter cold, then from too much sun as we reached the South. Now it posed a problem. We were stopped at the California State line and asked if we had any plant material with us. We couldn't have denied it even if we had wanted to; there it sat on the floor by the back seat, its newly formed bud beginning to show color. Donald got out of the car, lifted it out, and showed it to the inspector.

"Here's all we have," he said, "and isn't it going to be a beauty? We'll be on the road for several months, and decided to take it with us to enjoy."

The inspector looked at it dubiously, then at me, then at Donald.

"It ought to go into quarantine," he said, the emphasis on the "ought," but with a hint of indecision. Donald immediately took the initiative.

"I'm Dr. Barnhouse. You may have heard me on the radio. I'll be preaching in cities all the way up the state. We'll just have it in our car or in our motel room: it couldn't possibly cause any crop damage, if that's what's bothering you. I'm sure it will be all right." Confidently he put the plant back in the car.

"I'll tell you what," said the inspector, "If that's all you're going to do with it I'll give you a safe-conduct for it, so all you'll have to do is show that to the inspector at the next station you pass through and you won't have any trouble. What did you say your name is?"

He went back into the station, typed up something on a sheet of orange memo paper, and handed it to Donald. "Good luck!" he said. Donald handed the paper to me, waved a cheery good-bye to the inspector, and drove off before the man could change his mind.

"What does it say?" he asked.

It read: "Dr. D. G. Barnhouse has in his car (113087 Pa.) one Amaryllis bulb (growing) eastbound that he wishes to take northbound through your station."

"Thank You, Lord," Donald whispered.

The diet sheet that awaited us in San Diego was not as restrictive as Donald had feared. The meats and vegetables on this list were fortunately things he really enjoyed. I juggled pots and pans and a one-burner hot plate in our motel room. Feeling somewhat unsanitary about it, I washed dishes in the bathroom sink. I thought of all my friends working effortlessly at home with all the "conveniences." But I wouldn't have changed places with them for anything in the world.

During this time, Donald was trying to stockpile as many of the Romans sermons as possible, so we could be free for a trip around the world the following year. One evening in San Diego, when we returned to the motel after the meeting, he went to his typewriter to continue where he had left off that afternoon.

I said, "Why don't you wait until tomorrow? It's so late."

"Can't," he replied. "This is almost done, then if I get at least one more started, I'll be on schedule with the 'Romans' broadcasts." Already, his fingers were busily tapping the keys. I finished preparing for bed just as he pulled the page out of the typewriter. I went over and rubbed the back of his neck as I looked over his shoulder. He was already stacking the page behind the others he had written, so I couldn't see what it was. Oh, well, tomorrow was time enough for that.

For a moment he relaxed, flexed his neck, enjoyed the rubbing. Then he stretched, and like a swimmer about to plunge into the water, breathed deeply as he reached for one of the "sandwiches" of paper, carbon, and copy paper I had prepared for him.

"What are you working on now?" I left him and perched on the side of the bed.

"Romans 15:1, 'We then that are strong ought to bear the infirmities of the weak, and not to please ourselves.' He took another deep breath, ran his hand wearily over his face, and said, as if to himself, "But who will bear the infirmities of the strong?" For a moment he leaned his forehead against the typewriter. I knew he was praying, so I slipped quietly under the covers, leaving him to draw strength from the One who bore all his infirmities.

Several hours later he woke me as he came to bed.

"Marge, I found something terrific! It isn't 'the strong ought to bear the infirmities of the weak,' but 'the strong ought to *bear with* the infirmities of the weak!' This is how the *Revised Standard Version* translates it, and I found that is what the Greek actually says. This puts a whole new light on things. I don't know how I missed it all these years."

At the San Diego meetings, Donald hit hard at error in false religions, but there was a new note. Back in the Sarasota meetings he had talked about lodges, for instance, saying something like this: "If you want to wear funny hats in a parade and have special handgrips and passwords and sit with a sick friend so he won't have to die alone, God bless you. But if you tell me you can get to heaven by living up to any society's obligations, I'll fight you all the way to the gates of hell and watch you go through." Now he was saying, "*. . . I'll plead with you all the way to the gates of hell, and weep as you go through.*"

Monday through Friday evening Donald preached on Ephesians. "Don't let the preachers who say this is the 'Holy of Holies of the Bible,' 'the highest truth,' 'the deepest teaching,' scare you into thinking this epistle is over your head. To whom was it written? *Baby* Christians who had just come out of paganism and didn't know anything about the Bible.

"Some years ago I was traveling in the Orient with a missionary friend. He asked what I thought should be taught to new believers. I told him *God* tells us, here, what He wants them to know. In Ephesians 1 we find Paul saying that *as soon as he heard of their faith* he prayed that the God of our Lord Jesus Christ, the Father of glory, would give them the spirit of wisdom and revelation in the knowledge of Him, that they might know three things: one, the second coming of Christ ('the hope of his calling'); two, how much we mean to Him ('the riches of the glory of *his* inheritance in the saints'—us!); and three, the power of the Resurrection, available to us. If this is God's elementary doctrine, we too should understand these things. Turn now to the beginning of the Epistle of Paul to the Ephesians."

In this epistle, Donald was in his element, glorifying God the Father through the Lord Jesus Christ, and in the Holy Spirit. Every verse was rich with things to be opened to our understanding, by illustrations, by word studies, by comparing Scripture with Scripture.

He asked us to look at Ephesians 2:1, where, in the *King James Version,* three words are in italics: *"hath he quickened."* The italics, he explained, were the translators' way of telling us those words were not in the original Greek, but had been supplied to "make sense." Without them you have a sentence without a verb: "And you, who were dead in trespasses and sins."

He told how, when he had first studied this epistle in depth, he had decided to find the verb God intended for that sentence. Tracking back through the preceding verses, he had discovered it in verse 19. Here Paul ransacks the Greek vocabulary for words for which the English translation has only one word, "power." He wanted these new believers to know "what is the exceeding greatness of his power toward us who believe, according to the working of his mighty power, which he wrought *in* Christ, when he raised him from the dead. . . ." For the next three verses Paul goes into one of his great doxologies, then comes to chapter 2, verse 1: *"And you."*

"God wants us to know the mighty power He wrought *in* Christ when He raised from the dead *Him . . . and you,* who were dead in trespasses and sins!" Donald cried. *"In* Christ we were raised from the dead; *in* Christ we are at God's own right hand, in the heavenlies, far above. So start living your life from there! The problems of earth are nothing when looked at from the heavenlies!"

He had us circle "in" whenever it preceded a name or a

pronoun meaning "Jesus Christ," and told us to believe and claim the riches to which we are entitled *in* Him—all of grace. Access! Joy! Holy living! Family relationships raised to the relationship of the Godhead! The whole armor of God for protection; the "principalities and powers" power-less before that mighty resurrection power of Jesus. For me, it was all one big exclamation point of joy.

From San Diego we worked our way north, city by city where Donald had been scheduled to speak, through California and Oregon, arriving in Seattle, Washington, at the end of February. We were grateful for the "safe conduct" through California for our amaryllis, now in spectacular bloom.

One of the unforgettable pictures in my memory is of our arrival at Lake Tahoe where my daughter Carolyn and her new husband were staying: the picture of Donald, carefully wrapping our amaryllis in his enormous sweater—blossom, pot, and all—then cradling it like a child as he picked his way precariously to the cabin along a path tramped out in deep, newly fallen snow.

In Seattle, when Donald came to the end of his sermon on Sunday night, he said as usual, "Let us bow in prayer." I bowed my head, but it snapped right up again in astonishment as I heard him say, "While every head is bowed and every eye is closed. . . ." This was the standard introduction to an invitation in Baptist or Methodist churches—yet he *never* gave an invitation! What's more, we were in a Presbyterian church! What had come over him?

"Will those of you who already had the assurance of your salvation before you came in here tonight just slip up your hand, and put it down again?" All over the room hands went up. "Thank you. Thank you. Now, will you who to-night for the first time received the assurance that you are saved, once for all and forever, please slip up your hand?" A few hands were raised. "Aha!" cried Donald, "just as I thought. Most of you here tonight are already Christians.

For this we praise God. But now you must bring your *un-saved* friends under the ministry of God's Word. Come back tomorrow night and bring a friend with you. I'll be preaching on 'How to Know the Will of God.' And now our Father and our God, go with us as we go. If there be any here who have not been born again, accompany them with rest-less-ness, that they may know no peace until they rest in Thee. But upon all Thy redeemed own may Thy grace, Thy mercy, and Thy peace abide, and a new joy, *knowing* they are eternally Thine. In Jesus' precious name. Amen."

And without giving an "invitation" he let them go out into the night.

I knew what would happen. The Word had undoubtedly sunk deep. The illustrations would return to reinforce the remembered message; the rest-less-ness would build up like a head of steam and about two in the morning it would blow them wide open, and they'd let the Lord in.

In checking the record he kept of such things, Donald discovered that in Seattle, in other years, he had already preached several of the sermons he had been using on this winter's tour. He would have to substitute.

"What shall I give them on Thursday night?" he asked me.

"Why not 'Acceptable Prayer'?" I suggested. This was good, basic teaching that had helped me tremendously, although when I first heard it I had been as shocked as when I first heard his teaching on the Book of Hebrews.

He opened by telling about some of the nonsense people call prayer. Then he said, "I am asked, 'Do you believe in prayer?' I answer, 'No, I don't believe in prayer. I believe in God, and in the fact that God answers prayers according to certain rules.'

"If you just say, 'I believe in prayer,' period, that's as silly as saying, 'I believe in cashing checks.' Suppose I go down to the First National Bank and sign a counter check,

'Pay to the order of cash, 100 dollars,' then walk up to the teller and say, 'Give me five twenties, please.' He looks at it. 'Barnhouse. Do you have an account in this bank?' 'No, but I believe in cashing checks!' " Donald flashed a big, phony smile and batted his eyelids.

The audience roared with laughter.

"There are more rules about getting a prayer answered than about getting a check cashed," he continued. "Who has a right to pray?

" 'Oh,' says someone, 'doesn't everyone?' They have the nonsensical idea that they can get God down with a hammerlock and say, 'Now, God, produce!'

"In preparing this study I discovered that there are more verses in the Bible where God promises *not* to answer prayer than verses where God promises He *will* answer. This may be startling, but it is true. Take, for example, Proverbs 1:24 through 31. Here God says that because He called and you refused and you paid no attention when He stretched forth His hand and you wouldn't take His counsel or His reproof, He will laugh when terrible things happen to you. You'll call on Him then, but He won't answer.

"You say, 'But I don't want a God like that!' I don't care how you want God: God *is,* my dear friends. *He is sovereign,* and He is not subject to us. This is the most important doctrine in the Bible. God is right; God is just; and man cannot sin with impunity.

"If a man thinks he can live as he pleases and then come to God and pray, it's exactly as if you walked up to the bank to cash a check: *Do you have an account in the bank of heaven?* Has God ever heard the prayer of a Confucian or a Buddhist? Or of a Unitarian or any person who denies Christ? When a Mohammedan prays, 'Oh, Allah, Allah, Allah!' is he praying to the God and Father of our Lord Jesus Christ?

" 'Oh,' you say, 'you're terribly narrow.'

"I'm totally unconcerned with man's judgment of me. All I ask is, 'Is what I am preaching what the Bible says?' If it is, take it up with the Author! A minister cannot preach to you just the nice, pretty things in the Bible. There are also judgments. And I am under the great urgency of knowing that some day I will have to stand before God and hear Him ask, 'Did you obey my command, "Arise, go . . . and preach *the preaching that I bid thee"?'* So I'm not going to say, 'If you don't live in a certain way, when you pass on from this life you may go to a place of which you may possibly have heard the name.' No! I am going to say, 'If you die without Jesus Christ *you are going to hell.'* This you can understand!"

Suddenly he realized he had been thundering judgmentally. The tone of his voice changed and gentled. "I wouldn't be preaching here tonight if I were not sure that there may be someone listening to my voice who is going to spend eternity in hell, and I would do anything I could to stop him. I tell you the truth: I have said to God, 'Lord, if it were possible to send me to hell and thereby have some other people go to heaven, it would be all right with me.' I've faced this. So if I sound harsh to you at times it's merely because from speaking so often I have on my vocal chords something like the calluses that a ditchdigger has on his hands. But I love people. When I mention these people and say, 'God cannot hear your prayers,' I love the people but I hate the system." His voice was quiet, reasonable. "For instance, I love Christian Scien*tists,* but I know that anybody who believes 'Science and Health' is going to hell. They deny that Jesus Christ is the Lord Jehovah, God Almighty, and that He died on the cross, shedding His blood to save people by the redemption He provided there. And you can carry this on, through all religions. It was Jesus Himself who said that the only access to His Father was through Him and what He did on the cross. So prayers made in any other name do not get to God.

"Who collects those prayers?

"In the Psalms we learn that 'the gods of the nations are demons.' In Corinthians we are told that 'behind every idol is a demon,' and again, 'the things sacrificed to idols are sacrificed to demons.' So any prayer that is not prayed through Jesus Christ goes either to Satan under one of his many disguises or to demons.

"Now, my dear friends, I didn't write it! But you *know* that's what the Bible teaches. If you want to say 'the Bible is absolutely wrong and Dr. Barnhouse is duped by it,' all right. But I expect to stand one day before the Lord God Almighty and hear Him say, 'Well done, thou good and faithful servant. You took the side of My Book against all the rationale of men. No matter what they wanted to argue, you believed *Me!*'

"*And I do.* And I build my hope on 'the solid authority of the impregnable Rock of the Holy Scriptures,' as Gladstone called it.

"Let's come now to Christians. God definitely states that He does not answer *all* prayers of Christians. In Psalm 66:18 we read, 'If I regard iniquity in my heart, the Lord will not hear me.' The Hebrew of that word, 'regard' is 'to caress, to pet.' Suppose you are up late, working on your income tax report, and you think, 'I'll put down that I gave $200 to the church last year. True, I gave only $25, but I don't think they'll catch me and I'll get a deduction on the other $125 as well. Ho, hum: bedtime. Now, dear heavenly Father, bless me and mine, and give me this and that.' Do you think you can rob God and take an income tax deduction for it besides —and then come to Him in prayer? God says, 'I will not hear you.' Do you think that if you have a plan of known sin in your life you can expect to go to God and say, 'God, I'm in a jam. Please help me'? Turn from your sin, get back into God's will, and then you can begin to think about getting your prayers answered.

" 'Well,' says somebody, piously, 'if we ask anything according to His will, He'll do it.' But what does this mean? That phrase, 'if it be Thy will,' has become a face-saver for an awful lot of Christians. If what they pray for doesn't happen, they say, 'Well, I guess it just wasn't His will.' Maybe it *was* His will, but you weren't living according to the rules. In Psalm 84:11 it says, 'No good thing will he withhold from them that walk uprightly.' Now this is talking about believers, of course. The Psalms were not written to the Philistines or the Greeks or the Romans. They were written to Jews under the Old Covenant, and through the New Covenant they can be applied to believing Christians in our day and age—but they are not for the Mohammedans nor for the unsaved Presbyterian or Baptist or what have you who may have had some water applied to him in some fashion or another and may have gotten his name on a church roll. But Scripture says God will withhold no good thing from those *believers* that walk uprightly.

"Let's see how this works. As I said, we pray a lot of prayers that are nonsense. We're like little children. Here's Junior, age three. He sees the light shining on the butcher knife his mother is using in the kitchen to cut up something. He says, 'Mama, give me! I want to play with it!' She won't do it.

" 'Well, why can't I play with it? Am I not a good boy?'

" 'You are a lovely, good boy, but it's not a good thing for Johnny. You'd cut yourself.'

"Well, a lot of your prayers are just that stupid! 'Lord, gimme this! Gimme that!'

" 'Why?'

" 'Well, I *want* it!' But it's a butcher knife. Look back over your life. Aren't you glad the Lord didn't give you all the butcher knives you prayed for?

"Let's look at Junior again. One day he comes to Mama and says, 'Mama, I want a glass of milk and a cookie.'

" 'First, Junior, pick up your toys.'

" 'But I want a glass of milk and a cookie!'

" 'Junior! Pick up your toys!'

" 'Why can't I have milk and cookies? Aren't they good for me?'

" 'Yes, they're good for you.'

" 'Then why can't I have them?'

" 'Because you're not walking uprightly. Go pick up those toys!'

"And about now, mothers, is the time to use the Ping-

Pong paddle. In the Book of Proverbs it says, 'Foolishness is bound in the heart of a child but the rod of correction shall drive it far from him.' None of this Columbia University School of Pedagogy that teaches that the little dears must express themselves! If you let your little dears express themselves, you'll get exactly the same result as if you let your garden express itself: a fine crop of weeds. There has to be discipline.

"Then when Junior has picked up his toys, you can say, 'That's a good little boy. Now come have your glass of milk—and *two* cookies!'

"And that's the way God operates with us. 'No good thing will he withhold from them that walk uprightly.'

"But never think that prayer is just a cheap way of getting something for nothing. Again, we're at the bank. There is a sign in the window that says, 'If you present any check according to our rules, we will cash it.' That's about the equivalent of those verses in the Bible. 'If you ask anything according to his will, he heareth you.' and, 'If you ask anything in my name, I will do it.' To ask according to His will is to ask according to what He has set down in this Book; to ask in Jesus' name is to ask Him to endorse the check, and it has to be consistent with what Jesus is.

"Once someone saw me using a beautiful pen I had received for Christmas. I had seen the ads, so knew the price of it. My friend asked, 'How much did that pen cost?' Two answers: 'Nothing,' and '$25.' It didn't cost me anything, but it cost the donor something. All right: How much did your answer to prayer cost? It cost nothing, plus the death of the Lord Jesus Christ—because every prayer you ever had answered was bought and paid for by the blood of Jesus Christ shed for you on the cross. Don't ever think that God cheaply hands out something that doesn't cost Him anything. *In—order—to—bless—a—sinner—it—took—the—death—of—God's—Son.*

"Which brings us to the fifth rule for acceptable prayer.

Number 1 is: You must have an account to draw on in the bank of heaven. Jesus's own righteousness, imputed to you when you were saved, gives you the right to ask 'in Jesus' name.' Number 2: You must have no unconfessed sin and no planned future sin in your life. Number 3: You must ask according to His will as revealed in Scripture. Number 4: You must be walking uprightly.

"Now, number 5: God has forgiven your sins. If you will not forgive others, God will not hear you!

"What is the purpose of prayer? God wants to have fellowship with us. And if we don't come to Him often for fellowship, He sometimes puts us in a jam, to bring our attention back to Him. If you would pray more often, maybe you wouldn't be in so many jams!

"Prayer involves the whole Trinity: God the Father, God the Son, and God the Holy Spirit. If you have heard my coast-to-coast broadcast, you know my first sentence through all these years that I've been on the radio is: 'Through the Lord Jesus Christ we come unto Thee, our Father and our God, and in the Holy Spirit.' But of course personal prayer doesn't need to be formal. You are coming to a loving heavenly Father. It should be intimate conversation. Jesus said we were to call the Father 'Abba,' which is the Greek word for 'Papa.' That's how we should come to Him, lovingly, trustingly, but respectfully, knowing that 'him who cometh unto me I will in no wise cast out.' 'Oh,' you say, 'but it was Jesus who said that!' Jesus also said, 'I and the Father are one.'

"What does it mean to 'pray without ceasing'? When my wife and I travel, in the midst of a conversation one of us is apt to say, 'Lord, You are so wonderful!' and thank Him right then and there for something in the conversation. The Lord is a continual undercurrent beneath our thinking and speaking. Continual contact with Him is 'prayer without ceasing.' You don't have to mention each Person of the Trinity every time you pray, but as you come to the Father always be aware that you come through His Son. Therefore the power comes, not from talking to Him, but in being so related to Him that He will work in our behalf without violating His holiness and righteousness.

"And now, our Father, go with us as we go. . . ."

Our week in Seattle was exhilarating. In addition to enthusiastically received messages and good fellowship, we had the added joy of being taken up in a private plane from which vantage point we could see seven great mountain peaks. Donald knew the name of every one of them, and had interesting facts to tell me about each.

Friday morning we awoke to fresh snow and that sharp, clean, exciting air that accompanies it. A great week. It was here that Donald began adding to our evening devotions, "Lord, we know that before the foundation of the world you gave us X number of days to live. Thank You for a terrific day today. That's one less of the X number that can be bad!"

After Seattle, Donald had excellent Sunday-to-Sunday meetings in Spokane, leaving there after the Sunday morning service that ended the conference. We should have been in Salt Lake City by Monday night, with a whole week for Donald to catch up on his other work before his Salt Lake conference began in the First Presbyterian Church. But we ran into a blizzard and were snowbound for two days en route. Donald took this as a challenge.

"Satan is trying to block the meetings in Salt Lake, Marge! That's terrific! That means the Lord is really working, and we can expect great things! And I can catch up as well here as in our Salt Lake motel. Did we bring in that book by Pelikan I was reviewing? Ah, here it is!" and he was immediately immersed in his reading.

Finally the snow stopped, the roads were cleared, and we were on our way again. I could tell that for Donald this was to be a "time of refreshing."

"It's 'album' time. Let's play 'lakes'!"

"Crater Lake," I said instantly, that being the most recent. Closing my eyes, I could see the indigo depths, the little center island, the mirror-clear reflection of trees and cloud-puffs and the vast blue reaches of the sky. Peace. Tranquility. The wideness and depth of God's mercy translated into His creation. Donald's hand came softly upon mine and we shared wordlessly the remembered beauty. Then suddenly he threw back his head. Laughing with delight, he said, "Lake Mashu!"

Lake Mashu! Could I ever forget! We were on the island of Hokkaido in Japan back in 1956, driving through the amazing contradictions of that northernmost island's Akan National Park. Wild, wonderful scenery. Small lakes where you almost froze your fingers if you put them in the water. Yet a few feet up the banks you could dig in the rough sand and suddenly a hot spring would bubble up. At the turn of the road, a tribe of aborigines, cousins of the ones found in the mountains of Taiwan and in Australia and various skip-distances in between. In the center of the laughing circle, a trained bear dancing.

The road became steeper. Mists hung low on the horizon, hiding the Japan Sea which should have been visible from there. Our host, a Japanese doctor, looked distressed.

"I'm afraid we'll miss it. . . ."

"Miss what?" Donald asked.

"Lake Mashu. It is called the Lake of Mystery. On a rare clear day it is one of the most beautiful sights the human eye could behold. But most of the time it is shrouded in mists. Tourists come, they stay two, three days at the guest house, and go away without ever having seen it. Ah, well, the Lord knows."

The car swept up to a charming mountain resort and stopped. Below us lay a valley completely covered with thick, shifting mists.

We got out of the car and breathed in the sharp, moist

air. A busload of Japanese tourists was on the viewing platform below, peering hopefully into the misty depths. We descended the stairs and joined them.

I have never known quite how he accomplished it, but charmingly, without pushing, Donald always managed somehow to have us standing on the front row. He leaned over the guardrail and looked intently into the nothingness. By this time our host had joined us—a man as big as Donald, but with the same gift of insinuating himself through a crowd almost invisibly.

Donald began quietly, conversationally, to talk aloud: "Lord, here is one of the wonders of Your creation. We have come a long way to see it. We may never come back again. If You choose to keep it veiled, it's all right with us, but how wonderful it would be if You would let us see just a little glimpse of it."

I could hardly believe my eyes. Over to the left the great, thick layers of mist began to lift. Slowly, as if a mighty hand had flicked a blanket by the corner, it undulated upward and arched over an exquisite gem of a lake. Whereas Crater Lake is blue, this was green as an emerald, with a tiny, perfect island, and trees like Japanese etchings bordering it. A shaft of sunlight hit it like a spotlight. The tourists, who in twos and threes had been drifting sadly to their bus, gasped in astonishment and rushed back to the guardrail. An excited babble of Japanese voices surrounded us.

The blanket of mist began to settle back on the left, but the great undulation continued across the entire landscape with that finger of sunlight beneath it lighting the little tree-covered knoll, the green valley, the far meadows, and the sea! Glittering like a promise, the Japan Sea appeared for one moment, then the blanket, shaken and fluffed, settled back again. You would never have guessed what beauty lay beneath and beyond.

It wasn't until then I realized I had been holding my breath. I looked at Donald. His eyes were brimming with tears, and his face was radiant. "Lord, *thank You,*" he said quietly as his hand found mine.

As we drove on toward Salt Lake, remembering, that same joy and adoration again gripped us.

"Oh, Marge, Marge. Psalm 37:4. If people only *knew* how the Lord delights to delight those who delight in Him!"

V

In the Midst of Midst of Wrestle, Rest

TWENTY-ONE

In Salt Lake City, that stronghold of the Mormons, whose emphasis is on character and good works, Donald chose "The Scales of God" for his Sunday morning sermon. I marveled that, despite the many times he had preached this, it still came with freshness and power:

"I was born and brought up in California. When I was a boy there were no automobiles in California, no electric lights, no packaged groceries. Bread was not sliced nor wrapped; sugar was sold from a big barrel.

"I can remember being sent to the store to get a dollar's worth of sugar. The grocer took a big scoop and scooped some sugar into a paper bag, put the bag on one side of the old-fashioned scales, put some weights on the other side, then began pouring more sugar into the bag. My eyes were just even with the scales. I can remember that magic moment when the scales came just on balance; the grocer up-ended his scoop, dropped it back into the barrel, and I got my dollar's worth of sugar."

(All this time DGB had been suiting action to the words. You could almost see the scoop being lifted; you could see the imaginary sugar cascading into that invisible bag.)

"Now, how many pounds of sugar were in the bag?

Someone might say, 'Well, I remember my father telling me that his father told him there were eight pounds of sugar to the dollar.' Someone else says, 'No, no—I read in a book that at that time you could get ten pounds of sugar for a dollar.' Another person says, 'You're both wrong. I worked in a country store in Vermont and I personally weighed out twelve pounds for a dollar.'

"So now you have three denominations, one based on family tradition, one based on 'I read it in a book,' and one based on personal experience. But when I tell you the grocer put two five-pound weights, two two-pound weights, and a one-pound weight in this side of the scales, all your speculation is useless. Fifteen pounds of weights: fifteen pounds of sugar, postulating that the scales are correct. And all the eight-pounders, the ten-pounders, and the twelve-pounders are simply silly if they try to push their theory after they know what is in the other side of the scales.

"Now as I said, this is how denominations get started. Men know that one day they will be weighed in God's scales. They gather around this side of His scales and they don't look at what's in His side and they argue according to family tradition, 'I read it in a book,' or personal experience. 'Well, *I* think God wants this.' 'No, *I* think God wants that.' Well, who are you to think what God wants? He has revealed Himself, and if we go to the Bible we can *know* what is in His side of the scales.

"God Almighty has everywhere in His Word revealed that He is perfect. And if you're going to be in heaven you've got to balance that perfection: there'll be nobody in heaven who is not as perfect as God. Well, in myself I'm not, and you're not. Who then can be saved?

" 'Oh,' you say, 'I'll just do the best I can and God won't be too hard on me.' Well, in school they'll let you through on 70 percent passing. But if *God* passed you on 70 percent, heaven would be 30 percent dirty. And if God let you in on 99 percent, heaven would be 1 percent dirty. No, *no!* God's passing mark is 100 percent and it can't be anything less.

"All right, let's weigh the human race. There are three kinds of people in the world: the very bad, the ordinary, and the very good, according to human measurements. We'll put in God's side of the scales the pound of perfection, sixteen ounces. Now we reach out here and take a convict, a murderer. He robbed a bank and shot a policeman. But 'there's honor among thieves,' they say. We put him in the scales and he weighs two ounces. 'Oh,' says someone, 'everyone knows a guy like that can't measure up.' So we take him and all like him and we put him over here in a heap, and we write over him, 'LOST.' Now I'll show you later how he can be saved, but no man is going to be in heaven until first he has been in the heap marked 'LOST.'

"Now we take the next one. This is Joe Doaks, the average guy: you know, country club morality, good enough to keep out of jail, bad enough to do everything he wants to, smart enough to think he can get away with it. Put him in the scales: eight ounces. He ruffles up like a peacock and says, 'I'm four times better than that crook! He was two ounces and I'm eight ounces!' Then I come along and say, 'Wait a minute, Joe. You're not being measured by the crook. You're being measured against God.' So we take him and we put him in the same heap with the convict— and what a yell goes up!

"Now when you've weighed all the two ouncers and all the eight ouncers, there are very few left. But here is the honorable judge, upright and ethical. Twelve ounces! 'Oh!' says he, 'I'm six times better than the convict and one-and-a-half times better than the average guy.' And I say, 'But *wait* a minute, Judge. You're not being weighed against these. You're being weighed against God.' So we take him and we put him here in this same heap. And if you thought you heard a yell when the eight-ouncers went in with the convict, what you don't hear when you put the judge in with the convict! He says, 'Do you mean to say that God

Almighty isn't going to take any account of what I am and all the good I've done?'

"And here I say something that makes some people boil —but this is the heart of Christianity: your character can take you to hell but not to heaven. *God is not saving men by character.* Men say, 'Well, I'm not so bad. That one's good, and that one's bad, and I'm somewhere in the middle. If I work at it I can get better.' But *God* says, '*All* have sinned and come short of the glory of God.' 'There is none righteous, no, not one.' And I tell you that anyone is living in a fool's world who thinks that if he does good to humankind and does the best he can he will get by the judgment bar of God. He is a lost soul, under the condemnation of God, without hope, and dead in trespasses and sin.

"As we have seen, God *must* demand perfection, and none of us is perfect. God's solution to our problem was to send His only begotten Son into the world to provide us with a righteousness we do not have.

"When Jesus came into this world He made His friends among the two-ouncers, and the twelve-ouncers put Him to death. Why? Because in the Sermon on the Mount He said, 'Except your righteousness *exceed* the righteousness of the twelve-ouncers (the scribes and Pharisees) you shall in no wise enter the kingdom of heaven.' Then He thundered—and if anyone says his religion is the Sermon on the Mount, let this strike terror to your heart!—Jesus thundered at them, 'Be ye therefore perfect, even as your Father which is in heaven is perfect!' And they crucified Him because He taught that their twelve ounces wasn't enough, that *God's* standard is sixteen ounces.

"Someone says, 'But that means we are *all* sinners!' Exactly! This is where we begin, when we come to Christianity: we are *all* sinners. Someone objects, 'I'm afraid if I say I'm a sinner they'll think I've had my hand in the till.' Well, maybe not that, but you know, most of you cheat a bit on your income tax. You know: 'I only gave twenty dollars to the church, but I might as well take credit for two hundred. . . .' "

DGB paused as laughter rose from the audience, then said, "That laughter is very interesting. It is mass self-accusation: you know what I've been saying is true!

"So often people think we ministers don't know what life is. I have had three murders confessed to me; innumerable adulteries and broken homes; and more than one man has sat in my office, trembling, while the bank examiners were discovering his short accounts. His *reputation* had been eight ounces, and his *character* was about to be exposed as only two ounces. If you think we don't know what sin is: we've been dealing with you and your delinquent children. We *know*. I know what *my* 'old nature' is. If there is any difference between us, it is because I have faced the scales. And I know many here have also faced the scales. What I want the rest of you to do is face them, understand, and say, 'Oh, God, I don't have sixteen ounces. What do I do?'

"First you must admit that taking credit for your character can separate you from God and take you to hell, not to heaven: you must be born again. *This* is Christianity—not the good you do, not your ethics, not better milk for better babies and better slums for better slum dwellers.

"Don't misunderstand: we Christians will give blood; we'll give food to the starving; we'll do everything we can for others—we'll give our lives if need be. But we know this is not entered to our credit as part payment or down payment on our salvation. Salvation is by God's grace, through faith, plus nothing.

"So here we are, all in this heap marked 'LOST.' Now don't argue with me as to where you are in the heap. If someone objects, 'But Dr. Barnhouse, I'm twelve-and-a-half ounces!' so what? You aren't sixteen ounces. Empty your hands of your two ounces, eight ounces, twelve or twelve-and-a-half ounces and say, 'I *am* in the heap marked "LOST," but I believe that Jesus died for sinners and that he died for me.' Christ says, 'Come to me with your empty hands, and I'll fill them with Myself.'

"We sing it in the hymn, 'Rock of Ages, cleft for me,/Let me hide myself in Thee;/Let the water and the blood,/From Thy wounded side which flowed,/Be of sin the *double* cure:/ Save from wrath and make me pure.' And the cross of Jesus Christ becomes not a way *up,* to reform you, but a way *out,* to an absolutely brand new life. And in that new life your good works will grow from Christ, as their root, and will glorify Him.

"This is what salvation means. This is what the atonement means. This is God providing the pound of perfection that no one has.

"Now God will never, never, never say, 'Do the best you can and I'll make up the difference.' If so, some could say, 'God didn't have to do as much for me as He did for you!' and heaven would be a place of high pride. The second verse of 'Rock of Ages' says, 'Not the labors of my hands/ Can fulfill Thy law's demands;/Could my zeal no respite know,/Could my tears forever flow,/All for sin could not atone;/*Thou must save, and Thou alone.*' And the third verse says this: '*Nothing* in my hand I bring.' That's the hardest part, you see. Drop *everything* of your own doing that has made you a success in this world and that you think might earn salvation, and say, '*Nothing* in my hand I bring,/Simply to Thy Cross I cling;/Naked, come to Thee for dress,/ Helpless, look to Thee for grace;/Foul, I to the fountain fly;/Wash me, Savior, or I die.' And Christ washes away your sin and clothes you with His righteousness. Then when the judgment comes, and God says, 'I demand perfection, sixteen ounces in the pound,' you can say, 'Lord God, here's Jesus.' and you put Him in, and the scales balance. And you go into heaven not on your measurements but on Christ's measurements.

"Can you sing, 'My hope is built on nothing less/Than Jesus' blood and righteousness;/I dare not trust two ounces, eight ounces, twelve ounces,/But wholly lean on Jesus' name'?

"O Lord our God, may Thy Holy Spirit take these words to each heart here. Go with us as we go. If there be any here who have not been born again, accompany them with rest-less-ness. . . ."

During that week of meetings a feeling of satanic opposition persisted. Donald could feel the pressure, but he preached boldly, with authority, taking God at His word: "Submit yourself to God; resist the Devil and he will flee from you." As soon as the daily morning Bible studies on Galatians were over, I would walk back to the motel to prepare lunch according to Donald's diet; he would stay to speak to people, and come later.

Thursday night, as the crowd thinned out after the sermon, an angry little woman marched down the aisle. As she approached, I could see that Donald was aware of the battle flags. To disarm her, he stepped toward her and held out his hand. With a charming smile, he said, "I'm Dr. Barnhouse." She snapped back, "Well, I'm Mrs. Brandley. I'm one of those stupid Mormons you were talking about."

He leapt into the fray. "Do you know the Lord Jesus Christ?"

To my astonishment she answered, "Certainly I do!"

"Do you know Him as your personal Savior?"

"Certainly I do!"

"Do you have a knowledge of salvation? Are you saved?"

"Yes!"

"No, you're not!"

She glared at him in fury, then turned on her heels and walked away. Donald took the hand of the next person in line, but his eyes followed that proud back as she marched off.

Friday morning, just before the class was to begin, I saw her come in and stand hesitantly at the door, Then, spotting Donald and the pastor, she walked up and said something to them. The pastor gestured toward his study. Donald said something to her; she nodded and came down and sat in one of the few vacant chairs. I noticed that she was carrying a fat notebook, and I wondered what was in it.

She paid careful attention to what Donald was saying, as someone sizing up an opponent.

" 'Stand fast therefore in the liberty wherewith Christ has made us free, and be not entangled again with the yoke of bondage,' " he thundered. " 'Behold, I Paul (I, Donald Barnhouse) say unto you, that if ye be circumcised, Christ shall profit you nothing.' Doesn't that scare you? God says that if you add anything to Christ, He will subtract Christ. You have been saved by the shedding of His precious blood, *alone*. Don't try to add any of your filthy works to what He has done for you. Oh, sure, after you are saved, if you want to bring Him your works as a love gift, He'll accept it with joy, but not as a down payment on your salvation."

(I thought back to that week in Bradenton, when for the first time I had heard Galatians taught this way. How shocked I had been!) Then he explained how, when a believer sins, he falls *into* grace, not *from* grace. He showed how this had happened time and again, to Abraham, to David, to all the great heroes of the faith. And he proved that when you "fall from grace," you fall into *law*. He could make the complicated so simple!

Afterward I rushed back to prepare lunch, noting as I left that he and the little Mormon woman were going into the pastor's study. I began to pray for her, and for him!

Twelve noon came. Lunch was ready, but no Donald. It had been an hour: surely he had answered whatever her problem was by now. One o'clock. What could be keeping him? We had to pack the car that afternoon and leave as soon as he was finished preaching that night, driving as far as we could in order to be in Denver the following night.

Two o'clock! I began to worry. Then the door opened and in he came, the picture of jubilation.

"Marge," he said, exhilarated. "I have just seen the most remarkable conversion in my whole career. Do you realize

who that Mormon lady is? She holds the number three card
to the Mormon Temple; her husband is a high priest; she is
a teacher of teachers—and the Lord has just saved her!"

"*How* did you get through to her?"

"I didn't. The Lord did. She really knows her Bible. I
kept hammering away with the Word, making her read it
for herself, and the Lord suddenly broke through her false
interpretation, and everything became clear to her. It was
fantastic! We must pray for her." And right there we
prayed, while his lunch got cold.

Then he told me what had happened during those three
hours in the pastor's study. She had been incensed at his
teaching on Lucifer, and had brought her own lesson outlines on this, to "set him straight." He had taken her from
Scripture to Scripture, concentrating on the salvation verses
rather than on Satan. How that must have infuriated Satan!
"John 10:27 to 30 was what finally did it. 'My sheep hear
my voice, and I know them, and they follow me: and I give
unto them eternal life; and they shall never perish, neither
shall any man pluck them out of my hand. My Father,
which gave them me, is greater than all; and no man is able
to pluck them out of my Father's hand. I and my Father are
one.'

"She broke down then, and beginning to cry, said, 'I
never saw it this way before, but it's true! Oh, Dr. Barnhouse, what am I to do? A convention of twenty-five hundred women will be in Salt Lake on Monday, and I'm
supposed to teach them what to take back to their areas to
teach—but it's false doctrine! What am I to do?' "

He asked to see her lesson outlines. Wherever there was
a Scripture reference, he marked it and explained what it
meant from the Christian viewpoint. She said, "Why, that's
beautiful! Why didn't I see it this way before?" He told her
to stick with Scripture: "Faith cometh by hearing, and
hearing by the Word of God." She needn't mention Joseph
Smith, or the Book of Mormon: just teach positively from
God's Word, and trust Him to give the increase.

As soon as he finished preaching that night I slipped out the back of the church and met him at the car, which was packed and waiting. He had an envelope in his hand and was reading its contents.

"Marge, listen to this, from Mrs. Brandley. She gave it to the pastor to give to me. Listen!

Dear Dr. Barnhouse:
First, I am deeply grateful to the Lord for saving my soul. Second, [I am grateful] to you for your consideration and understanding, especially for your help in outlining the material for Monday. I have completed two [messages]: Scripture just seemed to come into my head almost faster than I could write it. I will forward you, as the originator, the talks when I have given them.

I truly thank the Lord for saving me, I know He is my Lord and Savior! This afternoon I have felt as though tons of hard cement had been removed from inside me. I am not weighed down, because I am His. Thank you.

Georgianne Brandley

Donald's eyes were full of tears. "Oh, Lord, bless her exceedingly abundantly above all she could ask or think—and protect her from the Evil One."

A year later Mrs. Brandley was in Philadelphia. In a taped interview, she told us of her encounter with DGB and how the Lord had opened her eyes to the truth of salvation by the shedding of Jesus' blood alone.

She remembered the Thursday night when DGB in a booming voice asked if she was saved and later declared loudly that she was not. "And here the church was about a third full of people. I could have gone through a hole. I was furious."

Georgianne had gone home and told her husband, who said, "You mean he contradicted you? Well, you have more authority than he'll ever have. He's a nobody. Go over there and pin his ears back."

"So the next morning," Georgianne recalled, "I took my lectures on Satan with me and went to his Bible class. At the close of the lesson we went into the pastor's study. He began to ask me questions, and I said that, yes, I was born and raised in the church. I was a descendant of the Prophet. I had graduated from the University of Boston. He said, 'I guess you know your Bible,' and I replied, 'I certainly do.' "

"Turn to Ephesians," he had said. "By grace are ye saved."

Georgianne said, "No, I don't accept that."

He continually brought her back to the subject of salvation. He asked her to read some Scriptures from Romans, and she did. "Now what does that say? The 'blood of Jesus Christ'?"

"Yes," she replied.

"And it does what?"

"It cleanses us from all sin."

"Now if the blood of Jesus Christ cleanses from all sin, and if you acquire this by grace—*what is it you're working for?*"

"We don't attain salvation any other way," she said. "We *have* to work for it."

Donald tried another approach. He directed her to John 10:28. " 'I give unto them'—what?"

"Eternal life."

"Turn to John 3:16—"

"Oh, I know that." Georgianne quoted the verse and came to the last part of it: " ' . . . whosoever believeth in him should not perish, but have everlasting—' "

"That *Georgianne Brandley* shall have everlasting life."

"I can't go along with that."

Donald persisted. " 'God so loved Georgianne Brandley that he gave his only begotten Son that if Georgianne Brandley believeth in him, Georgianne Brandley should not perish, but have everlasting life.' Say it."

"No," Georgianne had said, hanging her head.

After that Georgianne had refused to say anything, "I was stubborn. My Mormon back was really up and I wouldn't admit to this thing. This man had no authority. But he just kept at it and at it, and he'd keep shoving his chair forward and forward—and I'd keep backing off. And finally, instead of me pinning his ears back, he had *me* pinned against the bookcases. He said, 'This is the Holy Ghost that's dealing with you. Do you hear the voice of the Lord? Can't you accept this? *This* is salvation, and the Lord has it for you here and now.' "

Donald had then picked up a book, saying, "If I give you this, what is it?"

"It's a gift," Georgianne had replied.

Donald left the room and returned with his five volumes of *Romans.* "Mrs. Brandley, I want you to have these. They are a gift from me. No strings attached."

"Well, thank you. I really appreciate that."

"Then you accept the gift?"

"Yes, I do," Georgianne said. "And I do appreciate it."

"Then why don't you do the same thing with Jesus Christ?"

That was the breakthrough. Recalling that moment, Georgianne said, "I just broke. I went all to pieces. I wept all the way home, and after I got home I couldn't tell what happened to me. I had never had an experience like it before in my life. For weeks I had this wonderful feeling. I could never describe it. It seemed when I would read in the Bible about Jesus it was illumined for me. It was as though I had suddenly met someone I had never known, someone I had never even conceived of before."

As we drove away from Salt Lake City that Sunday night after we had read Georgianne Brandley's note (the one that said, "I feel as though tons of cement have just been removed...") the feeling of satanic opposition I had had all week seemed to weigh more heavily on me. Suddenly a large truck came roaring in from our left and cut across in front of us. Donald's quick turn onto the right shoulder of the road saved us from a bad accident. He drew the car farther off the road and stopped.

"Marge, do you feel a heavy oppression?"

"Oh, Donald, yes!"

He put his hand over mine. "Our heavenly Father, we come to You through the Lord Jesus Christ and in the Holy Spirit. We put ourselves into Your safekeeping this night. Beat back the powers of darkness that would attack us. Keep me alert to danger. Thank You for Your hand of protection on us just now. We praise You for what Your Word has accomplished here this week. Satan isn't happy that You have snatched Mrs. Brandley from his grasp and into the kingdom of Your dear Son. Oh, keep her standing firm. Guard her—and us. In Jesus' name. Amen."

The strange oppression lifted. We drove on, Donald breaking into a song of praise. I joined in, my heart once more light and free.

When we arrived home several weeks later, a letter from Georgianne Brandley awaited us. She wrote:

I am nearly finished with your second volume on the Book of Romans. Some I understand; the rest, the larger part, only vaguely. It is peculiar that two people can read the same book, and each see it differently, according to the way they have been taught. . . .

We are taught that we Latter-Day Saints are "the chosen generation, the royal priesthood, holy nation, and peculiar people." I haven't the knowledge to unravel that other than the way I have been taught it.

The proof of our gospel lies in Revelation 14:6, that "other angel flying in the midst of heaven, having the everlasting gospel" is Moroni—even though you did call Moroni a demon. (I wish you hadn't said that!) Sonship and brotherhood are interwoven in our teachings. Our priesthood are all sons of God and dwelt

with him before coming to mortal life . . . our choice prophets—
Joseph Smith, for example—were brothers of Jesus in the pre-
mortal or preexistent world.

Dr. Barnhouse, are you sure that your answers are the correct
ones? Couldn't you be mistaken? Why are you so positive? You
are! You speak, as do our authorities, with conviction and power.
When you speak I feel within me that you are right, but cannot
explain [why]. . . .

Thank you. . . . After talking with you, I called and had my
name removed from the list of those desirous of being baptized for
the dead.

> Gratefully,
> Georgianne A. Brandley

Donald looked up, shook his head, and said, "The Holy
Spirit is already leading her into all truth: we didn't discuss
baptism for the dead at all!"

A letter received from a Presbyterian woman who had
attended the Salt Lake meetings echoed Mrs. Brandley's
dilemma but came to different conclusions. It said:

Dear Dr. Barnhouse,

Perhaps shock is good for us—complacency is a terrible disease. . . .
I was deeply moved by many of the things you said in both of your
morning messages. . . .

However—and here two people who love God with all their
hearts and minds must part company. I love God with all my soul.
I pray for understanding, not only for myself, but that I may
understand others. I pray that I may understand you. That is why
this letter is being written.

If I understand . . . we do not worship the same God. He is
quite a different being—your God would consign to hell a son of
His, simply because that son believed what was taught to him by
those he loves and trusts. This is the case with many a Mormon or
Jew or Catholic or Presbyterian. . . . How could a just, loving,
forgiving God damn them? . . .

I believe with all my heart what you have said about Jesus

Christ's payment in full. I know *we cannot do anything of ourselves. But instead of a code of beliefs, or a doctrine, He said, "The spirit will lead you into all truth." You and I have asked and believed—how could the Spirit have led us on such different paths? . . .*

The Bible is your standard—Christ is mine. The Bible is a human *book, as well as a divine one. It is only the written Word; Christ is the Living Word. I know the Orthodox faith accepts the Holy Scriptures and Holy Tradition as equal authority. I know the Roman Church accepts the Holy Scriptures and the Church as equal authority. That is why I am not a member of either church, although I respect most humbly the devotion of their members. Perhaps Protestants have substituted the Bible as* only *authority. If this is so I must follow God all alone, for where Christ speaks louder than the Book, I will follow Christ! Luther called the Bible 'The cradle in which the Word of God is laid.' He can and* does *find us in many other ways also.*

Christ said, "Come unto me . . . and I will give you peace." How could I rest or live in His peace with the one He says is my neighbor outside the door? Won't He bring us all to Him in His own good time?

Regarding the woman's statement, "The Bible is your standard—Christ is mine," Donald wrote in an editorial, "She could not see that the Lord Jesus Christ cannot lie; what He has given in written revelation He never countermands by another revelation. Christ speaks no louder than the Bible, although He gives forth its truths with trumpet accompaniments."

Donald also wrote, "The writer did not want a God who would send any of his children to hell. . . . She did not want to believe any human beings were not children of God. . . . In other words, she was substituting the Christ of her imagination for the Christ of the Bible."

My heart ached for her. She would have to learn, as I had had to, that the God of the Bible is not only loving and forgiving, but also *holy,* and that His hatred of sin is as much a part of His character as His love of the sinner.

Her letter made me realize how far I had had to come in my comprehension of the holiness of God and the "sinfulness of sin." I was also reminded that Donald had a distance to go himself. Apparently, during those morning services which the Presbyterian woman had attended, Donald's old sarcasm had been evident and had wounded.

I thought of Mrs. Brandley. She had not only believed what she had been taught "by those she loves and trusts," but had taught it herself to other Mormons. She too had tried to "serve God the best that she knew," but when confronted with the true gospel, she had recognized all the others as false.

Another letter arrived from Georgianne Brandley. In part, it was a response to my invitation asking her to visit us. From it, Donald and I could tell that all her beliefs, the doctrines of her church, were being hauled out and re-examined under the guidance of the Spirit. Her letter showed that she was confused and yet enthusiastic and holding firm in her salvation.

When you speak of the gospel, you mean one thing; to us it is something completely different. The gospel to us is not the Bible or any part of it. The gospel is the Holy Priesthood and without that priesthood there is no church of Christ here on the earth.

The Dr. has me completely baffled when he talks of the Holy Ghost and the Holy Spirit. To us the Holy Ghost is one thing, then there is the Holy Spirit—how can there be so much misinterpretation?

Again, holiness—to achieve that is the ultimate. In view of it I have had many special anointings, and have made covenants with my heavenly Father. . . .

Last week was hectic. My Stake President is unhappy with me; my Bishop, with whom I have worked shoulder to shoulder for over a year—well, to quote: "You sound and smack of sectarianism." I've never been so insulted!

After I had given the lessons, the outlines of the lessons were accepted with enthusiasm by the authorities and I gave my per-

mission to have them run off for the benefit of all those present. Now they have been corrected and marked with a blue pencil. I have been told to change them. In this, for the first time in my life, I must be disobedient to authority. . . .

I cannot [change what I now know to be true]. Something different happened to me that day, and because of it I will not change the outlines.

She then told how, as she gave the lessons, the Holy Spirit came through her message with great power, and how afterward, to her astonishment, the entire audience of twenty-five hundred deeply moved women rose in silent standing tribute, then nearly hugged her to death as she came down from the platform.

I read on. She wrote about her family background and explained that when she, a widow, was sealed in the temple to her present husband, a widower, she had promised to acquiesce in the afterlife to his first wife, and so was "sealed for time and eternity in polygamy." She wrote: "You see, I am a polygamist. That is, I was—now I am not too sure. . . . I'd rather not think about it." And she had prefaced her letter with this: "If after reading this you had rather I did not visit with you, it will be quite all right, and I will understand perfectly."

Donald replied immediately:

Mrs. Barnhouse has shown me your letter, and I have it, and your previous one to me, to answer. How we rejoice in the manifest working of the Holy Spirit in your life, and for the assurance of your present possession of eternal life which He witnesses to you!

Then followed a whole page explaining how the English translation of the Bible was the only one in which two different words were used, interchangeably, to translate what in the original Greek was one word, *pneuma,* and that the "Holy Ghost" and the "Holy Spirit" were one and the same.

The fact that LDS leaders tried to distinguish between the two shows their unawareness of languages.

Now as to your statement that after we had read your family history we might not want to invite you!!! Dear Mrs. Brandley, the Lord is a Lord of love. We would love you and want you no matter what you were or had been. But I am sure the Holy Spirit is already teaching you, because you say, "I am a polygamist. That is, I was—now I am not too sure about it, I'd rather not think about it." But I say, in the light of the Bible, the only true Word of God, "DO THINK ABOUT IT!" You are not a second-class citizen. The Lord does not give to woman a place of inferiority. In Christ "there is neither male nor female" (Gal. 3:28). And Romans 7:1, 2 works both ways. First, it tells a woman that when her husband dies, she is free from the law of her husband. This definitely contradicts any thought of "sealing" for another world. Christ also taught this (Mark 12:25). Therefore, your husband's first wife was his only while she was here on earth. When she died he was a free man in the sight of God, and when married to you was your husband, and is your husband only at the present time. The whole doctrine of a woman's place being in heaven only because she is sealed to some LDS man is monstrous in the light of the Bible. You were redeemed by Christ Jesus and given eternal life; not conditional life, but eternal life and you belong in the promise recorded in 2 Corinthians 6:18. This verse does not say that you shall become an appendage to a man, but that you are His daughter even as a believer in Christ becomes a son (Gal. 3:26; John 1:12).

[You also speak] of holiness. How does holiness come about? Not through ritual anointings, but through the indwelling of the Holy Spirit. He is our holiness. Read John 17:17. . . . And the only anointing that the Bible knows anything about (except the ritual anointings of the Jewish Law, which were done away in Christ) is the anointing of the Holy Spirit. Read 1 John 2:26, 27. . . .

You speak of the difference in my use of the "gospel" and what you have been taught. The New Testament answer is in 1 Corinthians 15:1-4. ["I declare unto you the gospel which I preached

... by which also ye are saved.... that Christ died for our sins ... was buried, and... rose again."]

Do feel free to write fully about any problems that arise. Be assured that we will always be glad to hear from you, and that we are anticipating a good visit from you in June when your schedule is over and you are free.

I know the hard place you are in, but the Lord who has taken up His dwelling in your heart will give you the power and joy for every need. Galatians 5:1.

Yours faithfully,
Donald Grey Barnhouse

The next day the mailman picked up Donald's letter to Mrs. Brandley and left one for him from her. It contained several Latter-Day Saint publications, her outlines for the lessons she had given the Monday following her conversion, and a note which said:

"Regarding your outlines—I am in trouble! I have refused to change them, and so it stands. However, here are the first two."

She explained the LDS enclosures, to help him "see why I am confused.... I enclose the other things to show you that I am not a jack-Mormon [nominal], nor do I have any particular chip on the shoulder concerning my church. I am in good standing and have always been obedient to the voice of authority.

"My first act of disobedience has been in regard to my notes, your outlines. To change them would be to contradict the very thing I believe.

"Dr. Barnhouse... I am in really bad trouble. My husband is very disturbed about me and threatened to throw your books out if I didn't do it. Well, they are still here and here they remain. I love my husband and feel badly about the situation—but I also love the Lord. I have loved Him all my life and have always tried to be obedient to His commandments in all things. Please pray for me!"

Glad his own letter was on its way to her, Donald glanced through the LDS material, then picked up her lesson outlines and read them with amazement.

"Marge, the way she has grasped true doctrine is fantastic! Look how she has worked it out, from the sketchy notes I gave her!"

He passed the first set to me, then, looking at something she had written at the bottom of the other, read aloud, "I begin to see now that Joseph Smith reorganized the church of the Judaizers—everything in our church is under law: do this, do that, obey this commandment—I've been told to observe the law of the gospel since I was old enough to understand. The law, covenants, and oaths are given in the temple to be obeyed and followed. Christ did away with all this on the cross, when He said: It is finished! . . . I am very grateful to my Father in heaven that He gave me the curiosity (perhaps indignation) to hear the Dr. Look what I have gained: salvation and eternal life. . . . Thank you again and again!"

At Tenth Church the following Sunday, Donald told the story of her conversion, couching it in cautious language to conceal her identity, knowing it could get her into still more trouble if it were known. He told about her lesson outlines, then, using one of them, preached his sermon from it. It was so powerful, people were visibly shaken. Some came to him afterward and covenanted to pray for her.

From then on letters flew back and forth and the telephone lines between Doylestown and Salt Lake City were kept humming, as DGB would straighten out for Mrs. Brandley a point of Christian theology or vocabulary. I would hear snatches of the Doylestown end of the telephone conversations.

On one such occasion, when he hung up, I asked, "What was that in the beginning about her being forbidden to mention the blood?"

"Well, we had been talking about her classes. You know the Mormons believe that Jesus' crucifixion, death, and resurrection merely guarantee their resurrection, and His shed blood has nothing to do with their salvation. They must 'work out their own salvation.' Well, she told me that now, since her conversion, she has been teaching what the Bible says, that without the shedding of blood there is no remission of sin; that He who loved us washed us from our sins in His own blood; and other great passages. She said she had been reprimanded and forbidden to mention the blood anymore. . . ."

"So?"

"So instead of eliminating what is, of course, the very essence of salvation, she calls on women in the audience to read those passages aloud at the appropriate times. Women are being saved, and the authorities are very unhappy."

When she needed someone to talk to on a woman-to-woman basis, Mrs. Brandley would call me. We had sent her *Teaching the Word of Truth.* She had been ecstatic over it. Apparently it was doing for her what it had done for me. Her Christian growth was phenomenal as she studied her Bible in the new light of her salvation, gradually shifting from thinking according to LDS terminology to what God actually was saying in His Word in Christian terminology.

The "milk of the Word," which she so eagerly received, brought her quickly to the place where she was seeing Jesus Christ as He truly is: the unique, only-begotten Son of God. At the same time she was seeing herself compared to Him instead of compared to her people, where, in character and accomplishments, she had stood head and shoulders above the crowd. The closer she came to "the Wonderful Counselor, the Mighty God, the Everlasting Father, the Prince of Peace," the more horrified she became over what had been her Mormon concept of Him as merely a highly exalted man. According to their teaching, "As man is, God once was; as God is, man can become." Now she saw Jesus in all His majestic deity, stooping to take upon Him a human body and become a man in order to die to save her from her pride and self-righteousness.

In writing to us about what the Lord was teaching her,

she shared how one morning, as she was studying the material in DGB's *Romans,* the full impact of Romans 3:9 ("Jews and Gentiles . . . are all under sin") brought all of this into focus. She put it this way:

"Suddenly I couldn't go on. I was overwhelmed. I wept and wept until there were no tears left. Every word there was true. I was a sinner, lost, undone, unfit for anything; and stripped of my pride, I was Nothing—vile, unclean, fit for hell. In that time the Lord gave me a good look at myself. It wasn't pretty, not at all!" Her heart-cry continued for several pages, enumerating the teachings she had believed and taught others, the works she had done trying to achieve salvation as she had understood it, and concluding, "Truly I am a sinner, with nothing but pride, and now even that has been taken away—unclean, filthy, living in a cesspool of sin."

But, oh, her next paragraph where the marvelous grace of God in Christ broke through her despair! "But the blood of Jesus Christ has cleansed and saved me—not anything I have done: that's just works and of no use whatsoever. Jesus purchased my salvation by His great atoning work on Calvary, and never again can mere man make me cringe. I am saved! Once and for all and forever!"

Donald floated through the rest of the day.

But the pressures on Georgianne continued to build up. Her people couldn't understand what had happened to her, and kept trying various means to "bring her to her senses." A few weeks later she wrote:

"Your last two letters are the only tangible things I've had to hold onto. You will never, never know what this past week has been like. I wish I could wake up and feel it was a very bad dream—each day I wonder how much longer I can go on. I am so thankful my Savior's hand is strong or I would have dropped out long before this!"

We praised the Lord for His strong hand, and kept upholding her in prayer. She was never far from our thoughts.

TWENTY-TWO

In early May, Donald preached for a week in Bob Lamont's church in Pittsburgh. When we drove home from this conference, the night air was heady with the scent of flowering trees and shrubs. As we neared the rise from which we would see the house I felt the now familiar excitement welling up. There it was, every window glowing with light from within, welcoming us.

" 'Home is the sailor, home from the sea,/And the hunter home from the hill,' " I cried joyously. "How does that begin? I can't remember."

In a curiously flat voice he intoned, " 'Under a wide and starry sky.... Dig the grave and let me lie....' "

Appalled, I said, "How awful! I had forgotten...."

"Marge," he said, and his voice was infinitely weary, "there are times when I feel like the Apostle Paul. I am torn in so many directions.... I would so love to see Jesus and be with Him...." I was startled at the longing in his voice. He quoted Philippians 1:23, " 'I am in a strait betwixt two, having a desire to depart, and to be with Christ, which is far better. Nevertheless to abide in the flesh is more needful....' "

I could understand his depression. He had hoped to finish *The Invisible War,* but family problems and things in connection with the work kept pressing in on him. It looked as if Satan himself were behind the interruptions. In addition, Wanda, Donald's secretary, would be leaving shortly in order to be nearer her mother, who had suffered a heart attack. This was a real blow to DGB, who had come to depend on her, and to me, for she had become a dear friend.

We turned into the lane. Our headlights picked up the flowering cherry trees in full blossom along the fence. Donald's spirits lifted a bit. He stopped at the house, took out our bags, and noticed that the foundation of his long dreamed-of small greenhouse had been laid in our absence. Considerably cheered, he took the car to the garage.

Casting about for someone to replace Wanda, Paul Hopkins had found Sally Benton, who had taught school for ten years and was ready for a change. She was a good typist, was well organized, and was an excellent driver. She looked fragile and feminine but didn't fit the stereotype: she could even take apart and put together again the carburetor of her Model-A Ford. In addition, she *liked* to cook and keep house. But her main love was educational TV. She had a Sunday morning children's telecast over a local station for the Philadelphia Council of Churches. This for Donald was the frosting on the cake: she knew about producing a television show! Again the Lord had met our needs "exceeding abundantly."

And now it was time for Toshii's graduation from seminary and her return to Japan. We would miss her. All of us went to the airport to see her off; we hugged her tearfully. Then very solemnly, Donald slipped his hands down to his knees, making a formal Japanese bow, as her father had done when she had left him to come to us. Toshii giggled like a schoolgirl and bowed to him. Then she was on the plane, in the air, on her way back. America had not corrupted her.

We didn't know that Toshii was leaving with an aching heart. She and a fellow student—an American—had fallen deeply in love. But he had felt a call to chaplaincy in the navy; she felt she must go back to Japan and fulfill what she had been trained for, so after much prayer they had given each other up. But the Lord moves in mysterious ways: instead of being sent to the Mediterranean as he had thought, within a year the navy ordered Dick Moore to Tokyo, Japan! It was as if the Lord had tested them, then given them back to one another. (Dick and Toshii are now happily married and serving a church in New Jersey.)

June sped along, punctuated with the coming and going of many houseguests. One of the most enjoyable bonuses of the summer was having the grandchildren visit from time to time. Kathy and the girls were with us during June and July. They would tiptoe downstairs very early for their breakfast; Donald and I had ours later, in our bedroom, on the table set up for our games. After breakfast Donald would go downstairs and play some crashing chords on the piano, his signal for family worship. The little girls would come running and climb all over their granddaddy, with much hugging and kissing. Kathy would join us; then Donald would play a simple hymn and we'd all sing. There would be a Bible verse or two, then prayer. It didn't take more than five minutes, but it set a happy mood for the rest of the day. Each of us then would scatter to whatever we had to do.

Groups, such as the Geneva Cleric, an association of conservative pastors from the Philadelphia area, would often meet at the Farm for dinner and a time of discussion. Following such meetings Donald was frequently behind in his schedule and would stay at his typewriter until four or five in the morning, then sleep until noon. After a good brunch he would go out to mow the lawn, clad in a dizzy plaid shirt and his Texas ten-gallon hat, riding the big tractor-mower as if it were a prancing steed. He liked to do his thinking at these times: if anyone called, he couldn't hear over the roar of the motor, and the scent of new-mown grass was balm to his soul as his mind worked through knotty problems.

Then came the joyous news that Georgianne Brandley's

husband, Hal, had given his permission for her to come east for a visit. At the end of June, we met her train in Philadelphia and drove her to the Farm.

After dinner on the porch that evening, as we sat looking out over the rolling meadows and the little lake, Georgianne was pensive. She had been telling us of some of the methods that had been used by the authorities to bring her into line.

"I wish...." her voice trailed off. Then she said, "Dr. Barnhouse, I know they're going to put me out if I don't give up what they call 'this nonsense,' but now that I know the true Jesus I'll never give Him up. Do you suppose... could I become a member of Tenth Church while I'm here?"

"No, Georgianne...." She recoiled as if he had slapped her. "I'm sure Tenth would more than welcome you, but you've come this far in your witness to your people and you can't back out now. I know you are concerned about them. You must go back and be a missionary to the Mormons. You must stay until they put you out, *for Jesus' sake*. I promise you that when that happens you can come live with us and become a member of Tenth, but if you joined our church now, the Mormons could put you out for that, and your witness would be lost."

"How would they know?" Tears were near the surface.

"Do you think for one minute they aren't keeping watch on your every move? You're an important person, Georgianne. They probably have figured we'd try to persuade you to join Tenth, and I wouldn't be at all surprised if some Mormons showed up at church Sunday morning, to check up on you."

"Now, *really,* Dr. Barnhouse!"

Before Donald went up to his study for the evening, he gave Georgianne his guided tour of the house. Then she settled happily into the bedroom in the wing, surrounding herself with reference books Donald had supplied.

Sunday dawned hot and humid. The church building was

filling rapidly as we arrived. Donald went to his office for prayer with the elders before the service; I guided Georgianne to a spot under the left gallery in the auditorium where we could see and hear without being too noticeable. Taking a lively interest in everything, she studied the bulletin, looked up the Scripture lesson, and pored over the words of the hymns. Then Donald came onto the platform, and we stood as the service began.

Donald was about to begin the opening prayer when to my consternation he swayed slightly, turned deathly pale, grasped the edges of the pulpit to steady himself, then to my relief recovered and began to pray. It had taken only a moment, but in that same moment Georgianne whispered into my ear, "There they are!" I followed her glance to the opposite gallery. "Who?"

"The Mormons."

"How do you know?"

"The books."

I watched as two men and a woman made their way down the steep steps to seats in the front row of the gallery. Each had three books clasped to the breast. As they seated themselves they held these books in front of them on the gallery railing like a shield. "That's to protect them from what they believe to be the Devil in the pulpit," she whispered. "They're the *Book of Mormon,* the *Doctrines and Covenants,* and the *Pearl of Great Price.*"

I looked at Donald. The strange seizure of a moment ago had passed, but I realized he had been right: the Invisible War was indeed in progress, and the battle lines drawn.

During the last hymn we saw the three Mormons slip out of the church. As far as we knew, they were not there at the evening service.

Two nights later Georgianne called her husband, to check in and let him know how she was. He made a remark about something in Donald's sermon that made her realize they had indeed been checking up on her and must have reported back to the authorities in Salt Lake.

On Monday, the Fourth of July, Tenth Church had a picnic and conference at the recreation area of the Farm. With power and assurance, Georgianne gave her testimony, at Donald's request. We didn't know until afterward that she had been, as she put it, "frightened to death" because this was the first time that she had ever spoken before "Gentiles," as the LDS call all who are outside their fold. Our people were greatly moved. During prayer time many fervent prayers went up in her behalf.

At dinner she told us about her family. She had been a widow with four children when she married Hal. He had seven children, so she had been a busy mother. She and Hal were "rock hounds": they would go on field trips whenever they could, hunting the semi-precious stones that abounded in their part of the West. Hal would cut and polish these, and make them into beautiful jewelry. Georgianne had brought me a gift of lovely earrings he had made.

"How would he like some samples of Eastern gem-rocks?" asked Donald. Georgianne's eyes lit up. "I'll get him some," Donald said. He called a friend who knew about such things, and within a few days a good selection was on its way west. (As a result of this simple gesture of Donald's, showing a genuine interest in something that was so dear to Hal, something clicked, and the four of us enjoyed a pleasant camaraderie from then on.)

Thursday was a day of strange happenings.

At six-thirty A.M. Donald's hand on my shoulder woke me.

"Marge, do you smell gas?"

Instantly I was wide awake. I sniffed but could detect no odor of gas. I went into the bathroom, thinking it might be sewer gas backing up somewhere. I poked my head out the window: perhaps the septic tank had overflowed. Our home used no commercial gas, only electricity. Then it occurred to me that it was odd that he hadn't gotten up to check it himself.

He must have dreamed it, I thought, and crawled back into

bed, where he was lying with eyes closed. Then I saw that he was not asleep: he was praying. He turned to me.

"Marge, I am under satanic attack. I can feel it from every direction. We must pray!"

For over half an hour we prayed urgently, claiming the victory over Satan that Jesus had won by His death on the cross and His Resurrection, praising Him and glorifying His name. Then Donald said calmly, "Marge, I am about to go into a coma. Don't worry about me—everything is going to be all right." Whereupon he sank into a deep, deep sleep.

I was terrified. I flew down the stairs and called Georgianne, who, among her other accomplishments, was an R.N. I told her briefly what had happened. She came up to the bedroom with me, took his pulse, felt his forehead, lifted his eyelids, and looked at his eyes. "I'd get a doctor," she said.

"What do you think it is?"

She shook her head. "I really don't know. Let's see what the doctor says." (Years later she told me she would have diagnosed it as brain fever, but she didn't want to frighten me.)

Tom Durant, our regular doctor, was out of town. The local doctor Donald occasionally called was making his rounds at the hospital, so didn't arrive until several hours later. By then Donald was awake and had a splitting headache. The doctor left a prescription, and ordered ice packs for the headache, and a liquid diet. I had the uneasy feeling that he really didn't know what the trouble was. We called Bob Scott, the assistant pastor, and asked him to take prayer meeting, which in summer met on Thursday evenings at the recreation area of the Farm.

After lunch, Georgianne went to her room to type up some outlines of the commentary on the Book of John Donald had recommended. She asked me to call her fifteen minutes before dinner.

Kathy fed the children at five and tucked them in early. Prayer meeting would be at seven-thirty, so Kathy, Sally ton, Georgianne, and I planned to have our dinner at six o'clock.

Fifteen minutes before dinner I went to call Georgianne. She was stretched out on her bed, pale and frightened.

"Georgianne! What's the matter?"

"Oh, Margaret, I wish I knew." She sat up slowly and put her hand on the back of her head. "I was sitting there, typing, with my back to the door, when I became aware that someone was standing behind me. You know how you can sense this. I looked around, and there was no one there. I thought I must have imagined it and went back to my typing. In a few minutes I had that feeling again, only stronger. This time as I turned around I stood up, and I felt a blow on the head and there I was, flat on the floor. Yet *no one was here!* I crawled over and got up on the bed, and have been just lying here trying to figure it out." She sighed.

"Come get some dinner and you'll feel better," I said, helping her up.

At the table we discussed the events of the day. We wondered if Satan was behind all this, trying to stop Donald from exposing him (for Donald had been up late the night before, working on *The Invisible War*), and trying to frighten Georgianne into giving up her bold witness.

Sally said, "Ha! I'd just like to see Satan or anyone else pull something like that on me!"

We could see, coming up the lane, the first of the cars bringing people to prayer meeting. Kathy, Sally, and Georgianne went down to the recreation area; I went up to check on Donald. He felt better, but his head still ached.

At four in the morning I was aware that Donald was stirring restlessly. The ice in the ice bag had melted, so I went down to the kitchen, refilled it, and had just put it on his head when the telephone rang. It was Sally, calling from the cottage, a bunkhouse we had remodeled for a secretary's apartment.

"Marge, is everything all right? I saw lights over there...."

"Yes. I was just getting some ice for the ice bag—but you sound upset. Is everything all right there?"

"Marge—" (she was controlling her voice with difficulty) "I've just had the most awful experience. I never should have said that about any tricks played on me. I was sound asleep, when suddenly someone grabbed both of my feet and *shook* me, so hard it woke me and the bed was still shaking. I turned on the light. No one was in the room. I got up and peeked into the living room, then into the bathroom. Nobody. And the door and all the windows are closed and locked, because I had the air conditioner going. I can't figure it out!"

"Why don't you come over to the main house for the rest of the night?"

"No. I'll be all right. I just had to talk to someone and make sure I wasn't crazy. It's all right."

"Call me if anything else happens. And start praising the Lord! If it *is* Satan, he can't stand that!"

On Friday, things were back to normal. We did a lot of joyful praising to keep them that way.

Friday night, Donald and Georgianne delved more deeply into an examination of various Mormon beliefs and practices. Georgianne gave her permission to tape this discussion.

At one point Donald asked about the LDS wording of God's curse on Satan after the Fall and discovered that they quoted the first half of Genesis 3:15 straight out of the Bible: "I will put enmity between thee and the woman, and between thy seed and her seed."

"What about the rest of it?" Donald asked. " 'He shall bruise thy head and thou shalt bruise his heel'?"

"No, they don't say that."

"They don't?"

"No, that part's left out."

"Oh? The cross is left out. (This is, of course, the first prophecy of the cross.) *Very* interesting."

At the end of the interview, when it would have been

bedtime for most people, including Georgianne and me, Donald still had work to do.

"Well, God has delivered you," he said to Georgianne. "It's really amazing. I have seen some remarkable transformations in my life—multitudes of people saved—but I have never seen anything quite like this.

"Now, dear heavenly Father, we thank Thee and praise Thee that we do not have to be structured in an order of prayer, but as the Scripture says, 'We know not how to pray as we ought, but the Holy Spirit within intercedes with groanings that cannot be uttered.' And our hearts, O Lord our God, are appalled at this revelation of how Satan can twist the gospel and make it mean something else, and bring souls into slavery and bondage to men.... I thank Thee that our sins are cleansed not with the washing of water by men, but by the precious blood of Jesus Christ who gave Himself a ransom, that we might have eternal life. We worship Thee, we worship Thee.

"Our Father, we praise Thee for the deliverance that Thou hast given us. Our hearts are drawn to cry out for these women that Georgianne has been dealing with, especially the ones that are on the point of believing, Lord. May they look beyond anything in this life and see the Word of God and Christ in the Word, the Living Word, and be brought to the knowledge of eternal life. And we are thinking, Lord, of all the two thousand or more women who heard her speak on that March 28 and who went back to their wards to teach these lessons, that they too may turn to the Bible, that they may read and understand, they and those that hear them (for we want this Word to go on, Lord, from person to person to person, and spread as a fire). May it be, O Lord our God, so evidently Thy work it shall always be seen that no man had anything to do with it, that it was all of Thee, O God, Thou, the God and Father of our Lord Jesus Christ.

"Now bless us this night. Bless Georgianne. Give her quiet, sweet rest. We pray that as she sleeps Thou wilt give to her great comfort and joy and blessing. May we three together hold on to Thee, Lord, believing that Thou wilt save Hal and that Thou wilt in a wonderful way deal with him. We cannot do this, but Thou Lord, Thou canst beat back the powers of darkness through the blood of Jesus Christ. They overcame Satan 'by the blood of the Lamb, and by the word of their testimony.' And so we pray Thee, O God, that Thou wilt do this thing. O, hear us.

"Now give us rest, and give me quickness of mind for what work I have yet to do.

"Bless Marge, and I thank Thee for her. And all these things we ask in the name and for the sake of our Lord Jesus Christ. Amen."

Sunday we took Georgianne to the train, her spiritual batteries recharged for the witness she was determined to bear for her Lord.

After Georgianne's return to Salt Lake the telephone lines continued to hum between us. Frequently Hal would join in a jovial interchange with Donald. Donald and I continued to pray for Hal, sure the Lord was going to save him.

The theological problems for which Georgianne needed answers sparked Donald's thinking. His advice to her to stick with the Scriptures and not try to refute LDS teaching was making him think about his own approach to such things.

Late in July, Ralph came to the Farm to work with DGB on a companion booklet to *How to Mark Your Bible,* entitled *How to Study Your Bible.* They sat in his study, and with a tape recorder going, discussed DGB's methods of Bible study. DGB told how, as a boy of seventeen, he had been led into expository preaching by the excitement of his own discoveries on digging into God's Word. He recounted how a casual remark by Tom Hannay, the man who had brought him into the assurance of his salvation, had shamed him into putting down a newspaper he was reading and picking up his Bible, which, figuratively, he had not put down since. Then he discussed the main reference books there in his study.

Later, sitting in Donald's big study chair and listening to that tape, I realized that even though I had lived in this house for more than six years I had no idea what treasures of study helps were on those shelves. I looked around at the things that made Donald's work easier: the rolling book table, with its three-tiered movable shelves; the special storage space for his maps, in the corner where two low bookcases met; the handles placed on the edges of some of the wall bookcases so he could pull himself over, take out a book, and pull himself back to the typewriter without having to get up out of his chair. On the tape I could hear the chair squeaking slightly and could almost see him in action as he moved from place to place, showing Ralph what was there.

Next time I have a message to prepare, I thought, *I'll slip in here to do it.*

The plan of study Ralph Keiper had blocked out the year before for "B," as Ralph called him, worked well. They had marked on his calendar, a year in advance, the date each study in Romans or in the Summer Series would be broadcast, giving it a number or a key letter. As each was written, DGB would mark beside the number a *D,* "done." When it had been recorded he would add *&T,* "taped." Ralph would come to the Farm periodically to work with DGB, giving him outlines and idea sheets which he had researched, which DGB sometimes used, sometimes not, but they kept him flowing in the inevitable dry periods. For a weekly broadcast the deadlines were inexorable. Donald would assign himself a writing task and time himself with a kitchen timer, forcing himself to complete the task within the allotted time. The pressure from this was great, but he found himself producing more—and better—writing.

Donald plunged into the final study of his series on the Epistle to the Romans. It would be finished two whole weeks before he left for Costa Rica, leaving him time to catch up on other things. He was jubilant. This would complete ten years on the air in that epistle. By dinnertime he had finished his reference work, and planned to write the radio script that evening.

I was sure this last study would be a traumatic experience for him. Undoubtedly he would be working until all hours. We had our evening devotions, then as he sat down to the typewriter I left him and went to bed, with some private prayers of my own winging upward for him.

The next morning I slipped out of bed, leaving him sleeping, and tiptoed to the bathroom, eager to see the manuscript, which I knew would be waiting for me there as usual.

But where was it? I knew he had finished it, because he had roused me to tell me so when he had finally come to bed.

When he awakened a little later I asked him about it. He smiled at me tenderly.

"I have an appointment with Paul at the Foundation today. I thought you could drive me in, and I'd read it to you on the way."

Donald waited until we were on the open road, then drew the manuscript from his briefcase and started to read.

" 'To the only wise God be glory for evermore through Jesus Christ! Amen.' Romans 16:17.

"I put the paper into my typewriter to begin work on this study. At the top I typed the number series that makes it possible for us to identify this message. Suddenly my fingers trembled. I was trembling all over. I stopped typing and leaned back in my chair and looked at the paper, the typewriter, the open Bible beside me, the familiar volumes of research in my study, from floor to ceiling. Was it possible? I was typing the very last of my studies in the Epistle to the Romans."

His voice had trembled slightly as he began reading, but now was firm. He told how he had preached from nothing but this epistle for the first three-and-a-half years of his ministry at Tenth Church, and during that time had seen the church filled to capacity. When twenty years later he had begun these radio studies, he had destroyed those notes and started afresh.

"Now, some five hundred broadcasts later, with approximately four thousand large pages filled with small type, I am at the last benediction. It is a moment that is filled with deep gratitude to God. I know of almost a hundred men who have gone into the ministry as a result of the broadcast of these studies. I know of multitudes who have been richly blessed in their spiritual lives. . . . But far greater than any blessing that these studies have brought to others is their effect on my own life. I know that the epistle to the Romans has become the very fabric of my life. Here I have met God so many times that it would be impossible to remember them all.

"I believe that my emotion upon coming to the last verse in the epistle has helped me to understand it."

He then launched into a masterful exposition of the Scripture passage. How I wished I could watch his face instead of having to keep my eyes on the road! How I wished I could have had a recording of his voice as he read it, with all the power and emotion of this moment!

Then the exposition was over and he had come to the conclusion. Again his voice was trembling and had to be brought under control.

"As I sit at my typewriter working, I think ahead to eternity and when I shall be given some task to do by the Lord. I try to project myself forward and to know exactly how I shall go about it. For I say, 'Lord, I want to go about my present tasks in the same way that I shall work for Thee in the future.' And I say, 'Lord, I am Thy child. I have nothing in myself. All that is good in me is because Thy life is in me. I come to Thee for wisdom. Give me knowledge and power for the next moment, and then for the next moment. Show me Thy will. Teach me Thy way. Give me Thy power.' And now I know that anything effective that I ever do for the Lord is done after the completion of that process of surrender, filling, and action for Him. If I find that here on earth in the midst of a fallen creation, with my own outward man perishing, with the divine verdict written that 'if any one imagines that he knows something, he does not yet know as he ought to know' (1 Cor. 8:2, RSV), how much more shall it be that I shall follow this same process in eternity, when my fallen nature will be forever behind me, and I shall be like the Lord Jesus Christ in righteousness, wisdom and power.

"This is the wisdom of God: He has made it possible for men who were made lower than the angels to rise higher than the angels. He has made it possible for creatures to become sons. He has made it possible for those who were once bound by earth and all its forces of gravity in every field to be loosed from earth and to know the throne of God as eternal home.

"Is it any wonder that we cry, 'To the only wise God be glory for evermore through Jesus Christ!' To God be the glory. To God be all the glory. To God be all the glory for evermore. To God be glory through the Lord Jesus Christ.'

"I thank Thee, O Lord, that these are the last words of my feeble and humble work. To Thee be all glory through Jesus Christ. Whatever of weakness has been in the work comes from Donald Grey Barnhouse. Whatever of strength, power, love, grace and glory has been in the work has come from Thee. To God, the only wise God be glory for evermore, through the Lord Jesus Christ. Amen."

I glanced at him. Tears were streaming down his cheeks but his face was radiant. He put the manuscript down. I placed my hand softly over his.

TWENTY-THREE

In mid-August a visit from the Townsends (Cameron Townsend was head of Wycliffe Bible Translators) increased Donald's eagerness to be on his way to the Spanish Language School in Costa Rica, where at last his plans to perfect his Spanish would materialize. He was to be there on September 1, have four days to settle in, then on September 5 begin the actual studies that would enable him to preach in Spanish. I would not be with him at this time. My daughter Carolyn's first baby was due around September 2, so I would fly to California, stay with her for a week or two after the baby was born, then join Donald in Costa Rica.

DGB happily wound up his affairs: recording; writing two of his new radio series; seeing his dentist; giving Anton, the manager of the gardens and grounds at the Farm, instructions. The greenhouse was progressing well, and would be ready to use by late fall.

Sunday morning, August 28, Donald tried out on his congregation the first of his "First Things First" series, written that week and later to go out over the airwaves: "First, be reconciled to thy brother" (Matt. 5:23, 24). He opened with a quotation from the Apostle's Creed: " 'I believe in the forgiveness of sins.' Do you? If you do, then knowing God has forgiven you, you *must* forgive others." It was a searching-of-the-heart experience.

That evening his sermon was on Zephaniah 3:17: "The Lord thy God in the midst of thee is mighty; he will save, he will rejoice over thee with joy; he will rest in his love, he will joy over thee with singing." He is *personal* ("the Lord *thy* God"); He is *here* always ("in the *midst* of thee"), reachable, touchable. The Lord will meet with you; His Presence will go with you. He is *mighty* ("a Warrior who gives victory"). He has never known a defeat. Our battles have already been won by Jesus Christ on the cross, *then* fought out by us. He rejoices over us!

The message kept spiraling upward. We left the church feeling right up there in the heavenlies, beloved, surrounded by joy.

The next day Donald left for Costa Rica.

Carolyn's baby took its time about entering this world. On the eleventh of September Donald called me: "When are you coming down here? I miss you!"

"Donald, the baby isn't here yet. I'll let you know. I miss you, too!"

"Well, *my* daughters had their babies without their mother. . . ."

"Come on now, Donald," I said, laughing. "I promised Carolyn, and I'm going to be here as promised."

My little granddaughter arrived the next day. Max and Carolyn brought her home from the hospital two days later.

A week flew by. Donald called again. "Marge, when are you coming? You said you'd come after the baby arrived." He sounded like a petulant child.

I looked quickly at the calendar in Carolyn's kitchen. "Dear, I said 'a week *or two,*' but things are going so well here I think I'll be able to leave by Saturday." That was five days away.

"But I want you *now.* Marge . . . I don't feel well."

That rascal! Imagine his trying to play on my sympathies that way! "Donald, are you sticking to your diet?"

"How can I? I eat what the others eat: typical Spanish food."

"Now Donald, you get yourself into the city and get some lean meat and some of the vegetables on your list. You'll feel lots better, I know. I'll see you next weekend. Please take care of your diet! I love you!" *I've let him get much too dependent on me,* I thought. *Lord, make him behave himself!*

That was September 20. On September 22 Donald called again.

"Marge? I'm in Miami. I'm on my way home."

I was stunned. "Miami! But why?"

"I told you I didn't feel well. I thought I'd better get home and have Tom Durant look me over."

My conscience smote me. "Do you think it's the diabetes?"

"Could be. I'll be home tomorrow at six in the morning. I'm going to try to see Tom right away."

I was torn. I wanted to fly back home immediately, but if it should be something minor, and he should go right back to Costa Rica, there was no point in my leaving. I decided I'd wait for Tom's report.

The blood tests showed the diabetes was indeed flaring up. They put Donald into the hospital for observation, and started insulin, confident that it would bring things under control.

On Monday, Paul Hopkins called me and told me I'd better get home. Donald was not cooperating. Sugar, of course, was forbidden, but he'd buy candy bars whenever the cart with newspapers and candy came around. Because he was ambulatory, they couldn't watch him every minute. Maybe he'd listen to me.

For the first time I became alarmed. What I had thought was merely routine could be more serious. I was sorry I hadn't gone back when Donald first went home.

Sally Benton met me at the airport. She told me how he had insisted on driving himself to the hospital Saturday. He had parked his car in front of the hospital, taken his overnight bag, and signed himself in. Next morning the car was gone. They reported this to the police and found it had been towed away and impounded for illegal parking!

I was shocked when I saw him the next morning. His hair was disheveled; one side of his face looked odd. When Tom Durant, our doctor, came in I asked him whether Donald had had a slight stroke. He said they had tested for this, but the tests were negative. However, they were puzzled: they couldn't regulate the insulin. What was a correct dosage one day was wrong the next.

Donald begged to go home. Tom said he could if I would take him to the small emergency hospital in Doylestown every morning, have blood tests, then report to him, whereupon he would tell me what the insulin dosage should be. He showed me how to give the insulin injections and stressed the importance of keeping him on his special diet. *No* sugar in any form. He gave me some other instructions, then told me to report immediately any personality changes.

"Personality changes"? I wondered if Tom had told me everything. Donald walked out of the hospital, shuffling like an old man. I kept shooting little arrow prayers up to the Lord.

Once we were home, Donald seemed more like himself. We walked slowly around the lawns, enjoying the fall flowers in the borders and stopping to watch the birds.

That night we started a game of "Camelot." He took forever to make up his mind on the simplest moves.

In the morning I gave him his insulin a half-hour before breakfast, as instructed. I carried his breakfast up to him—and found him still in bed. He ate so slowly I began to get nervous: we were due at the hospital for blood tests at nine. He resisted being hurried into his clothes; he got belligerent when I told him we really must go. I brought the car around, and through the kitchen window I saw him snitch a cookie from the children's cookie jar. This was all so totally out of character I began to see what Tom had meant by "personality changes."

This was Sunday, and it seemed strange not to be in church. On the way to the hospital I switched on the radio, for the Bible Study Hour. Donald's interest perked up as he heard his voice, in the middle of a message he had written in January. He was talking about the confident plans the Apostle Paul was making (Rom. 15:22-24), which did not materialize. Donald's voice continued, about some of his own projected plans for 1961. Then he said:

"In spite of all this, I could dictate rapidly for an hour about events which might occur to cancel all these plans. The Lord might come. I might go to heaven through death. I might be alive but in the hospital. Some parts of the country might be unapproachable because of atomic fallout. I might lose my voice.

"It is not necessary to go farther. I have long since learned to live as though Jesus Christ were coming today, and to plan as though He were not coming for years. Everything I do and say is subject to the thought, sometimes expressed but always there even though unexpressed, that all is subject to the blessed will of God. . . .

"I think that God let Paul's plans go awry and his hopes fail in order to give great comfort to believers of all generations.

"Our trust is in the Lord, not in our plans. He is Lord of our lives and Lord of all our plans. He can do with us exactly what He pleases, and when, and where. And in our total commitment to His will lies our highest joy."

We arrived at the hospital just as the program ended. Donald was smiling. Suddenly I realized this was the first time he had really smiled since I had gotten back from California.

That night Donald woke me, complaining of severe pain in his neck. There was a gland in a certain spot that in the past had given him trouble: if I massaged it the swelling would go down. He asked me to do this. I couldn't feel any swelling, but the neck rub soothed him, and he went back to sleep.

Monday morning we went through the same agony over getting him up, having breakfast, dressing, and arriving at the hospital by nine. I hated to nag, but I had to. This only increased his hostility. As he got to his study door on the way downstairs he hesitated a moment, and told me to go on ahead. Then he slipped into his study and sneaked a fig out of the desk drawer where he kept his midnight "nibblings." I made a mental note to clear away all such temptations as soon as possible.

Monday night Donald wakened me, again around four, with what he called "constant pain" in his neck. Again, rubbing soothed him to sleep. However, the next morning the difficulty in rousing him for breakfast and his dawdling over everything were worse than ever. Sally had the car at the door this time, so we went straight out, giving him no chance at the cookies. He complained, "You steered me past the kitchen!"

After the blood test, he sat and talked interminably to the doctor, who listened patiently. Finally I got him on his feet. He leaned on my arm, going out slowly and saying, "This is my future. You're tied to an old man." "Silly!" I answered. "You've been *sick.*"

At home he wanted to work in the garden. When he tried to start the Rototiller, he couldn't do it.

"Do you want me to try?" I suggested.

"You couldn't." He sounded discouraged.

"Well, we'll get Anton to start it," I said.

From the kitchen window I watched Donald, usually so sure-footed, out in the field, trying to make a furrow, lurching as if slightly drunk. Finally I asked Anton, if he would try to persuade Dr. Barnhouse to let him take over. Donald turned the Rototiller over to him and came wearily to the house. He asked for some tea, then went to the porch. Again he said he had severe neck pain. After a while he asked for lunch, then wandered in, sat at the piano, and played some simple things, without his accustomed vigor. By this time he was too tired to sit at the table, so he lay down on the bed and had his lunch there.

That evening we tried "Camelot" again. He became so upset over not being able to win that I let him win a time or two. By this time I was truly concerned.

All this while, despite his confusion, he had had Georgianne on his mind. He had called her from the hospital when he was there for observation. Learning that on Wednesday, October 5, she was to speak before a convocation of five thousand women from all over the world, he promised to pray for her. As we were getting ready for bed he glanced at the calendar and said, "Tomorrow is Georgianne's big day." We prayed for her in our evening devotions.

That night, with the neck pain severe again, I asked what I could do to help. He cried out in frustration, "Fix my *cancer.*"

"Silly! Is that the trouble: you think you have cancer? Well, if that were true they wouldn't be fooling around with the diabetes: they'd operate immediately!" This seemed to relieve his anxiety. I felt the back of his neck and pressed that gland. "Is this where it hurts?"

To my astonishment, he said, "No."

Pressing gently, I moved my fingers around toward his ear. "Here?"

"No."

I moved up the base of the skull to the mastoid bone behind the ear. "Here?"

"Yes!" This was an alarming development.

I had been in daily contact with Tom, changing the insulin dosage as directed after he got the results of the blood tests. But this couldn't wait until tomorrow. I got up and called Tom, who told me to try hot compresses and call him first thing in the morning. The compresses helped and Donald drifted off to sleep.

Wednesday morning he was impossible. To his consternation, I burst into tears. "Oh, Donald, what on earth am I to do? I don't want to force you, but you *must* have breakfast within half an hour after the insulin shot, and you *must* finish in time to get to the hospital by nine or the blood tests won't go through in time for Tom to give me instructions on your dosage."

Wounded, he looked at me, his eyes begging for understanding. "Dear... I'm sorry.... I don't know what is wrong. Give yourself all the time you need for the breakfast... figure it out... call me five or ten minutes ahead, then keep giving me time checks.... If I am out of order, just whisper, 'Belligerent,' and I'll know what you mean. ... I'm sorry...." (From then on, that was what I did, and it worked.)

On the way home from the hospital Donald asked me what day it was. When I told him, he said, "Wednesday! Today is Georgianne's big day!"

There hadn't been time for devotions before we left, so when we got to the house we sat on the porch, prayed for our day and for Georgianne, then opened *Daily Light,* the wonderful little devotional book we used. It has an opening Bible verse, followed by a page full of related verses, for the morning and again for the evening of each day, the Bible's commentary on itself. "You read," said Donald.

The opening verse was Psalm 50:15, "Call upon me in the day of trouble: I will deliver thee, and thou shalt glorify me."

Donald interrupted. "That's for Georgianne!" He brightened as I continued to read. Most of the quotations for that day were from the Psalms, on how the Lord's goodness and mercy were to those who call upon Him. The last one, Psalm 116:1–4, read, "I love the Lord, because he hath heard my voice and my supplications. Because he hath inclined his ear unto me, therefore will I call upon him as long as I live. The sorrows of death compassed me, and the pains of hell got hold upon me: I found trouble and sorrow. Then called I on the name of the Lord."

Donald whispered, "That's for me."

David and Mary Alice and their three children were due to arrive late that afternoon for the brief vacation planned that summer. I had called and told them of the situation, but asked them to come anyhow, as planned, feeling it was in the providence of the Lord that David's vacation had fallen that week. I wanted his medical opinion of his father's condition. When I told Donald they were coming, he said with pleasure, "We must get out the puzzles."

"The puzzles" were intricately cut, thousand-piece jig-saw puzzles mounted on wood, part of his children's childhood. He knew the grandchildren would enjoy them. After dinner that night we all went into the living room and gathered around the table where David dumped the pieces out and the children turned them over so the picture side was up. Then we all started working it. All except Donald. He sat there, bewildered, staring at the pieces. He shook his head slightly, got up, went wearily over to the big chair, and sat there watching from afar. The others were too busy and excited to notice.

The next day I had a serious talk with David. He was deeply concerned and thought his father should go in for more tests. He had watched his father try to do a simple crossword puzzle in the daily paper that someone had brought in. Donald kept getting the horizonals and verticals mixed up. Yet only six weeks before this, at a gathering of his daughter Ruth's colleagues, he had worked a complicated anacrostic puzzle, and at the same time had carried on a conversation in French with a French guest, in Hebrew with a rabbi, and in English with the others. And all this with no more apparent mental effort than it would have taken me to carry on a simple conversation while knitting!

Amazingly, he could still play our eight-letter word game. The night before he went back to the hospital he was making a list of words with tricky letter combinations to use against me: "platypus," "rheostat," "tipstaff," and others.

The pain seemed to come more frequently and with increasing intensity. Friday afternoon it was decided Donald should go into the hospital Saturday morning for more tests. We didn't tell him about it for fear of upsetting and confusing him. Meanwhile, he had been on the telephone with our car salesman. Because of the hard use he gave it, Donald bought a new car every two years. He had decided that after his blood tests on Saturday he would go to the showroom, look over the new cars, and order one so it would be ready before we started on our winter conference tour. David said to me privately, "Marge, unless there's a miracle, Dad isn't going to be up to a winter conference tour this year. I'd soft-pedal the car."

I wrote a note to our salesman, telling him my husband was a sick man; he should write up the order, but do nothing about it until he heard from me. Donald had made an appointment with the man, so he was waiting for us. I walked up to the door slightly behind Donald, and motioned to the salesman; putting my finger to my lips, I pointed to my note. He held the door for us. As Donald shuffled through, the salesman took my note, glanced at it, then at Donald, nodded to me, and pocketed the note.

When we left, I started toward Philadelphia. It was five minutes or more before Donald realized we were not homeward bound. I explained, "Tom wants you to go in for some more tests, to see if they can do something about the pain." He looked relieved, then relaxed, and dozed a bit during the hour-long drive to Temple Hospital.

Tests revealed a massive tumor on the brain.

An immediate operation to remove it was indicated. I was glad David was there: he concurred. Donald gave his consent—anything to get rid of the pain.

The operation took seven hours. When it was over, the surgeon sought me out and found me in the coffeeshop. He sat down and very gently broke the news. He had removed a tumor the size of a grapefruit; it was malignant: on a scale of zero (benign) to four (a wild-fire growth), this was a three-plus. He had not been able to get all of it. To do so, he would have risked leaving Donald a "vegetable." He decided to leave that small bit and treat it with cobalt. The treatment would start when the incision healed and be given daily for about two weeks. Then we'd see. If the growth could not be checked, death would come swiftly. If it could be checked, Donald could go home to recuperate at the end of the treatments. It would be a while before they brought him down from the recovery room; he would undoubtedly be unconscious for several days. The surgeon had secured round-the-clock nurses and advised me to go home and get some rest. He laid a sympathetic hand on my shoulder, gave it an encouraging pat, then left.

I thought of the message in *Daily Light* that morning, October 8: "I will not fear what man shall do unto me. Who shall separate us from the love of Christ? . . . Nay, in all these things we are more than conquerors through him that loved us. . . ." I hoped these words had echoed in Donald's mind as he went into surgery. They sustained me as I started home. A loving heavenly Father had allowed this, for a purpose. No! He had *planned* it, before the foundation of the world. Ephesians 3:10 came immediately to mind: "To the intent that now unto the principalities and powers in the heavenlies might be made known by the church the manifold wisdom of God. . . ." Could what was happening to Donald be part of the Invisible War?

Right after Donald had gone into surgery I had wired his sisters, "SERIOUS NEWS DONALD AT MOMENT IN SURGERY BRAIN TUMOR PRAY." Now I sent a follow-up wire: "TUMOR REMOVED OUTLOOK BETTER KEEP PRAYING LETTER FOLLOWS." David had called his siblings and Uncle Toby's family; I called Mother and my children. Paul Hopkins notified the board of the Foundation, the church, and others. Round-the-clock prayer chains were set up. As soon as the Wycliffe people heard, they radioed the news to the tribes where Donald had preached the summer before, and primitive brothers in Christ joined their petitions to ours. Tenth's

Dial-a-Prayer service was turned over to daily bulletins on Donald's progress.

As I entered Donald's hospital room the next morning, a cheerful young nurse had just finished bathing him. He was lying absolutely still, tubes dangling from overhead attached to various parts of his anatomy, head bandaged, eyes closed, apparently in a deep coma. His arms lay motionless on top of the fresh covers. I leaned over and kissed him, then stood beside the bed, holding his right hand and talking to the nurse as she tidied the room. Suddenly I thought I felt a faint pressure from the hand I was holding. Quickly I looked at Donald's face. It was impassive. We talked for a while longer, and again I thought I felt a pressure, this time stronger. Looking at his expressionless face I felt foolish but I said, "Donald, can you hear me? If you can hear me, press my hand." This time the pressure was distinct. I said, "Does our chatter bother you?" I got a strong pressure. I was astonished. "Donald, would you like us to go somewhere else? Squeeze twice for no, once for yes." I received two squeezes. "Would you like me to stay and just stop talking?" One strong squeeze. The nurse gathered up the used bed linens and left excitedly to report this amazing happening. I said, "I love you," and kissed him, still holding his hand. Not a flicker of expression crossed his face but his hand gave me a strong squeeze.

I drew up a chair and sat beside him, holding his hand and studying his face. It occurred to me that hearing takes no muscular effort. Apart from motor responses, his mind could be functioning perfectly, and who would know? How awful for a thinking mind to be trapped inside a body that was unable to react, that couldn't lift an eyelid nor give a smile! I said, "Let's 'gild'!" He squeezed my hand. With my head next to his, I sang, "When morning gilds the skies, my heart, awaking, cries, 'May Jesus Christ be praised!' " I finished one verse, then felt a faint pressure. "Do you want to sleep now?" I asked. An even fainter pressure let me know he was already sinking to that deeper level of sleep.

Thus began my vigil. Knowing that despite the surgery his mind was functioning was very encouraging. Knowing he could communicate with me was thrilling. I was content to wait for the healing that would bring the rest of his body into function.

For a week he floated in and out of consciousness. Once or twice he spoke, calling the nurse or me, but his face continued to be expressionless. Then one day we noticed his eyes were ever so slightly open. The next day they were wide open, but his face was still motionless. Following my voice, his eyes looked at my face.

"Can you see me, darling?" I asked.

"Only . . . blobs . . . of dark . . . and . . . blobs . . . of light," he answered, closing his eyes again.

By October 19 the stitches were all out and the incision nicely healed. The daily cobalt treatments would begin the next day. Sitting at Donald's bedside day by day, I tried vainly to keep up with answering the mountains of mail that had been pouring in. A typical note read:

I am praying and believing for your recovery. I have been greatly blessed by your Bible teaching, even though I disagree with you theologically. However, I like to think that I have a spiritual heart fellowship with you.

Another letter read:

I am just one of thousands who have been blessed since way back in the 20's. . . . As the years whitened your hair, the love of God mellowed your heart, and more and more you have become characterized by the compassion of our beloved Savior.

Among many others there was a touching personal letter from Oswald Hoffman of the Lutheran Hour:

Dear Dr. Barnhouse:

Now you will find out how many friends you have. . . . There are many like myself who owe a great deal to you, because you have gone outside the wall to Him, have knelt at the foot of His cross, and have found forgiveness and life in His atonement, and have joyfully borne abuse and indignity for the sake of His Name. . . .

You have taught others how to take things patiently, and now you will have to take some of that instruction yourself. . . . We, your friends, are eager for the day when we shall again enjoy the warmth of your smile, even as you enjoy from day to day the warming smile of your Father that is His grace in Jesus Christ.

Cordially yours,
Oswald C. J. Hoffman

Day by day Donald's periods of consciousness became longer. He loved to have the Bible read aloud to him. He would pick up and complete the verses, although speech was still an effort. His eyes were focusing better, but he still recognized people more by their voice than by sight. His head had been shaved for the operation; now his white curly hair was growing back in a young-looking crew-cut effect. He was being fed by nose tube, and between the perfectly controlled diet of milk, juice, and vitamins and the complete rest, he was looking wonderful.

His mind apparently was floating freely among the various languages he knew. He would frequently use Spanish, that being the most recent acquisition, and the nurses would have to call in the Puerto Rican orderlies to interpret. One evening when Don, Jr., came in, the nurse reported that her patient "had been talking gibberish." Don listened to his father, then said, "Why, that's Hebrew he's speaking."

As Donald regained use of his body it became apparent that his left side was paralyzed. The useless arm and leg were exercised regularly. Gradually the leg began to function once more, but Donald still could not lift that arm. With his right hand he would massage the left hand, the arm, the shoulder, trying to bring life back into them.

His speech was still coming with difficulty. Much of

what he tried to say had to do with the unity of believers. One morning after our "gilding," I asked what he would like to pray for. He said, "We must pray for the Church— His body—the *whole* Church...." He paused, then said, "*We* know what the whole Church is." An answer seemed expected, so I said, "Yes, dear: each individual believer gathered together in Him."

"Yes," he replied, "each with his stuff and nonsense!"

Another time he seemed agitated. I stroked his forehead and asked what was troubling him. He said, "We must cry to the Lamb—He—is in us—and He will not be complete —until we are all in Him."

His daughter Dorothy flew from Germany to see him. When she walked through the door he smiled his first real smile. Such joy! During her stay, she and her brother Don would sing duets for their father, their beautiful voices blending and echoing through the hospital corridor, bringing clusters of nurses and visitors to listen at the door.

Leafing through the English Keswick hymnal they came to hymn 501, with words by Robert Murray McCheyne. As the glorious sound filled the room I saw tears well up in Donald's eyes at the second verse:

When I stand before the throne
Dressed in beauty not my own,
When I see Thee as Thou art,
Love Thee with unsinning heart:
Then, Lord, shall I fully know—
Not till then—how much I owe.

I had been recording it as they sang, thinking Donald might enjoy hearing it again after Dorothy had gone back to Germany. When I played the tape back that night, I heard his voice at the end, echoing the hymn in an agonized whisper, "I... owe...."

On Saturday, David came down from Rochester again to see his father. Donald was alert and glad to see him. David had brought Toby with him; they spent an enjoyable hour or two reading and talking with Donald. Dorothy came in late in the afternoon to join them.

As David was leaving, he took his father's right hand and said, "Dad, do you have any special words for your son?" With a hand squeeze, Donald answered, "Rest in the Lord." Then David took Dorothy's hand and leading her to the bedside asked, "How about for Dotty?" Their father's answer: "There is no rest except in the Lord."

On November 1 Donald's male nurse was able to get him out of bed and into a chair. On an impulse I put my lapboard across the arms of the chair and gave him paper and pen. He first made spirals as if to test the pen, then tried to write. His efforts looked like a baby's before coordination has been learned. Then I realized he didn't have his glasses on. I got them from the drawer and to my dismay discovered they wouldn't fit. The edema from the cobalt treatments had so distended that side of his head we had to have the glasses-bow curved to fit. From then on I gave him pen and paper each day, hoping that practice would help him learn to manage a pen once more.

The last of the cobalt treatments was scheduled for Saturday morning, November 5. Donald's improvement had been such that the doctors were considering the possibility of letting him go home. He could use the wing bedroom, where the back door was at ground level, opening onto the patio. It would be a simple matter to put him in a wheelchair and roll him out into the sunshine. When the greenhouse was finished we could lay a path to it from the patio; he could go there and enjoy his growing things. The nurse, a big, husky fellow, would be with him during the day to get him in and out of the wheelchair; I could take care of him at night.

The Thursday before the last cobalt treatment was due I had a strange conversation with Donald. His eyes had been moving back and forth as if he were planning something, thinking deeply about it. I sat beside him and asked, "What are you thinking about?"

"I'm writing a show."

"Oh?"

"Yes."

"Is this TV, or movies, or a play, or what?"

"Oh, any of them," he said.

His voice was not at all his normal voice. It sounded strange and sly. I asked, "What's it about?"

"Deceit."

"Deceit?"

"Yes—the deceitfulness of deceit."

"Tell me about it."

"It's to teach deceivers how to deceive." All the while he had been looking directly at me, as if by holding my eyes he could keep me from seeing him working his fingers under the bandage holding the nose-tube in place, a thing forbidden.

With a start I recognized the strange, sly voice, because at one time that same voice had spoken through me. When I was in my teens I used to read palms, as a parlor game. I became so good at it I was quite in demand at parties. For some reason I could see in a person's palm true things I had no way of knowing. At times like that I was aware that the voice saying these things through me *was not my voice*—and the voice coming from Donald sounded just like it. After I knew Jesus as my Savior, the Holy Spirit convicted me that I had been dabbling in the occult, and that the voice speaking through mine could well have been a demon. I had renounced the whole thing, in Jesus' name.

I took both of Donald's hands and began to pray. I claimed Jesus' own request from the Father, in His high priestly prayer of John 17:15, "I pray not that thou shouldest take them out of the world, *but that thou shouldest keep them from the evil.*" (The Greek says, "From the evil one.")

Immediately I was aware of the invisible warfare. Satan

had spoken through the Apostle Peter's vocal chords, and Jesus had rebuked him. I prayed to Jesus that this thing should likewise be rebuked and leave Donald. Satan works through subtle suggestion, and Donald's mind was so vulnerable at this point.

I was relieved to see the sly look vanish and the expression in his eyes return to normal.

On Friday the nurse got Donald out of bed and ready to sit in the chair. One strong arm supported him, while with the other hand the nurse pulled the chair up to him. Until now when Donald had gone through this procedure he had paid no attention to what was happening. This time was different. With a simple gesture of dignity and modesty he tried to pull down the hospital gown, which on his tall frame was ridiculously short. Then the nurse lowered him into the chair and put a cover over his lap.

My heart smote me. I thought, *What will it be like for this proud man to be confined to a wheelchair, unable to do anything for himself? To be aware of all the indignities of helplessness and have to suffer them? Thousands of others have, I know. Lord, if You want this for him, I'm sure it will work out for Your glory. But if You are keeping him here because I am clinging to him, and in Your grace you are letting him go through all this in order that I might not have to give him up, then I relinquish him to You, Lord. Whatever is Your will is all right with me. Lord, he is Yours, not mine.*

At that point Donald lifted his head, looked at me, and smiled. Really *smiled*. My heart leapt. Of course he was the Lord's and of course the Lord could still use him. I had visions of Donald in his wheelchair, rolling himself up a ramp onto the platform and preaching from that wheelchair as if from a royal throne. "Thus saith the Lord!" Strength was returning a little to his left arm: perhaps as time went on he'd even regain the use of it. Maybe the paralysis would clear completely—anything was possible with a God as big as ours!

I remembered Donald's illustration of why God lets seemingly terrible ordeals happen to His children:

"Suppose you are watching a movie. You see a mother and father walking along a road with their child between them. The father hits the child, who cries feebly, 'Oh, Daddy, don't!' Then the mother slaps the child, who begs, 'Please, please don't, Mommy!' whereupon the father grabs the little one's shoulders and shakes him. By now the child is sobbing.

"Oh, what cruel parents! you think.

"Then the curtains beside the movie screen slowly open, revealing a wide-angle cinemascope screen. Now you see the full scene: A blizzard is raging. A car, stuck in a snowbank, is in the foreground. The family is struggling up the road toward a house in the distance. The child, half frozen, just wants to lie down and die, but the parents, *in love,* are keeping his circulation going by slapping and shaking him into wakefulness, in order to save his life.

"If we could see the full scope of God's screen, we would understand why He lets these things happen. It may be that, as with Job, He is winning a skirmish in the Invisible War. Until we do understand, we just have to believe and trust our heavenly Father in all that He brings into our lives."

All I could see was a tiny portion of the screen. But I knew with deep certainty that out of this God would bring glory for the Lord Jesus Christ.

I placed the lap board across Donald's chair, and put his glasses on. I gave him a pen and a sheet of paper on which Ruth, the previous weekend, had written in large letters, "I LOVE YOU," signing it "Ruthie." He looked at that for a while, with a hint of a tender smile touching his lips. Then, after making a few tentative marks on the paper, he tried to print something specific. From the pressure of the swelling behind them, his eyes were not quite in line, so the letters did not land in the right places on the paper. But, put together in the sequence in which he wrote them, they spelled, "I ought." Then with great concentration he put his pen on the paper, not lifting it as he made very small cursive letters, and wrote something that apparently had meaning for him. The only word I could clearly make out was "Lord."

Before I left that night we read together the evening passages from *Daily Light* for November 4. My hand in his kept getting little squeezes as I read, "Through the tender mercy of our God. . . . the Dayspring from on high hath visited us. To give light to them that sit in darkness and in the shadow of death, to guide our feet into the way of peace. . . . These things have I spoken unto you that in me ye might have peace. In the world ye shall have tribulation; be of good cheer; I have overcome the world. . . . The peace of God, which passeth all understanding, shall keep your hearts and minds through Christ Jesus."

I floated home. Underneath were the Everlasting Arms.

Saturday morning I was later than usual leaving for the hospital. In case Donald did come home, I wanted to be caught up on laundry and get some other things out of the way in order to be able to give him my full attention. I was walking out the door when the telephone rang.

It was Tom Durant. "Marge, get here as quickly as you can. While Donald was having the cobalt treatment he suddenly went haywire and yanked out all the tubes. Apparently the cobalt has not been able to check that remaining bit of tumor and it has reached the cortex of the brain. He has calmed down now, but he won't last out the day. Come quickly!"

The car broke all records to Philadelphia. Donald was back in his room, tubes once more in place. I spoke his name and kissed him. He didn't open his eyes or give any indication that he knew I was there. Tom and some other doctors came into the room so I went out into the hall. I had to keep reminding myself of what I had said to the Lord when I relinquished Donald to Him.

Ruth, who had been flying down from Boston every weekend, arrived and was told the grim news. She went

into her father's room to join the other doctors. Soon thereafter they all emerged, looking solemn. Tom took me
aside. "We've done all we can, Marge. There's nothing at
all left to do."

"Nothing *at all?*" I echoed.

"I *could* put a shot of adrenaline into his heart. That
would keep him a little longer. . . ."

"How much longer?"

"Oh, maybe an hour."

(Within the corridors of my memory echoed Donald's
mocking voice, preaching on death and imitating a dying
man, " 'Doctor! Doctor! I've got $2,000 saved up, and I'll
give it all to you if you'll just keep me out of heaven two
weeks longer!' Oh, give it to the Bible Society and go ahead
and die! If the Lord is calling you home, why do you want
to cheat yourself out of one single moment of being in
heaven with Him?")

"No, Tom. Let's not interfere. . . ."

Ruth and I went back into Donald's room. A nurse was
fussing with one of the tubes.

"Can't they take those things out and let him go in
peace?" I asked Ruth, who looked at the nurse and said,
"Why not?" The nurse went out briefly, I suppose to get
permission, then came back to remove everything. What a
relief to have him look like himself! If only he would open
his eyes and look at me!

I sat down beside the bed, opened the Bible to John 14,
took his hand and started to read. I thought I felt a faint
pressure on my hand from his, but otherwise there was no
sign that he heard me. Remembering that morning after the
operation when indeed he was hearing, I went on.

"In my Father's house are many mansions: if it were not
so, I would have told you. I go to prepare a place for
you. . . ."

Suddenly my mind was illumined with the memory of
that time in Grand Rapids when Donald had said, "You are
not leaving me. You are coming to me!"

Lord, he will be there ahead of me, and I will see him there.

Lord, You are there, and his place is prepared, and he is coming to You. This isn't a departure, but an arrival!

" . . . and if I go and prepare a place for you I will come again to receive you unto myself, that where I am there ye may be also. . . ."

Ruth's hand was on my shoulder. Don, Jr., was in the doorway. I rose and went out so he could have his last private good-bye.

When I went in again some time later, Ruth was taking her father's pulse and looking very concerned. He was breathing with great difficulty.

(Oh, my Donald, is this the way you must go? Not, as Jacob, in full command, sitting up, leaning on his staff, blessing his children then lying back on the bed and dying with dignity? I had released you, yes, but I had not realized that in that instant the kite tail had been severed from the kite and that from then on all I could do was stand by, a spectator, as the kite, as if caught in a great tree, waited for the wind to loose it. . . .)

Tree! That word triggered the memory of the parable Donald had once written to explain to his children the "power" of Satan. This was a parable of a man who owned a great estate, and who had an enemy who hated him.

"The Enemy tried and tried to think of a way to get at the Estate Owner. The Estate Owner had a grove of beautiful trees on a knoll in the middle of the estate. He loved those trees, and often came to sit under their shade. 'I know!' cried the Enemy, 'I'll cut down one of his trees!'

"So in the dark of the moon, with axe and wedges, he crept to the grove. Furiously he worked all night, spurred on by his hate. Just as dawn was breaking, he heard hoofbeats in the distance and saw the Estate Owner and another man riding toward the grove. The Enemy, driven on by his fury, worked even faster. As the Estate Owner approached, the Enemy knocked out the wedges and the great tree tottered and fell. Twisting as it did so, it pierced the Enemy with one of its branches, pinning him to the ground. The Enemy shook his fist in the Estate Owner's face, screaming,

'Curse you! I may be dying, but I've cut down one of your trees! I've cut down one of your trees!'

"The Estate Owner spoke, gesturing toward his companion, 'This is my architect. I plan to build a great house in this grove. In order to do this it was necessary to cut down one tree. And that's the one you've been working on all night.'

"And you may be sure, that, just so, everything that Satan ever does ends in a mouthful of dust. Satan has never done anything apart from God's plan."

Donald's breathing was now coming in great tearing gasps, but except for the heaving chest his body was quiet. It was as if the Evil One were working as fast as he could, to cut down the tree before God could stop him, and Donald was quietly submitting to God's will.

Suddenly Donald seemed to hold his breath for a moment. Was the Holy Spirit, the holy Wind that blows where it will, gently lifting the kite? His soul and spirit seemed to respond, rising in that mighty updraft. Free at last, the kite sailed out of sight into eternity as with a last little sigh the tree began to fall. His body quieted and settled, and again, as at the moment of Doug's death, I was certain that the soul and spirit had departed first; then the body finished dying its physical death.

Through a light drizzle of rain I headed home to the Farm. All arrangements were in the hands of those most competent to carry them through. All the sacks of mail that had accumulated at the hospital for me to answer had been stowed away in my car, with the flowering plants and his personal belongings and the odds and ends that collect during a month's hospital stay. Ruth had insisted on taking me to dinner; then when she was convinced that I really was all right, she had gone on to Uncle Toby's to join her siblings, who were all going to the airport to meet David. My own responsibilities were over for the moment. My heart, bleak and gray and empty as the waning afternoon, was numb, not quite believing its long vigil was over, but accepting it, standing still, not looking forward or backward, just existing, as I drove the familiar shortcuts and back roads that led home.

Drizzling dusk had turned to lightly misting night as I turned into the lane. There were lights upstairs, and in the dining room and the kitchen, where I could see Kathy doing something at the stove. My feet carried me up the path, over the worn old doorstep, and through the door. Kathy—bless her!—greeted me not with gushing sympathy but with a cheery "Cup of tea, Marge?" holding out to me a fragrant steaming cup.

My spirits lifted. "I'd love it!"

Upstairs the children heard my voice and came tumbling down the stairs, interrupting one another eagerly as they came:

"Grandma! Have you heard the news? Granddaddy's in *heaven!*"

"Grandma, he's talking to Abraham—and David—and Lazarus—and Martha and Mary—and Peter and John and Andrew—"

"Grandma, *he can SEE Jesus!*"

Caught up in their excitement and joy, I hugged them and started laughing with them, and we began reminding each other of all the others there in heaven to greet him. As the names kept tumbling out I felt almost envious. Abundant entrance! "Oh, that will be glory for me...." How right the old hymn was. Donald was looking on His face, and seeing Him as He is. Joy!

TWENTY-FOUR

It was decided there would be a viewing on Tuesday night at the funeral parlor, a memorial service at Tenth Church Wednesday night, and a private burial in the Doylestown Cemetery Thursday morning. The "viewing" which I had dreaded, was, as one of his parishioners put it, more like a going-away party, and a wonderful time of strengthening fellowship. By Wednesday night—although it was strange to realize his body was resting in that closed casket in front of the pulpit instead of towering behind it, preaching—it was possible for all his family and mine to sing with joy,

For all the saints who from their labors rest,
Who Thee by faith before the world confessed,
Thy Name, O Jesus, be forever bless'd,
Alleluia, Alleluia.

For the memorial service, busloads of people came from New York and from Washington and from points west and in between. I wanted to greet each one personally afterward, but was whisked away and taken home to bed. I guess the strain of that month of vigil was showing. Thursday morning, with gray skies still weeping, we committed his body to the earth, and it was over.

On Friday one of the little girls asked, "Grandma, could I have a flower from Granddaddy's grave?" I could see no reason why not. Kathy gave her consent, so we three clambered into the car and drove the few minutes to the cemetery through brilliantly beautiful November sunshine.

I was glad I had come. Little birds flew about; a squirrel frolicked in the tree overhead; the whole world looked shiningly clean. Each of the little girls took a flower, still fresh because of the rain, and stood looking at the grave. For want of anything better to say, I said, "Isn't it nice that Granddaddy has such a cheerful place to be!"

Miss Five-year-old looked at me the way a mother would look at an exasperating child. "Grandma!" she cried, "Granddaddy isn't *here!* Just his old body that he's through with! Grandma, *Granddaddy's in heaven!"*

The mail came flooding in from all over the world, from friends, from colleagues, from radio listeners. Although many had never even seen him, most of them expressed a sense of overwhelming personal loss. He had become an intimate member of these households, and they needed comforting perhaps more than I. Many letters were addressed to me and the family, most to the Bible Study Hour. A few of the latter said such things as, "The Lord took him out of this world because he was using that Devil's translation of the Bible, the RSV"; or "I knew the Lord would have to judge him when he sided with the NCC and the WCC"; or "He shouldn't have said the Seventh-Day Adventists were true Christians." Most, however, were outflowings of grateful love. What one listener wrote sums it up:

I never saw Dr. Barnhouse, but I see Jesus Christ through his teachings. . . . He showed me how to study the Bible and to find pure joy in it. The Bible is no longer just the Bible—it is the Living Word.

In the providence of God, the board of directors of the Evangelical Foundation were in the middle of a board meeting in Philadelphia at the moment of Donald's death. The whole raison d'être of the organization had been to support his ministry. What to do now? In the midst of their shock and grief they finally came to a decision, which Executive Director Paul Hopkins disclosed in a letter to the Bible Study Hour listeners shortly thereafter:

Dear Friend in Christ,

"My father, my father,
  the chariot of Israel and the horsemen thereof!
The Lord's warrior has departed.
  Blessed be the name of the Lord!"

The telegrams, telephone calls and letters which have poured into our office in these past few days carry one clear message about this work which God has begun in Dr. Barnhouse: it must go on. . . .

With much prayerful consideration, our Board of Directors has adopted this resolution:

"Mindful of the stewardship which is ours to the unique ministry of Donald Grey Barnhouse, we the Board Directors of the Evangelical Foundation hereby resolve to devote our major effort to the continuation of a ministry of Bible teaching and exposition, grounded in faithfulness to the inspired Word of God as our authority for faith and obedience.

"The emphasis of the ministry of Dr. Barnhouse has been the centrality of Jesus Christ in all of life, coupled with a deepening sense of the necessity for unity in the Body of Christ in order that there be an effective Christian witness to the world.

"Be it further resolved that the future program of this Foundation be devoted to a ministry of reconciliation among those who love Christ through the continuation of the Bible Study Hour,

Eternity *magazine, and other channels, as the Lord may direct. . . ."*

We must and do pray that God will provide His Elisha to rise and pick up Elijah's mantle, mighty as he was in the Scriptures, to part the waters of doubt and unbelief for a new generation.

I looked up from that letter. Gripping me was an awareness that God was opening His cinemascope curtains and letting me glimpse something awesome: the whole sweep of His moving in sovereign grace through history, from person to person down through the ages. Donald Grey Barnhouse, large as he had loomed in my life, was just one small part. But he was one of the channels through whom the Lord had passed His message on to many others.

The curtains opened wider. It was as if I were present on one of the occasions when, as in Job 1:6, "The sons of God came to present themselves before the Lord, and Satan came also among them."

I could imagine Satan, enraged, ranting, "God, *I hate You!* You let me get at Donald Grey Barnhouse, but his body was all that fell. *He* is with You. *And now, look what is happening!"*

Indeed, what was happening was that the Barnhouse ministry was flourishing.

There were enough of the "Romans" broadcasts to continue the Bible Study Hour through the following spring, by which time a new speaker had been secured. The last three of Donald's messages, written but not taped by him, were read by Herb Ehrenstein for the broadcast. Then, over various stations the series, renamed "Dr. Barnhouse and the Bible," was started again from the beginning and has continued to be used over and over again to this day. The messages are so pertinent, so *alive,* that many listeners have written in with questions for him to answer, not knowing he has been gone for over twenty years. Now, via cassette tape, his sermons on Romans and many other subjects prepared for his summer radio series, are available from the

Evangelical Foundation (renamed "Evangelical Ministries" to state more accurately its function). Many of the messages he preached at Tenth and in pulpits all over the country have been put on cassette tape also, making it possible for listeners to catch the full flavor of his salty pulpit style of "Teaching the Word of Truth." Through these God is still using His gospel to dynamite false, man-made theologies, then as a dynamo to empower His children.

Donald had entrusted the production of *Eternity* magazine more and more to the able hands of his staff under Russ Hitt as editor. True, DGB as editor-in-chief was the primary contributor to the magazine, but enough of his articles and editorials were stockpiled to supply the need for many months to come. To this day *Eternity* has remained one of the leading evangelical publications.

By 1964, four years after DGB's death, the ten-volume "Exposition of Bible Doctrines, Taking the Epistle to the Romans as the Point of Departure" had been completed and published. In his preface to volume 5, *God's Grace,* the last one to be published before his death, DGB wrote, "This volume is copyrighted only to prevent its misuse. All truth belongs to the whole church of Christ, and I gladly allow any minister to preach any of these studies, with or without credit to me." Many times since then I have rejoiced on hearing excerpts, verbatim or adapted, used by others with telling effect. His other books, and new ones edited from tapes of his Bible readings at Tenth and his sermons, have enjoyed wide popularity.

What of Donald's book, *The Invisible War?* I can imagine how Satan must have chortled because Donald had been prevented from finishing it—but the last laugh was the Lord's. It was decided that if Schubert could have an Unfinished Symphony, DGB could have an Unfinished War (after all, the Invisible Battle is going to continue until the Lord puts an end to Satan's power and creates "new heavens and a new earth, in which dwelleth righteousness"). The series, as printed in *Eternity,* was made into a book that ends abruptly, but which most readers don't realize was "unfinished." It has brought blessing and power and comprehension of "Satan's devices" into many lives.

I could imagine how Satan, seeing that God was thwarting him, might have said, "Well at least I've knocked the props out from under Georgianne Brandley. She'll soon be in my pocket. You'll see!"

Not so! Elijah's mantle had touched her. She *knew* whom she had believed, and there was no turning back. As long as her husband did not repudiate her, there was nothing the LDS authorities could do to "bring her into line," except little by little to take her teaching assignments from her until only her classes in genealogy were left. She stood firm, maintaining a sure witness to the true Jesus Christ. When Hal died in 1978, she left the Mormon church and moved to Texas, where she bears a strong witness. The Lord's powerful hand continues to hold.

So the work of Donald Grey Barnhouse, both on a public and personal level, goes on, decades after his death. DGB's ideas, his expositions of Scripture, and his practical applications of the Word of God to real life, formulated so long ago, still remain current and fresh.

What makes his preaching and his writing contemporary and vibrant still? I believe it is because he had one purpose: to glorify the Lord Jesus Christ and, as the Presbyterian Shorter Catechism puts it, "to *enjoy* Him forever." Furthermore, DGB's ministry is based on the Bible, the "only infallible rule of faith and practice," God's love-letters to mankind. Man's basic needs have not changed, nor has God's love. The timeless gift of bringing the two together is DGB's great contribution to each succeeding generation.

Donald had often said, "Every Christian is like either the Sea of Galilee or the Dead Sea. The water flows into the Sea of Galilee and out again; it teems with fish, and green growing things flourish around it. But the water only flows *into* the Dead Sea. It just gets saltier and saltier; its shores are waste and barren, and nothing can live in it. Are you a Dead Sea, with the water of the Word pouring into you, but never shared with others? Or do you pass it on, experiencing its life and *dunamis* power as it gives life to those around you?"

Satan indeed managed to cut down the Lord's tree, but, as one of the letters that came in after his death said, using that same metaphor:

We shall all miss him, as a great tree that has fallen is missed when it no longer stands on a hill, tall against the sky. But through his tireless energy and absolute dedication, and through the constant care he had for the souls of others, that great tree has "set many seedlings" that now live to give witness and to bear fruit to the glory of the same living Christ, whom he served so well and whom he now sees face to face.

I thought of how a great, fallen tree in Fontainebleau Forest had once sheltered Donald Grey Barnhouse in his youth, as he struggled to die to self and live for his Lord, willing with all his new will to be yielded to Him, yet having to fight and conquer selfish ambition, the lusts of the flesh, the lusts of the eyes, the pride of life. These would rise again and again to tempt him. Satan would subtly use them to try to thwart in him that greater desire to show others God's methods for holy living. Planted by "the rivers of waters" of God's Word, Donald had indeed become a giant among the Lord's trees.

As in the parable of the Estate Owner and the Enemy, Satan might have gloated that a fallen Donald Grey Barnhouse was now powerless against him. But the Lord is building a great house, according to Hebrews 3:3, 4, 6, and in His sovereignty determined that in order to build it that tree had to fall. Who knows what other young men will find shelter beside it, seeking the Lord's will for their lives, or how many other great trees will grow from those seedlings he has set? God will use what Donald Grey Barnhouse let his Lord say and do and be, through him, to build His house.

EPILOGUE

I am Alpha and Omega, the beginning and the end, the first and the last... I Jesus....   Revelation 22:13, 16

The beginning and the end of this book is the Lord Jesus Christ. The whole life of Donald Grey Barnhouse was bound up in Him. Even as a teenager, Donald had written on the flyleaf of his Bible, following the autographs of some of the great men who had been his teachers, "I pray that Thy Name, O Lord, shall be written in my life."

His greatest theological battles were with those he thought were lowering even one iota the exalted position belonging to the Lord Jesus Christ alone. His life text, to which he gave all of his time and energy, expressed his goals:

That I may know him, and the power of his resurrection, and the fellowship of his sufferings, being made conformable to his death. Philippians 3:10

Now, Donald, you can truly know Him.

"The power of his resurrection," the *dunamis,* the dynamite of God that was the source of your energy here on earth, is now yours in fullness.

"The fellowship of his sufferings...." Ah, Donald, when you turned to embrace all men who were truly born again, when you insisted God was sovereign and chose whom He wished, the Pharisees of your day misunderstood you. You entered into His suffering, and now you enter into His full joy.

While you were on earth, He was conforming you to His death: like the Apostle Paul, you had to "die daily" in order that His life might possess you. Now that old, fallen nature is behind you and you are alive forevermore.

You once said you had nothing to leave me. But, oh, what more priceless heritage than the riches of God's grace in the pages of His Word! "The joy of the Lord is your strength." What joy you have left me, through His abiding life in me, nurtured by the insights He gave you! What strength is in Christ, our leaning post!

Unto Him that loved us,
And washed us from our sins in His own blood,
And hath made us a kingdom of priests unto God
    and His Father,
To Him be glory and dominion forever and ever. Amen.

A BARNHOUSE BIBLIOGRAPHY

The following is a partial list of published works by Donald Grey Barnhouse.

Acts (1979) Zondervan Corp.

Bible Truth Illustrated (1979) Shepherd Illustrated Classics, Keats Publishing.

The Cross Through the Open Tomb (1961) Eerdmans Publishing Co.

Genesis (1970, 2 vol.; 1973, 1 vol.) Zondervan Corp., 10th printing 1982.

God's Methods for Holy Living (1949) Revelation Publications. (Published jointly with *Life by the Son,* 1951, Eternity Book Service.)

Guaranteed Deposits (1949) Revelation Publications.

The Invisible War (1981) Zondervan Corp.

Let Me Illustrate (1967) Fleming H. Revell Co.

Life by the Son (1939) American Bible Conference Association Inc., Revelation Publications. (Published jointly with *God's Methods for Holy Living,* 1951, Eternity Book Service.)

The Love Life (1973) Regal Books.

Revelation (1971) Zondervan Corp.

Romans (1982) Eerdmans Publishing Co., 4 volumes.

Teaching the Word of Truth (1982) Eerdmans Publishing Co.

Thessalonians (1977) Zondervan Corp.

Words Fitly Spoken (1969) Tyndale House Publishers.

Your Right to Heaven (1977) Baker Book House.